An Index to African-American Spirituals for the Solo Voice

**Recent Titles in
the Music Reference Collection**

Wind Ensemble Sourcebook and Biographical Guide
Marshall Stoneham, Jon A. Gillaspie, and David Lindsey Clark

Guitar Music by Women Composers: An Annotated Catalog
Janna MacAuslan and Kristan Aspen, compilers

The Songs of Hans Pfitzner: A Guide and Study
Richard Mercier

Choral Arrangements of the African-American Spirituals:
Historical Overview and Annotated Listings
Patricia Johnson Trice

Twentieth Century Danish Music: An Annotated Bibliography and Research Directory
Lansing D. McLoskey

The Wind Ensemble Catalog
Jon A. Gillaspie, Marshall Stoneham, and David Lindsey Clark

Form and Analysis Theory: A Bibliography
James E. Perone, compiler

Sacred Latin Texts and English Translations for the Choral Conductor and Church
Musician
William Bausano, compiler

A Bibliographic Guide to Jazz Poetry
Sascha Feinstein

Library Resources for Singers, Coaches, and Accompanists: An Annotated Bibliography
Ruthann Boles McTyre

A Bibliographical Guide to Spanish Music for the Violin and Viola, 1900-1997
Laura Klugherz

Anton Rubinstein: An Annotated Catalog of Piano Works and Biography
Larry Sitsky

An Index to African-American Spirituals for the Solo Voice

Compiled by

Kathleen A. Abromeit

Foreword by François Clemmons

Music Reference Collection, Number 76

GREENWOOD PRESS
Westport, Connecticut • London

Library of Congress Cataloging-in-Publication Data

Abromeit, Kathleen A., 1962–
    An index to African-American spirituals for the solo voice /
compiled by Kathleen A. Abromeit : foreword by François Clemmons.
        p.   cm.—(Music reference collection, ISSN 0736–7740 ; no.
76)
    Includes bibliographical references.
    ISBN 0–313–30577–3 (alk. paper)
    1. Spirituals (Songs)—Indexes.   2. Afro-Americans—Music—
Bibliography.   I. Title.   II. Series.
ML128.S4A27   1999
016.78225′3—dc21   98–44409
                        MN
British Library Cataloguing in Publication Data is available.

Library of Congress Catalog Card Number: 98–44409
ISBN: 0–313–30577–3
ISSN: 0736–7740

First published in 1999

Greenwood Press, 88 Post Road West, Westport, CT 06881
An imprint of Greenwood Publishing Group, Inc.

Printed in the United States of America

The paper used in this book complies with the
Permanent Paper Standard issued by the National
Information Standards Organization (Z39.48–1984).

10 9 8 7 6 5 4 3 2 1

Contents

Foreword by Dr. François S. Clemmons   vii
Acknowledgments   ix
Introduction   xi

Bibliography   1

Title Index   9

First Line Index   77

Alternate Title Index   145

Topical Index
  Admonition/Judgement   179
  Aspiration   181
  Christmas   182
  Church   182
  Death   182
  Deliverance   184
  Easter   185
  Faith/Assurance   185
  Heaven   188
  Jesus   190
  New Testament   191
  Old Testament   191
  Praise   192
  Prayer   193

Foreword

From the time of the Civil War until the present, much has been written concerning the American Negro Spiritual. Some of it has been elucidating and inspiring, but much has been confusing. This is because some "official" historians have rejected outright this core cultural expression in our nation. To them, the Spiritual represented only the crude unlearned, and disorganized expression of a lowly, dejected people: Black, African-American slaves.

I firmly believe that the American Negro Spiritual has played a seminal and often overlooked role in our nation's history. These songs were present at every important occasion or event of plantation life: weddings, funerals, holidays, church services. They provided motivation and inspiration for run-away slaves and taught lessons about life in general. These messages were essential and universal for the entire slave population of the rural South, as well as a reflection of the nation's social and political mores at the time as a whole. Essentially, our history is reflected in our folk music.

There is something about this profound and often stunning body of work which baffles and eludes the impatient but well-intentioned scholar. Words just do not seem to come easily or do justice to its stark and awe-inspiring simplicity; its reliance on naive and persistent repetition; its unlearned dialect; its often unparalleled rhyme scheme; its child-like theology; a preponderance of demoralizing symbolism (as in "sometimes, I feel like a motherless child, a long way from home"); and its dogged utilization of the non-European syncopated rhythms. But inspite of what may seem like intellectual and musical limitations, this body of work is not only eagerly anticipated by audiences throughout the world, but has been the seed and germination of every important American musical genre since the 1870s. The secret has been and remains that this music, as with many other art forms, cannot be approached exclusively by the intellect. We must approach this music with our emotions, with our hearts.

In the early 1980s when I set about establishing the Harlem Spiritual Ensemble, I often felt that I was operating in a vacuum. I listened to many recordings, and I made an honest attempt at archival research by   visiting Fisk University, Tuskegee University, the Library of Congress, the Hampton Institute, Jackson State University, as well as Howard University and the Schomberg Library in New York City. In my research I painfully and reluctantly discovered that much great music is now out of print. To be sure, various arrangements, programs, photos and biographical materials were in private libraries and scattered around the country. Out of necessity, I established an informal network of friends and colleagues who were knowledgeable about the American Negro Spiritual, and who were willing to assist me. I received scores and books in the mail from complete strangers who had heard of my work and wanted to contribute.

Blessedly, we now have *African-American Spirituals for the Solo Voice: An Index* which should make the finding of these source materials a little easier. The young artist will not have to travel to numerous institutions and do many live interviews, as I did, to locate sources. This index will make the process of research and the assimilation of this music into the contemporary educational process that much easier. I recommend it to soloists, choral directors, arrangers/composers, writers, and historians alike. I feel that we have needed it for some time.

I would also like to applaud the timeliness of Kathleen Abromeit's index to the American Negro Spiritual. In society today, we face a disastrous drug crisis, the difficulties of single parenthood and unwanted pregnancies, the breakdown of the traditional family, the AIDS epidemic, and more.   I think this may in some way be similar to conditions in America before the Civil War, a state of national crisis in which American Negro Spirituals first appeared. I also think it is important to know that somehow, and in time, we can survive this crisis, and that our survival is part of a larger, cosmic plan. I hope this faith will give us hope and motivation to embrace the challenge of healing our wounded nation.

Dr. François S. Clemmons
New York, July 1998

Acknowledgments

This index has come to represent so much more than I could have anticipated at its conception. Most significant is the realization that the collective whole is so much more than the sum of its parts. Yet, I do want to attempt to thank those individuals who represent the parts. First, I would like to thank that Oberlin student, whose name I don't know, for coming to the reference desk at the Oberlin Conservatory Library, asking me to help her find "Hear de Angels Singin." Without her question this index never would have been compiled.

Research for this book was done at the Oberlin College Conservatory Library. There are many colleagues I want to thank. For financial support in my professional development, I am grateful to Ray English, Director of Oberlin College Libraries, and Karen Wolff, Dean of the Oberlin Conservatory of Music. For technical support, I am indebted to Alan Boyd, Assistant Director of Oberlin College Libraries, David Goldberg, Oberlin College Libraries, Systems Office, and Heather Smith, FileMaker Pro guru. For obtaining many items through ILL, I am thankful to Mark Kuestner, Diane Lee, Valerie McGowen-Doyle, and Michael Palazzolo. I am especially indebted to the following "reffies" for their many hours of computer work and their uncanny ability to find inconsistencies in the data: Bill Barrett, Teri Bartnicki, Sarah Clemmens, Sarah Day, Doug Kelly, Beth Levy, Stacy Nowicki, Mai-Linh Pham, Rosalie Sullivan, Phala Tracy, and Dan Wilder.

For creative support and encouragement, I wish to thank my colleague, friend, and mentor, Dan Zager, University of North Carolina-Chapel Hill. I am most grateful to François Clemmons, Jack Knapp, and Bill Sabin for their editorial expertise.

Special thanks to Allen, Terrie, Jeana, Mary, and Dick for having faith in their kid sister. I would also like to thank DeeDee Board and David Bower for their help with dialect and textual analysis.

Finally, for giving me roots and wings, I would like to thank my late parents Omajean Vivian Abromeit and Albert Carl Abromeit. Their wisdom and love continue to affect me deeply. I am forever thankful to John, my friend and husband, for his constant support, devotion to the walk and partnership in embracing the questions. I dedicate my efforts to my daughters Dyani and Brook. May you always *Chatter with de Angels* and help to create a world where all Life is known to be an expression of the Divine.

Introduction

African-American Spirituals for the Solo Voice: An Index began in November of 1993 as a solution to the highly problematic access to spirituals in the Oberlin Conservatory Library. It is an attempt to systematically index some sixty collections scored for solo voice represented at Oberlin, supplemented by a more comprehensive literature review in online databases. It is not intended as a current source of available materials - given that some titles have been reissued or reprinted. The reader is advised to consult bibliographic tools for availability of current editions. In choosing items for this book, I have endeavored to include significant collections, but inevitably there are anthologies I may have missed.

The first collection of slave songs appeared in 1843, without musical notation, in a series of three articles by a Methodist Church missionary known only as "c." Collections that included musical notation began appearing in the 1850s and proliferated following the Civil War. The earliest book-length collection of spirituals containing both lyrics and music was published jointly in 1867 by William Francis Allen, Charles Pickard Ware, and Lucy McKim Garrison. Their effort, *Slave Songs of the United States,* with a 38-page introduction, contains 136 songs, including seven in Louisiana French and African creole. This was to become one of the most important collections of spirituals of its time.

The next book-length collection was published in 1872 under the title *Jubilee Songs as Sung by the Jubilee Singers.* The Fisk Jubilee Singers of Fisk University, Nashville, Tennessee, founded just five years earlier, began to introduce the public to spirituals in their concert tours in order to raise money for their financially troubled school. A similar collection of 50 songs was published in 1874 by Hampton Institute under the title *Hampton and Its Students.* Tuskegee Institute followed suit in 1884 with *Tuskegee Normal and Industrial Institute, Its Story and Its Songs.* The last major collections were

James Weldon Johnson and J. Rosamond Johnson's *The Book of American Negro Spirituals* (1926), *The Second Book of Negro Spirituals* (1927), and William Arms Fisher's *Seventy Negro Spirituals* (1926). In the 1930s, the Cleveland Public Library published *Index to Negro Spirituals,* reprinted by the Center for Black Music Research in 1991. While the spiritual has been studied from a number of perspectives, and there is a wide-spread resurgence in its popularity, *African-American Spirituals for the Solo Voice: An Index* is the first index to be published in more than half a century.

TITLE INDEX

The main body is an alphabetical list of the spirituals indexed. Because of the various spellings and titles used for a given spiritual, the Title Index is searchable on the "uniform" title. If a spiritual is known by more than one title, a - *see also* - reference will suggest other entries to consult. In addition, some spirituals are known by one title with multiple versions of the text. Such spirituals include a text excerpt for easy identification.

Sample Entry:
Ain't That Good News (1)
"Ain't dat good news oh Lord..."
mci,59,AH
pet,205,C
Ain't That Good News (2)
"I've a crown up in the kingdom..."
cle,114,A
pet,205,C

This spiritual is found in the three sources represented by the symbols mci, pet, and cle, which are listed in the Bibliography pp 1-7. The number refers to the page number within that collection. Following each page number, abbreviations in capital letters identify specific information regarding that spiritual within a source:

A	Contains text, melody, and piano accompaniment
B	Contains text and chord symbols
C	Contains text only
D	Contains text, melody, and chord symbols
E	Contains text and melody
CH	Contains text and additional historical information on the spiritual
AH	Contains text, melody, piano accompaniment, and additional historical information on the spiritual
F	Uses Tonic Sol-Fa notation

FIRST LINE INDEX

As one might expect in working with songs that originate in an aural tradition, there are considerable inconsistencies in the identification of some spirituals. For example, *Down By the Riverside* frequently has the first line of text, "We'll wait till Jesus comes..." but is also known by the text, "When Christ the Lord was here below...." As a result, the user of this index may need to consult multiple listings in order to complete a comprehensive search for the desired title.

The first line of each spiritual is listed in alphabetical order followed by a " - *see* - " reference to the appropriate spiritual. All dialect has been included in the First Line Index.

Sample Entry:
Ain't dat a pity Lord ain't dat a shame - *see* - Sinner Man So Hard to Believe

ALTERNATE TITLE INDEX

Variant titles as well as any titles listed in dialect can be found in the Alternate Title Index with a " - *see* - " reference to the appropriate title in the Title Index.

Sample Entry:
Lil' David Play Yo Harp - *see* - Little David

TOPICAL INDEX

The spirituals have been separated into the following twenty topical subjects. Naturally, many could fit several categories, but for this index each spiritual has been assigned only one topic.

Admonition/Judgment
Aspiration
Christmas
Church
Death
Deliverance
Easter
Faith/Assurance
Heaven
Jesus

New Testament
Old Testament
Praise
Prayer
Rituals of Preparation for
    Renewal/Regeneration
Satan
Songs of Spiritual Journey
Suffering
Women
Work Songs

Bibliography

Abbreviations found in the left column of the Bibliography are also used in the index entries.

afr   *Afro-America Sings.* Detroit: Board of Education of the City of Detroit, 1971.

all   Allen, William Francis, Charles Pickard Ware [and] Lucy McKim Garrison. *Slave Songs of the United States.* New York: P. Smith, 1867.

and   Anderson, Walter F. *Look Away: 50 Negro Folk Songs.* Delaware, Ohio: Cooperative Recreation Service, n.d.

arm   Armstrong, M. F. *Hampton and Its Students. By Two of Its Teachers, Mrs. M. Armstrong and Helen W. Ludlow. With Fifty Cabin and Plantation Songs, Arranged by Thomas F. Fenner.* New York: G. P. Putnam's Sons, 1874.

bal   Ballanta-Taylor, Nicholas George Julius. *Saint Helena Island Spirituals.* New York: G. Schirmer, 1925.

bap   *Baptist Hymnal.* Nashville: Convention Press, 1975.

2   Bibliography

bar

Barton, William E.*Old Plantation Hymns.*   Boston: Lamson, Wolffe & Co., 1899.

blo

Blood-Patterson, Peter. *Rise Up Singing.* Bethlehem, Pennsylvania: Sing Out Corp., 1988.

bro

Brown, Lawrence. *Negro Folk Songs.* New York: Associated Music Publishers, 1930.

bry

Bryan, Ashley. *Walk Together Children: Black American Spirituals.* New York: Atheneum, 1974.

bry1

Bryan, Ashley. *All Night All Day: A Child's First Book of African-American Spirituals.* New York: Atheneum, 1991.

bur

Burleigh, H. T. *Album of Negro* Spirituals.   Melville, N.Y.: Belwin Mills, 1969.

bur1

Burleigh, H. T. *Plantation Melodies Old and New.* New York: G. Schirmer, 1901.

bur2

Burleigh, H. T. *The Spirituals of Harry T. Burleigh.* Melville, N. Y.: Belwin-Mills, 1984.

cha

Chambers, H. A. *The Treasury of Negro Spirituals.* New York: Emerson Books, 1963.

cle

Cleveland, J. Jefferson, and Verolga Nix. *Songs of Zion.* Nashville: Abingdon Press, 1981.

cou

Courlander, Harold. *Negro Folk Music, U.S.A.* New York: Columbia University Press, 1963.

det   Dett, R. Nathaniel. *Spirituals.* New York: Mills Music, 1946.

det1   Dett, R. Nathaniel. *The Dett Collection of Negro Spirituals: first group.* Chicago: Hall & McCreary Co., 1936.

det2   Dett, R. Nathaniel. *The Dett Collection of Negro Spirituals: second group.* Chicago: Hall & McCreary Co., 1936.

det3   Dett, R. Nathaniel. *The Dett Collection of Negro Spirituals: third group.* Chicago: Hall & McCreary Co., 1936.

det4   Dett, R. Nathaniel. *The Dett Collection of Negro Spirituals: fourth group.* Chicago: Hall & McCreary Co., 1936.

det5   Dett, R. Nathaniel. *Religious Folk-Songs of the Negro as Sung at Hampton Institute.* Hampton, Virginia: Hampton Institute Press, 1927.

dit   Diton, Carl. *Thirty-Six South Carolina Spirituals.* New York: G. Schirmer, 1928.

fen   Fenner, Thomas P., and Frederic G. Rathbun. *Cabin and Plantation Songs as Sung by the Hampton Students.* New York: G. P. Putnam's Sons, 1892.

fis   Fisher, William Arms. *Seventy Negro Spirituals.* Boston: Oliver Ditson Co., 1926.

fis1   Fisher, William Arms. *Ten Negro Spirituals.* Boston: Oliver Ditson Co., 1925.

4   Bibliography

gla

Glass, Paul. *Songs and Stories of Afro-Americans.* New York: Grosset & Dunlap, 1971.

gri

Grissom, Mary Allen. *The Negro Sings a New Heaven.* Chapel Hill: University of North Carolina Press, 1930.

hal

Hallowell, Emily. *Calhoun Plantation Songs.* New York: AMS Press, 1976.

hay

Hayes, Roland. *My Songs: Aframerican Religious Folk Songs.* Boston: Little, Brown & Co., 1948.

jac

Jackson, Irene V. *Lift Every Voice and Sing : A Collection of Afro-American Spirituals and Other Songs.* New York: Church Hymnal Corp., 1981.

jes

Jessye, Eva A. *My Spirituals.* New York: Robbins-Engel, 1927.

joh

Johnson, James Weldon. *The Book of American Negro Spirituals.* New York: The Viking Press, 1925.

joh1

Johnson, James Weldon. *The Second Book of Negro Spirituals.* New York: The Viking Press, 1926.

johg

Johnson, Hall. *The Green Pastures Spirituals.* New York: Carl Fischer, 1930.

johg1

Johnson, Hall. *Thirty Spirituals Arranged for Voice and Piano.* New York: G. Schirmer, 1949.

jon

Johnston, Richard. *Folk Songs North America Sings.* Toronto: E. C. Kirby, 1984.

ken Kennedy, R. Emmet. *Mellows: A Chronicle of Unknown Singers.* New York: A. & C. Boni, 1925.

ken1 Kennedy, R. Emmet. *More Mellows.* New York: Dodd Mead & Co., 1931.

kre Krehbiel, Henry Edward. *Afro-American Folksongs: A Study in Racial and National Music.* New York: Frederick Ungar, 1962.

lan Lanstaff, John. *Climbing Jacob's Ladder: Heroes of the Bible in African-American Spirituals.* New York: Maxwell Macmillan International, 1991.

lit Little, Charles F., Jr. *Praise Him With the Gospel.* Lexington, Kentucky: C.F.L. Music Publishing Co., 1983.

log Logan, William Augustus. *Road to Heaven: Twenty-Eight Negro Spirituals.* Tuscaloosa: University of Alabama Press, 1955.

lom Lomax, John A., and Alan Lomax. *American Ballads and Folk Songs.* New York: Macmillan, 1934.

lom1 Lomax, Alan. *The Folk Songs of North America.* Garden City, N. Y.: Doubleday, 1960.

lom2 Lomax, John A., and Alan Lomax. *Folk Song U.S.A.: The 111 Best American Ballads.* New York: New American Library, 1975.

lom3 Lomax, John A., and Alan Lomax. *Our Singing Country: A Second Volume of American Ballads and Folk Songs.* New York: Macmillan, 1941.

6 Bibliography

lud   Ludlow, Helen W. *Tuskegee Normal and Industrial School, for Training Colored Teachers, at Tuskegee, Alabama... Its Story and its Songs.* Hampton, Va.: Normal School Press, 1884.

mci   McIlhenny, E. A. *Befo' de War Spirituals.* New York: AMS Press, 1973.

naa   *Lift Ev'ry Voice: NAACP Song Book.* New York: National Association for the Advancement of Colored People, 1972.

new   Newman, Richard. *Go Down, Moses: A Celebration of the African-American Spiritual.* New York: Clarkson Potter, 1998.

nil   Niles, John J. *Seven Exaltations.* New York: G. Schirmer, 1929.

odu   Odum, Howard, and Guy B. Johnson. *The Negro and His Song: A Study of Typical Negro Songs in the South.* Westport, Connecticut: Negro Universities Press, 1968.

par   Parrish, Lydia. *Slave Songs of the Georgia Sea Islands.* New York: Creative Age Press, 1942.

pet   Peters, Erskine. *Lyrics of the Afro-American Spiritual.* Westport, Connecticut: Greenwood Press, 1993.

rel   *Religious Folk Songs of the Negro as Sung on the Plantations.* Arr. by the Musical Directors of The Hampton Normal and Agricultural Institute. Hampton, Virginia: The Institute Press, 1918.

san   Sandilands, Alexander. *A Hundred and Twenty Negro Spirituals*, 2d ed. Basutoland: Morija Sesuto Book Depot, 1964.

sew   Seward, T. F. *Jubilee Songs.* Chicago: Biglow & Main, 1872.

Note: *Jubilee Songs* has been reprinted in: (1) Pike, G. D. *The Jubilee Singers and Their Campaign for Twenty Thousand Dollars.* New York: Lee Shepard and Dillingham, 1873. (2) Marsh, J. B. T. *The Story of the Jubilee Singers With Their Songs.* New York: Negro Universities Press, 1969.

tob   Tobitt, Janet E. *A Book of Negro Songs.* Pleasantville, N. Y.: J. E. Tobitt, 1950.

whi   White, Clarence Cameron. *Forty Negro Spirituals.* Philadelphia: Theodore Presser Co., 1927.

worf   Work, Frederick J. *New Jubilee Songs as Sung by the Fisk Jubilee Singers.* Nashville: Fisk University, 1902.

worj   Work, John W. *American Negro Songs and Spirituals.* New York: Bonanza Books, 1940.

worj1   Work, John W. *Folk Song of the American Negro.* New York: Negro Universities Press, 1969.

worj2   Work, John W. *Ten Spirituals.* New York: Ethel Smith Music Corp., 1952.

Title Index

According to My Lord's Command
    ken1,47,CH
Adam in the Garden Pinning Leaves
    lom3,4,E
    mci,37,AH
    new,32,C
    pet,3,C
After a While
    odu,133,CH
    pet,156,C
Ain't Going to Tarry Here
    mci,47,AH
    new,72,C
    pet,112,C
Ain't Got Long to Stay Here
    jes,34,AH
Ain't Got Time to Die
    new,33,C
    pet,112,C
Ain't I Glad - *see* - I Ain't Going
  to Die No More
Ain't I Glad I've Got Out the
  Wilderness
    pet,342,C
    worf,18,A

Ain't That Good News (1)
    "Ain't dat good news oh Lord..."
    mci,59,AH
    pet,205,C
Ain't That Good News (2)
    "I've a crown up in the
    kingdom..."
      cle,114,A
      pet,205,C
Ain't You Glad You Got Good
  Religion
    pet,205,C
All I Do the Church Keep
  Grumbling
    bal,70,A
    joh1,130,A
    pet,3,C
All I Do the People Keep
  Grumbling
    dit,29,A
    pet,3,C
All I Want Is a Little More Faith
  - *see* - Little More Faith in
  Jesus

All My Sins Are Taken Away
    bal,11,A
    mci,67,AH
    pet,206,C
    san,90,F
All My Sins Done Taken Away
    odu,60,CH
All Night All Day - see - Angels
  Are Watching Over Me
All Night Long
    lom1,486,D
    see also - Paul
      and Silas
All Over This World
    mci,51,AH
    pet,264,C
    worj1,57,CH
All the Way to Calvary
    hal,64,A
    pet,306,C
Alleluia
    afr,53,A
Almost Done Toiling Here
    joh1,140,A
    pet,236,C
Almost Done Traveling
    arm,215,A
    fen,43,A
    pet,29,C
    rel,43,A
Almost Over
    all,74,E
    pet,156,C
Am I a Soldier
    naa,30,D
Am I Born to Die
    hal,31,A
    new,120,C
    pet,4,C
Amazing Grace
    cle,211,D
    hal,50,A
    jac,114,A
    lit,6,A
    lom2,436,AH

    pet,342,C
Amen
    and,7,A
    cle,147,A
    jac,28,A
Anchor Believer Anchor - see -
  Anchor in the Lord
Anchor in the Lord
    pet,52,C
    san,20,F
And I Cry
    jes,16,AH
Angel Band - see - Band of
  Angels
Angel Done Changed My Name
    mci,45,AH
    pet,306,C
Angel Roll the Stone Away
    bal,80,A
    joh1,118,A
    pet,156,C
Angel's Waiting at the Door
    pet,157,C
    worj1,58,CH
Angel's Waiting at the Tomb
    ken1,20,E
Angels Are Watching Over Me
    and,25,A
    bal,23,E
    bry1,8,D
    new,121,C
    pet,52,C
Angels Done Bowed Down
    new,34,C
    pet,4,C
Angels Done Changed My Name
    ken,36,E
    new,128,E
Angels in Heaven Going to Write
  My Name
    bal,37,A
    joh1,128,A
    pet,382,C
Animals a Coming
    pet,206,C

Ante-Bellum Sermon - see -
Joshua Fought the Battle of
Jericho
Anybody Here - see - Is There
Anybody Here
Anyhow My Lord
bal,57,E
pet,382,C
Appolyon and the Pilgrim
det3,11,A
Archangel
mci,49,AH
pet,52,C
Archangel Open the Door
all,32,E
pet,343,C
Are You Ready
mci,53,AH
pet,264,C
Around About the Mountain
hay,85,AH
As I Went down in the Valley to
Pray
san,23,F
At the Bar of God
pet,264,C
At the Judgment Bar
bal,51,A
pet,265,C
Auction Block - see - Many
Thousand Gone
Away Down in Sunbury
all,99,E
Away in the Kingdom
gri,18,E
pet,336,C
Away in the Middle of the Air
odu,105,CH
Aye Lord Don't Leave Me
bal,13,A
pet,157,C
Aye Lord Time Is Drawin' Nigh
- see - Lord Time Is Drawing
Nigh

Baby Mine
odu,261,CH
Babylon's Falling
arm,248,A
det5,2,A
fen,76,AH
pet,265,C
rel,76,A
Baby's in Memphis
odu,248,CH
Balm in Gilead
and,4,A
bap,205,A
blo,208,B
bur2,111,A
cha,14,A
cle,123,A
det1,8,A
det5,88,A
johg1,44,A
new,123,C
pet,53,C
worj1,43,AH
worj2,6,A
Band of Angels
dit,30,A
odu,104,CH
pet,208,C
Band of Gideon
arm,242,A
det5,56,A
fen,70,AH
joh,156,A
pet,158,C
rel,70,A
san,108,F
Band of Music
hal,56,A
pet,208,C
Baptism
det4,6,A
Baptizing
mci,57,AH
new,35,C
pet,306,C

Baptizing Hymn
        pet,208,C
Battle Hymn of the Republic
        cle,213,A
Be Still and Listen
        cha,89,A
Be With Me
        new,124,C
        pet,5,C
Bear Your Burden
        bal,16,A
        odu,82,CH
        pet,113,C
        whi,24,A
Been A-Listening - *see* - I've Been
    Listening All Night Long
Been Down Into the Sea
        bar,44,E
Been Washed in the Blood
        mci,61,AH
        pet,307,C
Before I'd Be a Slave
        bar,25,E
Before This Time Another Year
        lom,586,E
        new,125,C
        pet,5,C
        worf,31,A
        worj1,52,CH
Behold That Star
        bry1,17,D
        bur2,123,A
Believer I Know
        par,131,E
Bell Done Ring
        mci,85,AH
        par,164,CH
Bell Done Rung (1)
    "I know member know Lord..."
        all,34,E
        pet,158,C
Bell Done Rung (2)
    "I know that the bell done
    rung..."
        pet,382,C

Belshazzah Had a Feast
        johg1,24,A
Better Walk Steady
        ken1,89,E
Big Camp Meeting in the Promised
    Land
        bar,29,E
Big Fish
        odu,141,CH
Black Bird and the Crow
        bur1,10,A
Black Sheep Where You Left Your
    Lamb
        fis,4,AH
Bless My Soul and Gone
        jes,20,AH
Blessed Hope
        odu,146,CH
Blessed Quietness
        cle,206,A
Blind Man Lying at the Pool
        hal,62,A
        new,53,C
        pet,6,C
Blind Man Stood on the Road and
    Cried
        bur,14,A
        bur2,99,A
        hal,29,A
        joh,108,A
        johg,36,A
        ken,106,AH
        lom,596,E
        lom1,473,D
        odu,136,CH
        pet,6,C
        pet,158,C
        whi,92,A
Blood Done Sign My Name
        bal,65,A
        dit,20,A
        odu,122,CH
        pet,383,C
Blood-Strained Banders
        lom3,24,E

Blood Will Never Lose Its Power
cle,184,D
Blow Gabriel
log,8,E
odu,86,CH
whi,107,A
Blow Your Gospel Trumpet
bal,43,A
pet,209,C
Blow Your Trumpet Gabriel
all,3,E
fis,8,AH
pet,159,C
Book of Life
new,126,C
pet,307,C
Bound for Canaan Land
mci,42,AH
new,73,C
pet,343,C
Bound for the Promised Land
lom2,442,AH
Bound to Go
all,22,E
pet,343,C
Bow Low Elder
ken1,89,AH
worj1,74,CH
Brethren Rise and Shine
san,91,F
Bright Sparkles in the Churchyard
arm,200,A
det5,174,A
fen,28,AH
pet,53,C
rel,28,A
Brother Guide Me Home
all,86,E
pet,209,C
Brother Have You Come
san,26,F
Brother Moses Gone
all,49,E

Brother You'd Better Be a Praying
odu,80,CH
Brothers Don't Get Weary
all,95,E
pet,88,C
Brothers Don't Stay Away
san,92,F
Built a House in Paradise
all,29,E
pet,209,C
Burden Down
and,5,A
But He Ain't Coming Here to Die
No More
det5,103,A
By and By (1)
"By and by I'm going to see
them..."
bap,506,A
bur,23,A
bur2,103,A
cha,16,A
cle,164,A
det4,9,A
det5,124,A
fis,12,AH
joh,98,A
new,126,C
odu,144,CH
pet,6,C
san,93,F
whi,12,A
worf,45,A
worj1,70,CH
By and By (2)
"By and by we all shall meet
again..."
worj,228,A
pet,7,C
Bye and Bye
"Lord I wonder..."
hal,60,C
pet,114,C

Calinda
    all,111,E
Calvary
    cle,87,A
    hal,35,A
    joh,112,A
    pet,265,C
    whi,96,A
Calvary's Mountain
    det3,26,A
Can't Hide Sinner
    bal,35,A
    par,142,A
    pet,265,C
Can't You Live Humble
    joh1,138,A
    pet,159,C
    worf,25,A
Certainly Lord
    and,6,A
    cle,161,A
    det3,15,A
    johg,5,A
Changed My Name
    cle,118,A
Chatter With the Angels
    bry1,9,D
Children Did You Hear When
  Jesus Rose - *see* - Did You Hear
  When Jesus Rose
Children Do Linger
    all,51,E
    pet,344,C
Children Go Where I Send Thee
    and,42,E
    blo,208,B
Children We All Shall Be Free
    det5,107,A
    sew,13,A
Children You'll Be Called On
    pet,114,C
    sew,19,E
Chilly Water
    joh1,114,A
    pet,54,C

Choose You a Seat and Set Down
    lom3,34,E
Christ Is All
    cle,180,A
Christians Hold Up Your Heads
    pet,217,C
    worf,29,A
Christians' Hymn of the
  Crucifixion
    bar,39,E
Church of God
    arm,199,A
    fen,27,A
    pet,54,C
    rel,27,A
City Called Heaven
    cle,135,D
    pet,7,C
City of Babylon
    ken1,133,AH
Climb Up Ye Little Children
    san,27,F
Climbing Up the Mountain
    cle,120,A
Coffin to Bind Me Down
    bar,22,E
Cold Icy Hand
    bar,8,E
Come All of God's Children
    san,28,F
Come Along
    bar,13,E
Come Along Moses
    all,104,E
Come and Go
    and,8,A
Come and Go With Me
    mci,44,AH
    new,71,C
    pet,383,C
Come By Here - *see* -
  Kum Ba Yah
Come Come Come and Go With
Me
    bal,66A

pet,345,C
Come Down
   pet,160,C
Come Down Angels
   pet,266,C
   san,29,F
Come Down My Lord
   san,30,F
Come Down Sinner
   det5,132,A
   pet,55,C
   rel,138,A
Come Go With Me
   all,57,E
   pet,345,C
Come Here Jesus If You Please
   new,43,C
   pet,7,C
Come Here Lord
   joh1,176,A
   pet,7,C
Come Let Us All Go Down
   pet,345,C
Come Let Us All Go Down
  - see also - Good Old Way
Come On Sinner *- see -* I'm All
  Wore Out Toiling for the Lord
Come Out the Wilderness
   cle,136,A
Come Sinner Come
   odu,78,CH
Come to Me
   jac,1,A
Come Trembling Down
   new,127,C
   pet,56,C
Come Unto Me
   det4,20,A
   gri,50,E
   pet,308,C
Comfort in Heaven
   bar,12,E
Coming Again By and By
   mci,64,AH

pet,115,C
Coming Down the Line
   mci,71,AH
   pet,266,C
Coming Here Tonight
   bal,36,E
   pet,346,C
Communion
   det4,7,A
Conviction of the Wise Men in
  Jerusalem
   ken1,41,CH
Cotton Needs Picking
   and,46,E
Couldn't Hear Nobody Pray *- see -*
  I Couldn't Hear Nobody Pray
Cross Me Over
   mci,75,AH
   odu,89,CH
   pet,384,C
Crowned Him Lord of All
   bar,29,E
Crucified *- see -* Were You
  There
Crucifixion *- see -* He Never Said a
  Mumbling Word
Cruel Jews
   mci,38,AH
   pet,8,C

Daniel *- see -* Didn't My Lord
  Deliver Daniel
Daniel Daniel Servant of the Lord
   pet,56,C
Daniel Saw the Stone (1)
  "Daniel saw the stone rolling..."
   det1,9,A
   det5,54,A
   joh1,162,A
   jon,91,E
   pet,115,C
   rel,157,A
   san,31,F

Daniel Saw the Stone (2)
   "Daniel saw the stone hewn out
   of the mountain..."
      pet,209,C
Daniel's in the Lion's Den
      bal,42,A
      mci,77,AH
      pet,160,C
Danville Chariot
      arm,183,A
      fen,11,A
      pet,161,C
      rel,11,A
Dark Was the Night
      cou,251,E
Day I Left My Home
      odu,259,CH
Day of Judgment
      all,53,E
      pet,267,C
Death Ain't Nothing But a Robber
      pet,8,C
Death Come to My House He
   Didn't Stay Long
      joh1,108,A
      pet,384,C
Death Is in This Land
      odu,109,CH
Death's Going to Lay His Cold Icy
Hands on Me (1)
   "Cryin' oh Lord cryin'..."
      joh1,96,A
      johg,35,A
      new,186,C
      pet,385,C
Death's Going to Lay His Cold Icy
Hands on Me (2)
   "Death t'row thy sting away..."
      mci,73,AH
      pet,385,C
Death's Going to Lay His Cold Icy
Hands on Me (3)
   "Death is going to lay his cold
   icy hands on me..."
      bal,75,E

joh1,93,A
      pet,161,C
Deep River
      and,3,A
      blo,208,B
      bry,27,E
      bur,11,A
      bur2,74,A
      cha,19,A
      cle,115,A
      det5,167,E
      fis,20,AH
      fis1,2,A
      hay,24,AH
      joh,100,A
      lom,594,E
      new,30,E
      pet,162,C
      san,32,F
      tob,20,E
      whi,124,A
Did You Hear How They Crucified
   My Lord
      det5,104,E
      rel,141,A
Did You Hear My Jesus
      arm,230,A
      fen,58,A
      pet,346,C
      rel,58,A
Did You Hear When Jesus Rose
      afr,23,A
      hay,123,AH
      new,185,C
      pet,383,C
Didn't It Rain (1)
   "Didn't it rain some fo'ty nights
   an' days..."
      bur2,26,A
      hal,6,A
      new,177,C
      pet,287,C
Didn't It Rain (2)
   "Didn't it rain oh didn't it rain..."
      pet,287,C

Didn't It Rain (3)
  "Didn't it rain children..."
    lan,2,D
    lom1,477,D
    pet,267,C
Didn't My Lord Deliver Daniel
    blo,208,B
    bro,3,A
    bry,17,E
    bur2,184,A
    cha,23,A
    cle,106,D
    hay,45,AH
    jac,73,A
    joh,148,A
    jon,158,E
    lan,16,D
    naa,5,D
    new,78,E
    pet,162,C
    san,33,F
    sew,16,E
Didn't Old Pharaoh Get Lost
    joh,60,A
    pet,210,C
    sew,64,A
Didn't You Hear
    cou,241,E
Die in the Field
    joh,68,A
    pet,115,C
Dig Deep Children
    log,33,E
Divers Never Gave Nothing to
  the Poor
    ken1,51,CH
Dives and Lazarus
    lom,583,E
Do Don't Touch My Garment Good
  Lord
    bal,8,A
    joh1,68,A
    pet,211,C
Do Don't You Weep for the Baby
    fis,30,AH

new,177,C
    pet,8,C
Do Lord Remember Me
    blo,208,B
    cle,119,D
    gri,68,E
    jac,69,A
    lit,11,A
    mci,82,AH
    mci,186,AH
    naa,6,D
    new,38,C
    odu,92,CH
    pet,9,C
    pet,57,C
Do What the Spirit Say Do
    naa,38,D
Does You Call That Religion
    nil,2,AH
Done Been Sanctified
    bar,31,E
Done Carry de Key an' Gone - *see* -
  Too Late
Done Found My Lost Sheep
    hal,10,A
    joh,167,A
    pet,57,C
Done Found the Way at Last
    mci,92,AH
    pet,58,C
Done Made My Vow to the Lord
    jac,42,A
    naa,7,D
    pet,346,C
Done Written Down My Name
    johg1,22,A
Don't Be Weary Traveler
    all,75,E
    bur2,18,A
    det5,113,E
    fis,32,AH
    new,39,C
    pet,308,C
    rel,127,A

Don't Call the Roll
    det1,19,A
    det5,119,A
    pet,163,C
    rel,150,A
Don't Come Oh Lord
    log,27,E
Don't Get Weary
    bal,87,E
    det5,114,A
    new,129,C
    pet,58,C
Don't Leave Me Lord
    det5,31,E
    new,130,C
    pet,58,C
    rel,117,A
Don't Let the Wind Blow Here No
More
    bal,39,A
    pet,267,C
Don't You Grieve After Me (1)
    "Who is that a-coming..."
    pet,59,C
Don't You Grieve After Me (2)
    "When I'm dead and buried don't
you grieve after me..."
    mci,91,AH
    pet,116,C
Don't You Grieve for Me
  - see - Angel's Waiting at
the Door
Don't You Have Everybody for
Your Friend
    bal,71,E
    pet,347,C
Don't You Hear the Lambs - see -
Hear the Lamb's Crying
Don't You Let Nobody Turn You
Around
    johg,10,A
    naa,8,D
    new,74,C
    pet,59,C
    whi,60,A

Don't You See - see - I Got a Home
in That Rock
Don't You View That Ship Come
Sailing
    arm,226,A
    det5,220,A
    fen,54,A
    pet,163,C
    rel,54,A
Don't You Want to Go
    bar,31,E
Don't You Weep After Me
    blo,208,B
    see also - Mother Don't
      You Weep
Don't You Weep When I'm - see -
Mother Don't You Weep
Don't You Wish You Were in
Heaven
    mci,97,AH
    pet,385,C
Down By the River (1)
    "We'll wait till Jesus comes..."
    pet,116,C
Down By the River (2)
    "When Christ the Lord was here
below..."
    det5,55,A
    naa,9,D
    pet,211,C
    rel,167,A
Down By the River (3)
    "Yes we'll gain this world..."
    bar,13,E
Down By the Riverside
    jac,43,A
    new,75,C
    pet,163,C
Down in Hell
    det3,24,A
Down in the Valley to Pray
    bar,4,E
Down on Me
    new,39,C
    pet,10,C

worj2,10,A
Downward Road
    lom1,485,D
Downward Road Is Crowded (1)
    "Downward road is crowded with
    unbelievin' souls..."
        det5,14,A
        new,178,C
        odu,73,CH
        pet,10,C
        rel,119,A
Downward Road Is Crowded (2)
    "Downward road is crowded
    crowded the wind blows east..."
        pet,347,C
Drinking of the Wine
    odu,136,CH
Drive Satan Away
    hal,70,E
    pet,309,C
Dry Bones
    cha,26,A
    hay,34,AH
    ken,53,AH
    new,131,C
    pet,348,C
Dry Bones Going to Rise
    mci,62,AH
    odu,102,CH
    pet,309,C
Dum-A-Lum
    hal,9,A
    pet,386,C
Dust and Ashes
    arm,251,A
    bal,92,E
    det5,213,A
    fen,79,A
    rel,79,A

Eagle's Wings
    bal,38,A
    pet,386,C

Early in the Morning
    all,44,E
    new,132,C
    odu,260,CH
    pet,60,C
Elder You Say You Love King
Jesus
    san,34,F
Elijah Rock
    pet,60,C
End of That Morning
    hal,25,A
Enlisted in the Field of Battle
    hal,32,A
    pet,133,C
Enlisted Soldiers
    det5,180,A
    pet,117,C
    rel,145,A
Even Me
    cle,174,A
Every Day
    odu,119,CH
Every Day Will Be Sunday
    pet,164,C
Every Hour in the Day
    all,58,E
    pet,10,C
Every Little Step Goes Higher
    dit,47,A
    pet,387,C
Every Time I Feel the Spirit
    and,22,A
    bal,88,E
    bur,6,A
    bur2,5,A
    cha,32,A
    cle,121,D
    det5,169,A
    dit,10,A
    fis,39,AH
    fis1,6,A

jac,44,A
joh,142,A
johg1,78,A
new,179,C
pet,309,C
rel,169,A
whi,38,A
Everybody Got to Die
cha,31,A
Everybody Wants to Know Just
How I Die
bal,22,E
pet,348,C
Everywhere I Go My Lord
cou,247,E
Ezekiel Said Here Was a Wheel in a
Wheel
dit,42,A
pet,11,C
Ezekiel Saw the Wheel (1)
"Wheel oh wheel..."
joh1,144,A
new,40,C
Ezekiel Saw the Wheel (2)
"Ezekiel saw the wheel way up in
the middle of the air..."
and,10,A
cle,84,A
det5,60,A
hay,26,AH
lan,14,D
pet,387,C
rel,164,A
san,35,F
whi,85,A
Ezekiel's Wheel
gri,32,E
pet,388,C

Faint Not
lud,13,A
Fairest Lord Jesus
naa,30,D
Faith of Our Fathers
naa,31,D

Fare Ye Well
all,47,E
new,40,C
pet,310,C
Farewell My Brother
new,76,C
pet,164,C
Farewell My Dear Mother
worj1,52,CH
Father Abraham
det3,28,A
joh,144,A
mci,93,AH
pet,348,C
Fighting On
fen,93,A
new,76,C
pet,118,C
rel,93,A
Fisherman Peter
dit,37,A
Five of Them Were Wise - *see* -
There Were Ten Virgins
Fix Me Jesus
bal,83,A
cle,122,A
dit,45,A
new,41,C
pet,310,C
Fly to My Jesus' Arms
lud,3,A
Fold My Hands and Tie My Feet
log,14,E
Footprints of Jesus
cle,200,A
For I Ain't Going to Die No More
par,190,C
For My Lord
odu,90,CH
For the Lord
hal,42,A
pet,164,C
Forty Days and Nights
odu,127,CH

Four and Twenty Elders
    det5,71,A
    pet,249,C
    rel,105,A
    tob,17,E
Foxes Have Holes in the Ground
    san,127,F
Free at Last
    bry,21,E
    cle,80,A
    gla,49,D
    jac,51,A
    joh1,158,A
    ken,38,E
    mci,95,AH
    naa,10,D
    new,77,C
    pet,212,C
    pet,228,C
    worj1,46,CH
Free Free My Lord
    odu,68,CH
Freedom Train Coming
    cle,92,D
From Every Graveyard
    pet,268,C
    sew,12,A
Funeral Chant
    dit,38,E

Gabriel's Trumpet Going to Blow
    pet,268,C
Galman Day
    log,29,E
Gambler Get Up Off of Your Knees
    joh,122,A
    pet,287,C
General Roll
    pet,212,C
    sew,53,E
General Roll Call
    det5,166,A
    fen,91,A
    pet,349,C
    rel,91,A

General Roll Call - *see also* -
    When the General Roll is Called
Get in the Union
    odu,85,CH
Get on Board Little Children
    and,12,A
    bur,34,A
    bur2,115,A
    bry1,25,D
    cha,21,A
    cle,116,A
    det5,131,A
    joh,126,A
    pet,171,C
    rel,134,A
    tob,28,E
Get on Board Old Ship of Zion
    ken1,141,CH
Get on the Boat Little Children
    mci,69,AH
    pet,60,C
Get on the Evening Train
    bar,33,E
Get Your Ticket
    gri,48,E
    pet,272,C
Getting Ready to Die
    pet,213,C
    san,38,F
    sew,53,E
Gideon's Band
    fen,70,AH
    pet,165,C
    rel,70,A
Gift of God Is Eternal Life
    mci,81,AH
    pet,61,C
Give Me a Clean Heart
    cle,182,A
Give Me Jesus
    bur2,30,A
    cha,36,A
    cle,165,A
    fis,46,AH
    jac,117,A

joh,160,A
mci,102,AH
pet,61,C
sew,19,E
worf,40,A
Give Me Jesus When I Die
mci,115,AH
pet,62,C
Give Me That Old Time Religion
- *see* - Old Time Religion
Give Me the Wings
worj2,14,A
Give Me Your Hand
det1,14,A
joh1,86,A
pet,63,C
Give Up the World (1)
"Sun give a light in the heaven
all around..."
all,27,E
pet,166,C
Give Up the World (2)
"My brother won't you give up
the world..."
hal,73,E
new,179,C
pet,311,C
Give Way Jordan
det5,96,A
fen,23,A
hay,38,AH
pet,138,C
pet,165,C
rel,23,A
Glad I Got Religion
odu,70,CH
Glory and Honor (1)
"Got glory an' honor praise
Jesus..."
mci,104,AH
pet,63,C
Glory and Honor (2)
"Live humble humble humble
yourselves..."

fen,87,A
pet,349,C
rel,87,A
see also - Live Humble
Glory Glory Hallelujah
bal,53,A
cle,98,D
johg1,76,A
Glory Hallelujah to the New-Born
King
johg1,80,A
Glow Within
cha,121,A
Go and I Go With You
odu,135,CH
Go Chain the Lion Down (1)
"Go chain the lion down before
the heaven doors close..."
pet,118,C
sew,59,E
Go Chain the Lion Down (2)
"Go chain the lion down..."
pet,166,C
Go Down Death
ken,60,AH
Go Down in the Valley and Pray
pet,350,C
Go Down Moses
and,13,A
bry,13,E
bur2,42,A
cha,38,A
cle,112,A
cle,212,A
det1,15,A
det5,108,A
fis,99,AH
gla,23,D
hay,22,AH
jac,107,A
joh,51,A
johg,25,A
lan,8,D
lom2,464,AH
mci,235,AH

naa,11,D
new,68,A
pet,166,C
rel,153,A
san,145,F
sew,22,A
tob,31,E
whi,75,A
Go Elijah
　　log,22,E
Go in the Wilderness
　　all,14,E
　　pet,168,C
Go Mary and Toll the Bell (1)
　　"Go Mary and toll the bell who's
　　all them come dressed in
　　white..."
　　　　det5,153,A
　　　　hal,14,A
　　　　lud,8,A
　　　　new,180,C
　　　　pet,215,C
　　　　rel,113,A
Go Mary and Toll the Bell (2)
　　"Go Mary an' toll the bell..."
　　　　pet,215,C
Go on Brother
　　det,8,A
Go Round Go Round
　　bal,27,E
　　pet,217,C
Go Tell It on the Mountain (1)
　　"Go tell it on the mountain..."
　　　　and,40,A
　　　　bap,82,A
　　　　cle,75,A
　　　　jac,29,A
　　　　naa,12,D
　　　　new,34,C
　　　　pet,217,C
Go Tell It on the Mountain (2)
　　"When I was a seeker I sought
　　both night and day..."
　　　　bal,90,E
　　　　bry,7,E

bur2,152,A
det1,25,A
det5,III,A
fis,56,AH
pet,351,C
rel,174,A
tob,15,E
God Be With You
　　cle,203,A
　　naa,31,D
God Don't Like It
　　lom3,28,E
God Has Smiled on Me
　　cle,196,D
God Is a God
　　cle,140,A
　　pet,63,C
God Knows It's Time
　　odu,71,CH
God Moves on the Water
　　lom3,26,E
God of Elijah
　　lud,10,A
God's Amazing Grace
　　cle,195,A
God's Going to Set This World on
Fire
　　new,77,C
　　pet,269,C
God's Going to Straighten Them
　　pet,268,C
　　worj,230,A
God's Going to Trouble the Water
　　- see - Wade in the Water
God's Going Wake Up the Dead
　　odu,75,CH
God's Got Plenty of Room - see -
Plenty Good Room (1)
Going Away to See My Lord
　　mci,65,AH
　　pet,388,C
Going Down to Jordan
　　odu,124,CH
Going Home in the Chariot
　　pet,213,C

Going Lay Down My Life for My
  Lord
          odu,91,CH
Going Over on the Other Side of
  Jordan
          bar,5,E
Going to Follow
          all,18,E
          pet,350,C
Going to Heaven
          det5,152,A
          fen,92,A
          pet,311,C
          rel,92,A
Going to Hold Out to the End
          worf,27,A
Going to Live Humble to the Lord
          det5,6,A
          rel,135,A
Going to Outshine the Sun
          odu,109,CH
Going to Pull My War Clothes
          dit,24,A
          pet,118,C
Going to Quit All of My Worldly
  Ways
          hal,69,E
          pet,350,C
Going to Ride Up in the Chariot
          bro,10,A
          joh1,121,A
          pet,167,C
          pet,389,C
          san,39,F
          sew,20,E
Going to Roll in My Jesus' Arms
          hal,5,A
          pet,312,C
          whi,32,A
Going to Set Down and Rest
  Awhile
          fis,49,AH
          new,83,C
          pet,65,C

Going to Shout All Over God's
  Heaven
          and,17,A
          bur2,79,A
          cha,47,A
          cle,82,A
          det5,126,A
          fis,41,AH
          fis1,8,A
          hal,58,E
          hay,70,AH
          joh,71,A
          ken,155,AH
          new,133,C
          pet,213,C
          rel,168,A
          san,62,F
          whi,20,A
          worj1,48,CH
Going to Sing All Along the Way
          joh,128,A
          pet,214,C
Going to Write to Master Jesus
          san,40,F
Going Up
          arm,216,A
          cle,181,D
          det5,34,A
          fen,44,A
          joh,118,A
          pet,389,C
          rel,44,A
Gold Band
          all,83,E
          pet,269,C
Golden Altar
          all,77,E
          pet,65,C
Gone Along
          bar,8,E
Good Bye
          all,52,E
          new,221,C
          pet,169,C

Good Bye Brother
"Good bye brother good bye
brother..."
all,47,E
pet,65,C
Good Bye Brothers
"Good bye brothers good bye
sisters..."
new,135,C
pet,66,C
san,41,F
Good Bye City of Babylon
ken1,12,E
Good Bye Mother
lom,592,E
Good Lord Done Been Here
ken1,28,CH
mci,55,AH
pet,66,C
Good Lord I Done Good
pet,350,C
Good Lord Shall I Be the One
hal,48,A
new,134,C
pet,169,C
Good Lord Shall I Ever Be the One
det5,32,E
pet,351,C
rel,123,A
Good Lord When I Die
worj1,63,CH
Good Morning Everybody
pet,216,C
worf,3,A
Good News
hay,79,AH
pet,216,C
Good News Angels Bring the
Tidings
bal,10,A
san,42,F
Good News in the Kingdom
and,14,A
Good News Member
all,97,E

pet,216,C
Good News the Chariot's Coming
and,15,A
arm,224,A
cle,124,A
det5,90,A
fen,52,A
pet,169,C
rel,52,A
san,43,F
worj1,49,CH
Good Old Chariot - see - Tell My
Jesus Morning
Good Old Chariot Swing So - see -
Swing Low Sweet Chariot
Good Old Way
all,84,E
pet,313,C
sew,42,E
Gospel Train
fis,52,AH
gla,18,D
johg1,74,A
ken1,40,CH
mci,107,AH
new,118,A
odu,113,CH
pet,170,C
san,129,F
sew,36,A
see also - Get on
Board Little Children
Got a Home at Last
jes,74,AH
Got Glory and Honor
ken1,73,AH
Got My Letter
pet,313,C
worj,224,A
Got Religion All Around the
- see - Christians Hold Up Your
Heads
Got to Go to Judgement
pet,269,C

Grace Before Meat at Hampton
>det5,179,A
>rel,143,A
Grade Song
>odu,252,CH
Graveyard
>all,15,E
>new,138,C
>pet,11,C
Great Big Stars
>bry1,45,D
Great Camp Meeting - *see* - Walk
Together Children
Great Day
>cle,142,A
>joh1,56,A
>johg1,14,A
>naa,16,D
>new,84,C
>pet,119,C
Great Day for Me
>cou,17,D
Great Gittin' Up Mornin' - *see* - In
That Great Getting Up Morning
Great Judgment Day
>odu,99,CH
Green Trees
>and,44,A
Grey Goose
>and,45,E
Guide My Head
>pet,172,C

Hail Hail Hail
>arm,177,A
>det5,185,A
>fen,4,A
>pet,218,C
>rel,5,A
Hail John's Army Bend Down and
Died
>mci,99,AH
>pet,172,C
Hail Mary
>all,45,E

>pet,119,C
Hail Sinners Hail-lo
>log,16,E
Hail the Crown
>fis,68,AH
>kre,158,A
>pet,351,C
Hail the King of Babylon
>johg,34,A
Half Has Never Been Told
>ken1,37,CH
Hallelu
>worj,225,A
Hallelu Hallelu
>all,50,E
>pet,218,C
Halleluiah to the Lamb
>mci,110,AH
Hallelujah (1)
"Hallelujah hallelujah..."
>pet,218,C
>worf,47,A
Hallelujah (2)
"Hallelujah an'a hallelujah..."
>joh,172,A
>johg,8,A
>pet,313,C
Hallelujah King Jesus
>johg,39,A
Hallelujah to the Lamb
>pet,270,C
Hammer Keeps Ringing
>pet,12,C
Hammering
>pet,12,C
Hammering Judgment
>hal,60,E
>pet,270,C
Hand Me Down My Silver Trumpet
>and,47,A
>pet,389,C
Handwriting on the Wall - *see* -
There's a Handwriting on the
Wall

Hanging Over Hell
　odu,88,CH
Happy Morning
　all,10,E
　pet,219,C
　pet,67,C
Hard to Rise Again
　bar,11,E
Hard Trials (1)
"Foxes they have holes in the
ground..."
　arm,213,A
　cle,107,E
　det5,222,A
　fen,41,A
　lom,600,E
　new,139,C
　pet,12,C
　rel,41,A
Hard Trials (2)
"Ain't that hard trials..."
　mci,105,AH
　pet,352,C
Hard Trials (3)
"Been a lis'nin' all de night
long..."
　bur2,157,A
Has Anybody Here Seen My Lord
　fis,63,AH
　pet,173,C
Have You Got Good Religion
　jac,120,A
He Arose
　jac,40,A
　see also - Jews Killed
　Poor Jesus
He Is King of Kings
　det5,146,A
　jac,79,A
　pet,220,C
　rel,99,A
　worj,218,A
　worj1,68,CH
He Is the Lord of Lords
　det5,151,A

fen,96,A
　san,147,F
He Is Waiting
　odu,83,CH
He Knows Just How Much We
Can Bear
　cle,202,A
He Locked the Lion's Jaw
　lud,5,A
He Never Said a Mumbling Word
　cha,39,A
　cle,101,D
　det2,21,A
　fis,1,AH
　hay,121,AH
　jac,34,A
　joh,174,A
　ken,126,AH
　lom,587,E
　lom2,448,AH
　new,181,C
　par,165,CH
　pet,15,C
He Raised Poor Lazarus
　det5,66,A
　pet,69,C
　rel,116,A
He Rose From the Dead
　cle,168,A
　pet,221,C
　san,45,F
Heal Me Jesus
　odu,139,CH
Healing Waters
　lom,581,E
Hear Gabriel Blow in That Morn
　hal,45,E
　pet,271,C
Hear Me Praying
　joh1,166,A
　pet,352,C
　pet,366,C
Hear the Angels Singing
　arm,246,A
　det5,206,A

fen,74,A
pet,219,C
rel,74,A

Hear the Lamb's Crying
arm,210,A
bal,30,E
bro,8,A
cle,128,A
hay,110,AH
jon,359,E
pet,9,C
pet,13,C
san,149,F

Hear the Lambs Crying
bur2,167,A
det5,224,A
fen,38,A
rel,38,A

Heave-A-Hora
odu,265,CH

Heave Away
all,61,E

Heaven
odu,98,CH

Heaven Bell Ring
all,20,E
pet,271,C

Heaven Bells
all,79,E
pet,272,C

Heaven Bells Ringing and I'm
Going Home
bar,20,E

Heaven Bells Ringing in My Soul
bar,10,E
fis,70,AH
pet,14,C

Heaven-Bound Soldier
joh,54,A
pet,353,C

Heaven Is a Beautiful Place (1)
"Heaven is a beautiful place I
believe..."
bal,16,A
pet,68,C

Heaven Is a Beautiful Place (2)
"Heaven is a beautiful place I
know..."
gri,22,E
pet,68,C

Heaven Is Going to Be My Home
bal,55,A
pet,353,C

Heaven Is Shining
arm,219,A
det5,94,A
fen,47,A
mci,109,AH
pet,220,C
pet,238,C
rel,47,A

Hell and Heaven
lom,588,E

He'll Understand and Say Well
Done
cle,178,A
naa,39,D

He's a Mighty Good Leader
pet,69,C
worj,231,A

He's Got His Eyes on You
pet,272,C

He's Got the Whole World in His
Hands
and,36,E
bry,19,E
bry1,29,D
cle,85,A
naa,14,D
pet,69,C

He's Just the Same Today
bur2,106,A
cha,40,A
hal,30,A
joh,80,A
pet,70,C

He's the Lily of the Valley
det5,145,A
fis,74,AH
gri,96,E

new,42,A
pet,70,C
pet,71,C
san,47,F
sew,48,A
He's the Lord of Lords
pet,313,C
rel,96,A
sew,33,A
Hide Me
gri,66,E
pet,273,C
Hint to the Wise
odu,257,CH
His Eye Is on the Sparrow
jac,3,A
His Love Comes Trickling Down
log,31,E
His Name So Sweet
cle,90,A
Ho Every One That Thirsts
det4,16,A
Ho-Ho
odu,261,CH
Hold On
cle,86,A
nil,8,AH
pet,173,C
Hold Out
bal,66,A
pet,120,C
Hold Out to the End (1)
"I'm goin' t' hol' out to de en'..."
mci,112,AH
pet,120,C
Hold Out to the End (2)
"All them Mount Zion
member..."
all,57,E
pet,120,C
Hold Out Your Light
hal,37,A
pet,390,C
Hold the Wind Don't Let It Blow
joh1,178,A

lom1,474,D
pet,121,C
pet,121,C
Hold Your Light
all,10,E
pet,121,C
Holy Baby
lom1,482,D
Holy Bible
new,176,C
pet,16,C
worf,6,A
Holy Holy You Promised to
Answer Prayer
bal,14,A
dit,8,A
new,84,C
pet,16,C
Holy Is My God
hal,44,A
pet,314,C
Hope I Join the Band
mci,117,AH
pet,71,C
Hour is Come
lud,6,A
House That's Built Without Hands
mci,114,AH
pet,72,C
How Can I Pray
bal,18,A
pet,314,C
san,48,F
How I Got Over
cle,188,A
How Long
new,141,C
pet,16,C
How Long Has the Train Been
Gone
bal,12,A
johg1,17,A
pet,174,C
whi,54,A

How Long Watchman
    bar,36,E
How You Do Believer
    bal,75,A
    pet,390,C
Howdy Howdy
    bar,4,E
Humble
    pet,315,C
Humble Yourself the Bell Done
  Ring
    joh1,183,A
    pet,274,C
Hunting for a City
    all,18,E
    pet,174,C
Hunting for the Lord
    all,13,E
    pet,122,C
Hush Hush Somebody's - see -
  Hush Somebody's Calling My
  Name
Hush Somebody's Calling My
  Name
    cle,100,D
    new,166,C
    pet,292,C
    san,49,F
Hymn
    lud,11,A
Hymn to Parnassus
    det,10,A
Hypocrite and the Concubine
    new,185,C
    pet,221,C

I Ain't Going to Die No More
    pet,221,C
    san,89,F
    sew,57,E
I Ain't Going to Grieve My Lord
  No More
    bal,64,A
    dit,14,A
    new,140,C

    pet,353,C
I Ain't Going to Study War No
  More
    and,37,A
    bur2,68,A
    cha,12,A
    cle,138,A
    det3,29,A
    fis,60,AH
    odu,101,CH
    pet,214,C
    pet,252,C
    tob,22,E
I Ain't Going to Trust Nobody
    mci,118,AH
    pet,275,C
I Ain't Got Weary Yet
    pet,122,C
I Am Bound for the Promised Land
    bal,36,A
    new,85,C
    pet,222,C
I Am Coming to a King
    ken1,36,CH
I Am Free
    mci,124,AH
    new,86,C
    pet,122,C
I Am Going Over There
    bal,54,A
    pet,226,C
I Am Going to Join in This Army
    det5,120,A
    pet,354,C
    rel,128,A
I Am Hunting for a City
    bal,48,A
    pet,174,C
I Am Not Afraid to Die
    bal,68,A
    new,44,C
    pet,72,C
I Am Seeking for a City
    arm,228,A
    bur2,129,A

det2,17,A
det5,36,A
fen,56,A
johg,28,A
pet,123,C
rel,56,A
san,51,F
see also - I Don't Feel No
   Ways Tired
I Am the Light of the World
   odu,64,CH
I Am the True Vine
   pet,315,C
I Am the Truth and the Light
   mci,120,AH
   pet,222,C
I and Satan Had a Race
   all,40,E
   pet,122,C
I Believe I'll Go Back Home
   gri,36,E
   pet,316,C
I Believe This Is Jesus
   pet,72,C
I Belong to the Union Band
   det3,23,A
I Cannot Stay Here By Myself
   new,97,C
   odu,115,CH
   pet,27,C
   see also - Lord I Cannot
     Stay Here By Myself
I Can't Stand the Fire
   all,42,E
   new,186,C
   pet,17,C
I Can't Stay Away
   jes,65,AH
   johg,32,A
   mci,133,AH
   new,142,C
   pet,73,C
I Can't Stay Behind (1)
   "I can't stay behind there's room
   enough in the heaven..."

all,6,E
pet,123,C
I Can't Stay Behind (2)
   "I can't stay behind the roses
   bloom ..."
   dit,49,A
   pet,175,C
I Come This Night
   san,53,F
I Couldn't Hear Nobody Pray
   and,9,A
   bur,30,A
   bur2,83,A
   cha,42,A
   cle,78,A
   det5,202,A
   det5,X,A
   jac,54,A
   joh,89,A
   johg1,30,A
   lom1,473,D
   new,184,C
   pet,17,C
   rel,160,A
   san,22,F
   worj1,24,AH
   worj1,51,CH
I Do Know God Don't Lie
   bal,72,E
   pet,73,C
I Do Love the Lamb
   log,15,E
I Done Been Home
   hal,43,A
   pet,390,C
I Done Done - *see* - I Done What
   You Told Me to Do
I Done What You Told Me to Do
   det1,24,A
   hal,21,A
   joh,180,A
   pet,280,C
   pet,354,C
I Don't Care for Riches
   odu,108,CH

I Don't Care What the World
  May Do
      cle,176,A
I Don't Feel No-Ways Tired
      cle,175,A
      see also -- I Am Seeking
          for a City
I Don't Feel Weary
      all,70,E
      pet,124,C
I Don't Want to Stay Here No
  Longer
      bur1,3,A
      det5,38,A
      san,107,F
I Don't Want You Go on and Leave
  Me
      bar,23,E
I Feel Like Dying in This Army
      mci,131,AH
      pet,354,C
I Feel Like My Time Ain't
  Long (1)
  "Went to the graveyard the
  other day..."
      joh1,174,A
      lom3,31,E
      new,44,C
      pet,18,C
I Feel Like My Time Ain't
  Long (2)
  "I feel like I feel like my time
  ain't long..."
      cle,148,A
      pet,275,C
I Fold Up My Arms and I Wonder
      ken,111,AH
I Found Jesus Over in Zion
      gri,88,E
      pet,391,C
I Going Put on My Golden Shoes
      odu,107,CH
I Going Try the Air
      odu,106,CH

I Got a Hiding Place
      gri,90,E
      pet,391,C
I Got a Home
      odu,95,CH
I Got a Home in That Rock
      bur2,21,A
      cha,44,A
      dit,16,A
      joh,96,A
      ken,88,AH
      pet,73,C
      pet,395,C
      whi,104,A
      worj2,15,A
      tob,8,E
I Got a Key to the Kingdom
      gri,98,E
      pet,393,C
I Got a Letter This Morning
      bal,27,E
      pet,222,C
I Got a Light
      det1,3,A
I Got a Mother in the Bright
  Shining World
      bal,76,A
      new,187,C
      pet,74,C
I Got a New Name
      new,45,C
      pet,317,C
I Got a Robe - *see* - Going to
  Shout All Over God's Heaven
I Got My Religion on the Way
      mci,149,AH
      pet,223,C
I Got My Sword in My Hand
      gri,65,E
      pet,124,C
I Got Shoes
      bry,9,E
      det3,14,A
I Got to Lay in Yonder Graveyard
      par,196,C

I Got Two Wings - *see* - Two
Wings
I Have a Leader Over There
bal,24,E
pet,318,C
I Have Another Building
new,143,C
pet,75,C
worf,26,A
worj1,61,CH
see also - I Know I Have
Another Building
I Heard a Voice Couldn't Tell
Where
mci,135,AH
pet,355,C
I Heard From Heaven Today
all,2,E
pet,223,C
see also - Peter Go Ring
Them Bells
I Heard of a City Called Heaven
whi,118,A
I Heard the Angels Singing
odu,140,CH
par,140,E
I Heard the Preaching of the Elder
det5,62,A
joh1,90,A
pet,355,C
worf,33,A
I Hope I'll Join the Band
worj1,63,CH
I Hope My Mother Will Be There
arm,218,A
det1,13,A
det3,19,A
det5,130,A
fen,46,AH
pet,75,C
rel,46,A
I Know de Udder Worl' Is Not
- *see* - Run Mary Run
I Know I Have Another Building
whi,16,A

see also - I Have Another
Building
I Know I Would Like to Read
det5,40,A
new,90,C
pet,176,C
rel,148,A
I Know My Jesus Loves Me
hal,36,A
pet,223,C
I Know My Road Is Rough and
Rocky
worj2,8,A
I Know My Time Ain't Long
odu,119,CH
I Know That My Redeemer Lives
pet,75,C
I Know the Lord
and,18,A
I Know the Lord Has Laid His
Hands on Me
bur2,90,A
cle,166,A
det1,29,A
det5,207,A
fis,76,AH
hal,74,A
jac,103,A
joh1,164,A
new,48,C
pet,356,C
rel,166,A
san,96,F
worf,7,A
worj1,64,CH
I Know When I'm Going Home
all,30,E
pet,125,C
I Look for Jesus All My Days
odu,79,CH
I Love Everybody
cou,27,E
I Love My Blessed Savior
bal,78,E
pet,18,C

I Love the Lord
  pet,125,C
I Mean to Lift Up the Standard for
  My King
  gri,30,E
  pet,394,C
I Must Walk My Lonesome - *see* -
  Lonesome Valley
I Never Felt Such Love in My Soul
  Before
  pet,357,C
I Never Intend to Die in Egypt Land
  hal,66,A
  pet,128,C
I Saw the Beam in my Sister's Eye
  all,17,E
  new,188,C
  pet,358,C
I Saw the Light
  whi,94,A
I Shall Not Be Moved
  jac,110,A
I Stood on the River of Jordan
  bry1,24,D
  bur2,95,A
  cle,149,D
I Stood Outside the Gate
  gri,76,E
  pet,22,C
I Thank God I'm Free at Last - *see* -
  Free at Last
I Thought I Had a Friend
  odu,250,CH
I Want God's Heaven to Be Mine
  joh1,88,A
  pet,358,C
I Want Jesus to Walk With Me
  cle,95,A
  jac,17,A
I Want to Be a Christian - *see* -
  Lord I Want to Be a Christian
I Want to Be Ready
  and,21,A
  blo,212,B
  bur2,195,A

  cha,50,A
  cle,151,A
  det1,30,A
  det5,33,A
  jac,81,A
  johg,18,A
  naa,16,D
  pet,230,C
  rel,163,A
  san,64,F
  tob,6,E
  whi,116,A
  see also - Walk in
    Jerusalem Just Like
    John
I Want to Climb Up Jacob's - *see* -
  Jacob's Ladder
I Want to Die Easy When I Die
  and,39,E
  bal,20,E
  joh1,46,A
I Want to Die Like Lazarus
  all,98,E
  new,189,C
  pet,321,C
I Want to Die Shouting
  bar,12,E
I Want to Go Home
  all,46,E
  new,91,C
  pet,24,C
I Want to Go Where Jesus Is
  bar,13,E
I Want to Join the Band
  all,95,E
  pet,178,C
I Want to Live So God Can
  Use Me
  gri,62,E
  pet,320,C
I Want to See Jesus in the Morning
  mci,144,AH
  new,150,C
  pet,321,C

I Went to the Hillside
    san,65,F
I Will Be There in the Morning
 - *see* - I'll Be There in the
 Morning
I Will Overcome
    new,49,C
    pet,178,C
I Will Pray
    pet,322,C
I Will Sleep Away
    log,28,E
I Wish I Been There
    all,29,E
    pet,132,C
I Wish I Had Been There - *see* - I
 Wish I Been There
I Wish I Had Died in Egypt Land
    pet,24,C
    worf,32,A
I Wish I Have Had an Eagle's
 Wings
    dit,6,A
    pet,396,C
I Won't Die No More
    mci,142,AH
    pet,396,C
I Won't Stop Praying
    pet,132,C
I Would Like to Read - *see* - I
 Know I Would Like to Read
If Anybody Ask You Who I Am
    ken,45,E
If I Got My Ticket Can I Ride
 - *see* - If I Got My Ticket Lord
If I Got My Ticket Lord
    lom3,32,E
    pet,175,C
If I Had a Hammer
    naa,40,D
If I Had Died When I Was a Babe
    det4,20,A
If I Have My Ticket Lord
    gri,82,E
    pet,276,C

If I Keep Praying On
    odu,98,CH
If I Was a Mourner
    odu,73,CH
If the Lord Calls You
    log,21,E
If You Ask Him
    cle,186,A
If You Can't Come Send One
 Angel Down - *see* - Send One
 Angel Down
If You Don't Like the Way I Work
    odu,256,CH
If You Love God Serve Him
    arm,178,A
    det5,8,A
    fen,6,A
    pet,235,C
    rel,6,A
If You Want to Get to Heaven
    det5,134,A
If You Want to See Jesus
    arm,184,A
    fen,13,AH
    new,50,C
    pet,317,C
    rel,12,A
    worf,42,A
I'll Be Sleeping in My Grave
    gri,24,E
    pet,276,C
I'll Be There
    bar,19,E
I'll Be There in the Morning
    det5,121,A
    fen,104,A
    pet,225,C
    rel,104,A
I'll Fly Away
    cle,183,A
I'll Hear the Trumpet Sound - *see* -
 You May Bury Me in the East
I'll Make Me a Man
    hay,17,AH
    pet,224,C

I'll Meet You Way Up Yonder
hal,18,A
pet,176,C
I'm a Child of Grace
whi,112,A
I'm a Poor Little Orphan
jes,50,AH
I'm A-Rolling - *see* - I'm
Rolling
I'm a Soldier in the Army of the
Lord
gri,60,E
mci,55,AH
pet,125,C
pet,130,C
I'm a Soldier in the Army of the
Lord - *see also* - In the Army of
the Lord
I'm a Soldier of the Cross
ken,146,AH
I'm All Wore Out Toiling for the
Lord
fis,84,AH
new,192,C
pet,19,C
I'm Almost Done Traveling
mci,137,AH
pet,76,C
I'm an Everyday Witness
gri,58,E
new,193,C
pet,393,C
I'm Crossing Jordan River
cou,258,A
I'm Going Back with Jesus
pet,176,C
I'm Going Down to the River of
Jordan
bal,82,E
pet,225,C
I'm Going Home
all,84,E
pet,126,C
I'm Going Home Children
lud,4,A

I'm Going Home on a Cloud
ken,65,AH
I'm Going to Do All I Can
pet,126,C
worj1,109,AH
I'm Going to Eat at the Welcome
Table
bry1,20,D
dit,22,A
jac,55,A
pet,76,C
I'm Going to Join the Band
bar,28,E
pet,356,C
worf,12,E
I'm Going to Join the Great
Association
arm,173,A
det5,122,A
fen,1,AH
new,160,C
pet,239,C
rel,1,A
san,56,F
I'm Going to Lay Down My Life
for My Lord
worf,36,A
I'm Going to Live With Jesus
pet,76,C
sew,58,E
I'm Going to See My Loving
Father When I Get Home
bal,21,E
pet,226,C
I'm Going to Sing
and,30,E
bar,27,E
bry1,37,D
cle,81,A
pet,226,C
san,97,F
worj,226,A
I'm Going to Sit at the Welcome
Table
new,112,C

tob,35,E

I'm Going to Stay in the Battlefield
   mci,122,AH
   pet,126,C

I'm Going to Tell God All My
Troubles
   new,91,C
   pet,20,C

I'm Going to Wait Until the Holy
Ghost Comes
   bal,52,A
   pet,318,C

I'm Going to Walk With Jesus By
Myself
   bar,30,E

I'm Going Up to Heaven Anyhow
   joh1,126,A
   pet,127,C

I'm Going Where There Ain't No
More Dying
   mci,127,AH
   new,144,C
   pet,20,C

I'm in Trouble
   all,94,E
   new,196,C

I'm Just Going Over Jordan
   fis,88,AH

I'm Just Going Over There
   pet,395,C
   worj,221,A

I'm Mighty Tired
   fen,80,AH

I'm on My Journey Home
   odu,99,CH

I'm Rolling (1)
   "I'm a rolling I'm a rolling..."
   fis,86,AH
   pet,19,C
   rel,94,A
   sew,14,A

I'm Rolling (2)
   "I'm a-rollin thro an unfriendly
world..."
   and,19,A

cle,150,A
det5,185,A
fen,94,A
fis1,16,A
joh,145,A
new,36,A
sew,14,A

I'm Running for My Life
   bal,26,A
   new,92,C
   pet,127,C

I'm Running On
   gri,86,E
   pet,227,C

I'm So Glad (1)
   "I'm so glad the angels brought
the tidings down..."
   pet,356,C
   san,57,F

I'm So Glad (2)
   "I'm so glad done just got out of
that Egypt land..."
   mci,139,AH
   pet,177,C

I'm So Glad (3)
   "I'm so glad I'm so glad..."
   gla,17,D
   pet,227,C
   pet,318,C
   sew,40,A

I'm So Glad (4)
   "I am so glad I've been in the
grave and rose again..."
   worf,28,A

I'm So Glad Jesus Lifted Me
   jac,6,A

I'm So Glad Troubles Don't Last
Always
   det5,235,E
   whi,14,A

I'm Traveling to the Grave
   det,17,A
   det5,187,E
   fen,95,A
   pet,177,C

rel,95,A
sew,27,E
I'm Traveling to the Land
bal,63,A
pet,225,C
I'm Troubled in Mind (1)
"I'm troubled in mind..."
all,30,E
hay,69,AH
new,47,C
pet,21,C
I'm Troubled in Mind (2)
"I'm troubled I'm troubled..."
det5,236,E
fis,90,AH
joh,120,A
pet,76,C
san,58,F
sew,58,E
worj1,51,CH
I'm Working on the Building
new,195,C
pet,127,C
In Bright Mansions Above
det5,42,A
johg,9,A
pet,178,C
rel,124,A
san,59,F
worj1,62,CH
worj2,5,A
In God We Trust
cle,214,A
In His Hands - *see* - He's Got the
Whole World in His Hands
In My Heart
lud,17,A
In Some Lonesome Graveyard
par,193,AH
In That Beautiful World on High
- *see* - I Hope My Mother Will
Be There
In That Day
fis,96,AH
pet,277,C

In That Great Day
bar,43,E
In That Great Getting Up
Morning (1)
"In that great getting-up
morning..."
lom2,456,AH
pet,277,C
In That Great Getting Up
Morning (2)
"I'm going to tell you about the
coming of the Saviour..."
arm,235,A
det5,154,A
fen,63,AH
joh1,40,A
new,145,A
pet,278,C
rel,63,A
tob,10,E
In That Morning - *see* - You May
Bury Me in the East
In That Old Field
par,175,E
In the Army of the Lord
hal,54,A
new,194,C
pet,178,C
see also - I'm a Soldier in
the Army of the Lord
In the Kingdom
det5,92,A
pet,77,C
rel,108,A
In the Mansions Above
all,59,E
pet,131,C
In the Morning
mci,140,AH
odu,100,CH
pet,228,C
In the New Jerusalem
pet,228,C
In the River of Jordan
pet,319,C

pet,331,C
san,60,F
sew,38,A
see also - Pray On
In This Field
  gri,70,E
  pet,357,C
In This Land
  new,92,C
  pet,21,C
Inching Along - *see* - Keep Inching
  Along
Is It True
  ken1,45,CH
Is Massa Going to Sell Us - *see* -
  Mother Is Master Going to Sell
  Us Tomorrow
Is There Anybody Here
  bar,21,E
  bry,25,E
  det4,19,A
  pet,22,C
Is There Any Body Here Getting
  Ready to Die
  lud,9,A
Israelites Shouting
  cou,248,E
It Just Suits Me
  odu,121,CH
It May Be the Last Time
  gri,42,E
  pet,279,C
It's Getting Late in the Evening
  cou,234,E
It's Going to be a Mighty Day
  pet,289,C
  worj,232,A
It's Me O Lord - *see* - Standing in
  the Need of Prayer
It's Moving Day
  odu,250,CH

I've a Message From My Lord
  mci,146,AH
  pet,229,C
I've Been in the Storm So Long
  bur2,162,A
  cle,144,D
  fis,94,AH
  new,93,C
  pet,23,C
  worj2,3,A
I've Been Listening All Night Long
  arm,247,A
  bal,84,A
  det5,170,A
  fen,75,A
  mci,126,AH
  pet,5,C
  pet,17,C
  pet,23,C
  rel,108,A
  san,25,F
  sew,25,A
I've Been Rebuked
  cle,143,E
  jes,24,AH
  new,192,C
  pet,17,C
I've Been Redeemed
  pet,319,C
I've Been Toiling at the Hill
  det5,226,A
  pet,229,C
  rel,142,A
I've Been Trying to Live Humble
  dit,48,A
  new,51,C
  pet,358,C
I've Done What You Told Me
  - *see* - I Done What You Told Me
  to Do
I've Got a Home in the Rock Don't
  - *see* - I Got a Home in That
  Rock

I've Got a Mother in the Heaven
    det5,123,A
    new,149,C
    pet,77,C
    rel,137,A
I've Got a Robe - *see* - Going to
Shout All Over God's Heaven
I've Just Come From the Fountain
    jac,98,A
    pet,319,C
    san,63,F
    sew,18,A

Jacob's Ladder (1)
"We are climbing Jacob's
ladder..."
    and,5,D
    bap,147,A
    bry,11,E
    cle,205,A
    det2,25,A
    det5,118,A
    hal,33,A
    jac,123,A
    joh,59,A
    lan,6,D
    lom1,453,D
    naa,23,D
    pet,397,C
    rel,118,A
    san,138,F
    tob,14,E
    worj,220,A
Jacob's Ladder (2)
"I want to climb up Jacob's
ladder..."
    all,96,E
    bal,61,A
    dit,2,A
    new,151,C
    pet,321,C
    pet,359,C
Jacob's Ladder Long and Tall
    hal,16,A
    pet,322,C

Jay Gooze
    odu,248,CH
Jehovah Hallelujah
    all,2,E
    pet,230,C
Jehovah Has Triumph Messiah Is
King
    ken1,35,CH
Jerusalem Morning
    rel,68,A
    see also - Sweet Turtle
      Dove
Jesus Ain't Coming Here to Die No
More
    pet,230,C
    rel,151,A
Jesus Blood Done Make Me Whole
    bal,79,E
    new,54,C
    pet,322,C
Jesus Done Bless My Soul
    odu,65,CH
Jesus Done Just What He Said
    bal,25,E
    pet,78,C
Jesus Going to Make Up My
Dying Bed
    ken1,103,AH
    par,178,E
    pet,78,C
Jesus Got His Business Fix
    log,10,E
Jesus Healed the Sick
    kre,160,A
Jesus Is Listening
    odu,81,CH
Jesus Is Risen From the Dead
    pet,231,C
    worf,35,A
Jesus Locked the Lion's Jaw
    hal,19,A
    pet,79,C
Jesus on the Waterside
    all,28,E
    new,152,C

pet,79,C
Jesus Rides That Milk-White Horse
   dit,12,A
Jesus Rolling in His Arms
   mci,150,AH
   pet,79,C
Jesus Sitting on the Waterside
   whi,62,A
Jesus Won't You Come By and By
   all,60,E
   pet,359,C
Jesus Wore the Crown
   odu,108,CH
Jews Killed Poor Jesus
   pet,13,C
   san,130,F
   sew,45,A
   see also - He Arose
Jews They Took Our Savior
   fis,36,AH
   pet,24,C
Job
   lom3,14,E
Job Job
   cou,225,E
John Brown's Body
   new,87,A
   san,66,F
John Done Saw That Number
   gri,38,E
   lom3,16,E
   new,197,C
   pet,281,C
John John
   par,145,E
John John of the Holy Order
   all,16,E
   pet,25,C
John Saw the Holy Number
   arm,196,A
   det5,63,A
   fen,24,A
   jes,44,AH
   joh,158,A
   mci,157,AH

pet,80,C
rel,24,A
John Saw the Number No Man
   Could Number
   bal,46,A
   pet,281,C
John the Bunyan
   hal,61,A
   pet,359,C
John the Revelator
   lom1,480,D
John Was Writing
   lom3,22,E
John's Gone Down on the Island
   bur2,133,A
John's on the Island on His Knees
   mci,154,AH
   pet,132,C
Join the Angel Band
   all,39,E
   pet,133,C
Join the Army of the Lord
   mci,152,AH
   pet,179,C
   see also - Reign Oh Reign
Join the Heaven With the Angels
   odu,103,CH
Join Them
   all,21,E
   pet,80,C
Jordan's Mills
   pet,323,C
Joshua Fought the Battle of Jericho
   bur1,16,A
   bur2,192,A
   cha,52,A
   cle,96,A
   joh,56,A
   johg,31,A
   lan,10,D
   lom2,466,AH
   new,94,C
   pet,231,C
   tob,32,E

Jubilee
    cle,109,A
    joh1,142,A
    pet,282,C
Judgment
    det5,158,A
Judgment Day Is Rolling Around
    arm,206,A
    fen,34,A
    pet,282,C
    rel,34,A
    san,68,F
    sew,34,A
Judgment Day Is Trying Time
    mci,158,AH
    pet,282,C
Judgment Will Find You So
    pet,283,C
    sew,47,A
Just Above my Head
    new,37,C
    pet,179,C
Just As I Am
    cle,208,A
Just Behold That Number
    san,69,F
Just Going Over in the Heavenly
Land
    bar,42,E
Just Let Me Get Up in the House
    - see - Let Me Get Up
Just Like John - see - Walk in
    Jerusalem Just Like John
Just Now
    all,67,E
    pet,323,C
Just to Behold His Face
    cle,187,A

Keep in the Middle of the Road
    pet,360,C
Keep Inching Along
    and,20,A
    cle,93,A
    det5,10,A

    fis,79,AH
    hal,7,A
    joh,134,A
    johg1,32,A
    lom1,456,D
    naa,17,D
    new,148,C
    odu,89,CH
    pet,128,C
    pet,359,C
    rel,154,A
    san,70,F
    worj1,66,CH
Keep Me From Sinking Down
    det1,21,A
    det5,228,A
    det5,XII,A
    fen,73,A
    joh,154,A
    new,174,A
    pet,397,C
    rel,73,A
    san,99,F
    sew,26,A
    worj1,50,CH
Keep Moving
    san,71,F
Keep the Ark Moving
    mci,159,AH
    pet,323,C
Keep Your Hand on the Plow
    lom2,468,AH
Keep Your Lamps Trimmed
    pet,180,C
Kind Savior
    hal,59,A
    pet,180,C
King David
    cou,236,E
King Emanuel (1)
    "Who do you call the King
    Emanuel..."
        arm,197,A
        det5,147,A
        fen,25,A

pet,80,C
rel,25,A
worj1,68,CH
King Emanuel (2)
"My King Emanuel..."
all,26,E
pet,231,C
King Jesus Built Me a House
Above
pet,81,C
worj,227,A
King Jesus Is Listening
cle,152,A
jac,84,A
King Jesus Is My Only Friend
bal,6,A
new,200,C
pet,81,C
King Jesus Is the Rock
odu,92,CH
King Jesus Sitting on the Water
Side
mci,167,AH
pet,323,C
King of Kings
and,23,A
bry,51,E
Kum Ba Yah
afr,43,E
and,27,E
cle,139,D
jac,94,A
naa,37,D
new,81,C
pet,54,C

Lamb Beautiful Lamb
pet,328,C
Lamb's Blood Done Washed Me
Clean
mci,163,AH
pet,360,C
Land I Am Bound For
san,110,F

Last Call
ken1,38,CH
Last Supper
hay,115,AH
pet,25,C
Lay This Body Down
all,19,E
lom,577,E
new,154,C
pet,398,C
Lead Me to the Rock
pet,324,C
Lead on O King Eternal
naa,32,D
Lean on the Lord's Side
all,100,E
pet,232,C
Leaning on That Lamb
johg1,42,A
Leaning on the Lord
det5,208,A
L'Envoi
det5,XIII,A
Let God's Saints Come In
all,76,E
Let Me Fly
jon,123,E
Let Me Get Up
pet,183,C
pet,367,C
san,98,F
sew,59,E
Let Me Ride
cou,250,E
Let Me Shine
bal,28,A
pet,401,C
Let My People Go - see - Go Down
Moses
Let the Church Roll On
gri,100,E
mci,161,AH
new,201,C
pet,361,C
pet,398,C

Let the Heaven Light Shine on Me
    det2,20,A
    det5,44,A
    johg1,66,A
    pet,361,C
    rel,132,A
    san,72,F
Let Us Break Bread Together
    afr,26,A
    and,1,A
    bal,67,A
    cle,88,A
    jac,102,A
    joh1,63,A
    naa,18,D
    new,55,C
    pet,106,C
    pet,398,C
    san,73,F
Let Us Cheer the Weary Traveler
    and,28,A
    bur2,176,A
    det5,30,A
    joh,184,A
    new,202,C
    pet,81,C
    san,74,F
    tob,37,E
    worf,37,A
Let Us Go Down to Jordan
    mci,164,AH
    pet,324,C
Let Us Praise Him
    det5,195,A
    pet,232,C
Lift Every Voice and Sing
    cle,210,A
    naa,33,D
Like a Feather in the Wind
    log,30,E
Like a Rough and a Rolling Sea
    det5,229,A
Listed in the Battlefield - see -
    Enlisted in the Field of Battle

Listen to the Angels
    pet,133,C
Listen to the Lambs
    cha,55,A
    det5,136,A
    fis,102,AH
    joh,78,A
    new,54,C
    pet,26,C
    rel,158,A
    san,75,F
    tob,13,E
Little Black Train Is Coming
    gri,10,E
    pet,283,C
Little Boy
    hay,103,AH
    pet,82,C
Little Boy Named David
    ken1,124,AH
Little Children
    log,7,E
Little Children Then Won't You Be
Glad
    all,87,E
    pet,232,C
Little Children You Better Believe
    mci,170,AH
    pet,325,C
Little David (1)
    "Lord called David..."
        afr,28,A
        bar,26,E
        bry,3,E
        bur2,60,A
        cha,58,A
        cle,94,A
        hay,30,AH
        joh,65,A
        mci,58,AH
        pet,82,C
        pet,284,C
        san,77,F
        tob,14,E
        worf,41,A

worj1,73,CH
Little David (2)
"Little David play on your harp..."
    det4,5,A
    det5,64,A
    ken,160,AH
    lan,12,D
    mci,172,AH
    pet,233,C
    rel,139,A
Little David (3)
"Lit' David play on yo' harp..."
    new,95,C
    pet,399,C
    whi,81,A
Little Innocent Lamb
    pet,134,C
Little More Faith in Jesus
    cha,11,A
    pet,180,C
    san,19,F
    sew,63,A
    worj1,61,CH
Little Talk With Jesus Makes It Right
    joh1,74,A
    pet,83,C
    worf,24,A
Little Wheel Turning in My Heart
    det5,168,A
    fen,100,A
    fis,104,AH
    fis1,18,A
    pet,325,C
    rel,100,A
    san,133,F
Live Humble
    cle,108,A
    det5,12,A
    hay,107,AH
    pet,362,C
    worf,4,A
    worj1,54,CH
    worj1,74,CH

Living Humble
    par,152,E
Lonesome Valley
    all,5,E
    bur2,87,A
    gri,2,E
    ken,98,AH
    lom2,444,AH
    new,111,C
    pet,21,C
    pet,362,C
    pet,373,C
    worj1,53,CH
Look at How They Done My Lord
    bal,56,A
    joh1,168,A
    pet,26,C
Look Away - *see* - Some of These Mornings
Look Away in the Heaven
    and,26,A
    dit,54,A
    pet,27,C
Look What a Wonder Jesus Done
    bal,69,A
    new,96,C
    pet,326,C
Lord Answer My Prayer
    mci,183,AH
    pet,138,C
Lord Bless the Name
    odu,67,CH
Lord Don't Move This Mountain
    cle,173,D
Lord Have Mercy
    det5,236,A
    mci,189,AH
    pet,34,C
Lord Heal Him
    ken1,25,CH
Lord Help Me to Hold Out
    cle,194,A
Lord How Long
    ken,93,AH

Lord I Cannnot Stay Here By
   Myself
         mci,178,AH
         see also - I Cannot Stay
            Here By Myself
Lord I Done Done
         fis,130,AH
         fis,130,AH
Lord I Just Got Over
         odu,66,CH
Lord I Want to Be a Christian
         and,29,A
         bap,322,A
         cha,49,A
         cle,76,A
         det1,32,A
         det5,50,A
         jac,118,A
         joh1,72,A
         new,56,C
         pet,362,C
         rel,156,A
         san,78,F
         worf,17,A
         worj1,131,AH
Lord I Want Two Wings - *see* -
Two Wings
Lord I Wish I Had Come
         pet,27,C
         san,79,F
Lord I'm Hungry
         new,102,C
         pet,35,C
         worj2,7,A

Lord Is My Shepherd
         pet,83,C
         worj,223,A
Lord Is This Heaven
         mci,174,AH
         pet,234,C
Lord Keep Me From Sinking -
   see - Keep Me From Sinking
   Down

Lord Lord Lord
         and,24,A
Lord Make Me More Patient
         all,52,E
         pet,363,C
Lord Remember Me
         all,12,E
         pet,400,C
Lord These Bones of Mine
         bal,70,A
         new,205,C
         pet,329,C
Lord Time Is Drawing Nigh
         par,185,A
Lord Touch Me
         cle,199,A
Lord Until I Reach My Home
         det3,32,A
         pet,134,C
         rel,171,A
Lord Write My Name
         hal,49,A
         new,159,C
         pet,401,C
Lord's Been Here
         pet,326,C
Lord's Prayer
         cha,84,A
Lordy Lordy Lordy
         odu,257,CH
Love and Serve the Lord - *see* - If
   You Love God Serve Him
Love Come Trickling Down
         ken,119,E
         worj1,65,CH
Love Feast in Heaven
         pet,84,C
Love King Jesus
         lud,15,a
         san,34,F
         worj1,69,CH
Love the Lord
         odu,94,CH
Low Down Chariot
         lom3,36,E

Made My Vow to the Lord
worj1,67,CH
Man Goin' Round - *see* - There's a
Man Going Around Taking
Names
Many Thousand Go
all,48,E
lom,577,E
Many Thousand Gone
cle,137,A
det1,31,A
det5,233,A
fen,95,A
fis,110,AH
jon,60,E
lom1,455,D
new,115,A
pet,135,C
rel,95,A
san,87,F
sew,27,A
whi,26,A
March Along
log,26,E
March Down to Jordan
jes,40,AH
March On
johg,38,A
naa,20,D
pet,135,C
sew,51,A
worj1,71,CH
Marching up the Heavenly Road
pet,135,C
Mary and Martha
and,2,A
cle,162,A
det1,23,A
joh1,81,A
new,182,A
pet,235,C
san,80,F
sew,56,A

Mary Don't You Weep
cle,153,A
fis,127,AH
johg,26,A
new,55,C
pet,88,C
pet,91,C
tob,33,E
worj2,12,A
Mary Had a Baby
bal,5,A
bal,40,A
bal,40,A
bal,41,A
bry,15,E
joh1,124,A
johg1,46,A
new,203,C
pet,28,C
Mary Wept and Marthy Moaned
gri,34,E
pet,181,C
Mary What You Weeping About
ken,135,AH
Mary Where Is Your Baby
ken,73,AH
Master Going to Sell Us - *see* -
Mother Is Master Going to Sell
Us Tomorrow
May Be the Last Time
dit,28,A
new,155,C
par,166,CH
pet,29,C
Meet Oh Lord
all,43,E
pet,284,C
pet,284,C
Meet You in the Morning - *see* -
Shine Shine I'll Meet You in the
Morning
Members Don't Get Weary
joh1,155,A
pet,84,C

Michael Row the Boat Ashore
    all,23,E
    new,204,C
    pet,363,C
Mighty Day
    bar,20,E
Mighty Fortress in Our God
    naa,29,D
Mighty Rocky Road
    bar,6,E
    worj1,70,CH
Milk-White Horses - *see* - Band of
    Gideon
Missionary Baptist Song
    ken1,43,CH
Moan Member Moan
    lom,578,E
Moanin' Dove - *see* - Sometimes
    I Feel
Moaning
    lom,579,E
Moses Smote the Water
    bal,86,A
    pet,181,C
Mother Don't You Weep
    bur2,180,A
    pet,91,C
    worf,40,A
Mother Is Master Going to Sell Us
    Tomorrow
    det5,230,A
    fen,86,A
    fis,92,AH
    new,101,C
    pet,21,C
    pet,28,C
    rel,86,A
Motherless Children Have a Hard
    Time
    dit,27,A
    pet,30,C
Mount Zion
    pet,364,C
Move Along
    new,158,C

    pet,182,C
Move Me
    cle,185,D
Move Members Move
    cou,230,E
Murmuring Word - *see* - He Never
    Said a Mumbling Word
My Army's Crossing Over
    all,38,E
    pet,182,C
My Body Rock Along Fever - *see* -
    My Body Rocked a Long Fever
My Body Rocked a Long Fever
    all,32,E
    pet,30,C
My Brethren Don't Get Weary
    arm,180,A
    fen,8,A
    pet,84,C
    rel,8,A
My Brother I Do Wonder
    det1,18,A
My Brother's Died and Gone to
    Heaven
    fis,108,AH
    pet,236,C
My Faith Looks Up to Thee
    cle,215,D
    naa,34,D
My Father How Long
    all,93,E
    pet,182,C
My Father Took a Light
    fis,112,AH
    pet,400,C
My God He Is a Man of War
    gri,28,E
    pet,85,C
My God Is a Rock
    par,161,AH
    pet,85,C
My God Is So High
    cle,105,E
    hay,83,AH
    johg,6,A

pet,379,C
My Good Lord Done Been Here
   bry,5,E
   cle,163,A
   worf,11,A
My Good Lord's Been Here
   pet,326,C
   san,81,F
   sew,62,A
My Head Wet With the Midnight
  Dew
   bal,49,E
   pet,327,C
My Little Black Star
   nil,12,AH
My Little Soul
   pet,242,C
My Little Soul's Going to Shine
   worj1,56,CH
My Lord Delivered Daniel
   arm,193,A
   det5,65,A
   fen,21,A
   rel,21,A
   san,82,F
My Lord God Rocking in the
  Weary Land
   ken,40,E
My Lord Is Riding All the Time
   fen,98,A
My Lord Says He's Going to Rain
  Down Fire
   joh1,28,A
   pet,284,C
   pet,284,C
My Lord What a Morning
   and,30,A
   arm,176,A
   bur2,30,A
   cha,60,A
   cle,145,A
   det2,22,A
   det5,157,A
   det5,VIII,A
   fen,4,A

   fis,116,AH
   jac,105,A
   joh,162,A
   johg1,68,A
   lom1,454,D
   new,136,A
   pet,286,C
   rel,4,A
   san,83,F
   whi,114,A
My Lord What Shall I Do
   ken1,81,AH
   mci,187,AH
   pet,89,C
My Lord What Should I Do - *see* -
  My Lord What Shall I Do
My Lord's Coming Again
   odu,74,CH
My Lord's Going to Move This
  Wicked Race
   pet,285,C
   worj,217,A
My Lord's Riding All the Time
   det5,150,A
   pet,285,C
   pet,285,C
   rel,98,A
My Lord's Writing All the Time
   joh,123,A
   johg,24,A
   pet,285,C
My Lord's Writing Down Time
   bur1,6,A
My Loving Brother
   and,2,A
My Merlindy Brown
   bur1,12,A
My Mind Stayed on Freedom
   new,100,C
   pet,86,C
My Mother Got a Letter
   odu,120,CH
My Mother's in Heaven
   log,3,E

My Name's Been Written Down
cou,244,E
My Name's Written on High
pet,237,C
worf,13,A
My Ship Is on the Ocean
joh1,150,A
pet,183,C
san,84,F
sew,50,A
My Sin's Been Taken Away
pet,327,C
My Sister Ain't You Mighty Glad
ken1,110,AH
My Sister You'll Be Called On
mci,168,AH
pet,136,C
My Soul Is a Witness - see -
Witness for My Lord
My Soul Is a Witness for My Lord
cha,62,A
My Soul Wants Something That's
New
det5,105,A
hal,47,A
pet,30,C
pet,365,C
rel,147,A
My Soul Wants to Go Home to
Glory
ken,141,AH
My Soul's Been Anchored in the
Lord (1)
"My soul's been anchored in the
Lord..."
pet,364,C
worf,43,A
My Soul's Been Anchored in the
Lord (2)
"In the Lord my soul's been
anchored in the Lord..."
cle,74,A
joh1,37,A
pet,401,C

My Soul's Determined
mci,181,AH
pet,136,C
My Soul's Going to Heaven
odu,101,CH
My Time Is Come
bal,59,A
pet,31,C
My Trouble Is Hard
odu,130,CH
My Way's Cloudy
bur2,172,A
det1,28,A
det5,231,A
fen,97,A
joh,92,A
pet,31,C
pet,32,C
rel,97,A
san,85,F
sew,52,A

Negro Lullaby
bur1,14,A
Never a Man Speak Like This Man
kre,159,A
Never Leave Me Alone
dit,26,A
pet,87,C
Never Me One
bal,43,A
pet,184,C
Never Said a Mumbalin - see - He
Never Said a Mumbling Word
Never Saw Such a Man
pet,87,C
New Born Again
bap,474,A
bar,7,E
fis,119,AH
new,60,C
pet,327,C
New Born Baby
fis,24,AH
pet,87,C

New Burying Ground
    bar,35,E
No Condemnation in My Soul
    gri,92,E
    pet,365,C
No Devil in Our Land
    mci,129,AH
    pet,237,C
No Hiding Place
    cle,141,A
    par,151,E
No I Ain't Ashamed
    mci,191,AH
    pet,328,C
No Liar Can Stand
    mci,193,AH
    pet,286,C
No Man Can Hinder Me
    all,10,E
    new,99,C
    pet,137,C
No More Auction Block - *see* -
Many Thousand Gone
No More My Dear Brother
    bal,42,A
    pet,365,C
No More Rain Fall to Wet You
    all,46,E
    pet,237,C
No-Ways Tired - *see* - I Don't Feel
No-Ways Tired
Noah Hoist the Window
    par,134,A
Noah Noah
    cou,246,E
Nobody Knows the Trouble I Feel
    pet,32,C
Nobody Knows the Trouble I
  See
    bry,45,E
    cha,65,A
    cle,170,A
    fis,124,AH
    fis1,13,A
    joh,140,A

    joh1,34,A
    kre,164,A
    log,32,E
    pet,33,C
    sew,9,A
    whi,9,A
    worj1,50,CH
    worj1,57,CH
Nobody Knows the Trouble I See
  Lord
    cle,171,A
    det3,31,A
    new,46,E
    san,86,F
Nobody Knows the Trouble I've
  Had
    all,55,E
Nobody Knows the Trouble I've
  Seen
    and,31,A
    arm,181,A
    bal,89,E
    blo,211,B
    bur,2,A
    bur2,119,A
    det1,17,A
    det5,232,A
    fen,9,AH
    jac,67,A
    pet,33,C
    rel,9,A
Nobody Knows Who I Am
    new,57,C
    pet,34,C
    worf,39,A
Not Weary Yet
    all,12,E
    pet,137,C
Now Let Me Fly
    bry1,44,D
Now We Take This Feeble Body
    det,14,A
    pet,34,C
    san,88,F
    worj1,59,CH

Number Me One
    par,188,A

O Adam Where Are You - *see* -
  What a Trying Time
Ode
    lud,14,A
Official Song of the NAACP - *see* -
  Lift Every Voice and Sing
Oh Daniel
    all,94,E
    pet,183,C
Oh Freedom
    bry,53,E
    cle,102,A
    det5,110,A
    jac,109,A
    johg1,10,A
    lom2,462,AH
    naa,22,D
    new,103,C
    pet,138,C
    rel,114,A
    san,94,F
Oh Glory
    pet,88,C
Oh Graveyard
    johg1,64,A
Oh Holy Lord
    pet,238,C
Oh Holy Lord
    san,95,F
    sew,43,E
Oh Holy Savior
    det4,32,A
Oh Jerusalem
    det5,190,A
    pet,366,C
    rel,111,A
Oh Lawd How Long - *see* - Before
  This Time Another Year
Oh Look-a Death - *see* - Never a
  Man Speak Like This Man

Oh Mary
    afr,30,A
Oh Mary Oh Martha
    gri,14,E
    pet,89,C
Oh Redeemed Redeemed
    hal,52,A
    pet,330,C
    pet,403,C
    san,103,F
    sew,31,A
Oh Shout Away
    pet,243,C
Oh Sinner
    gri,44,E
    pet,288,C
Oh the Robe
    par,180,AH
Oh the Sunshine
    odu,67,CH
Oh Yes (1)
  "Oh yes oh yes..."
    arm,186,A
    det5,210,A
    fen,14,A
    pet,240,C
    rel,14,A
Oh Yes (2)
  "I come this night to sing and
  pray..."
    joh1,105,A
    pet,241,C
    pet,402,C
Old Ark Is Moving Along (1)
  "Old ark's moving moving
  moving..."
    and,32,A
    cle,113,A
    joh1,25,A
    johg,20,A
    lom1,475,D
    fen,77,A
    lud,20,A
    new,206,C
    pet,368,C

tob,18,E
worf,19,A
worj1,73,CH
Old Ark Is Moving Along (2)
"Just wait a little while..."
    arm,249,A
    det2,24,A
    det5,58,A
    pet,90,C
    rel,77,A
Old Man Devil Gotta Go Some
    cha,94,A
Old Satan
    pet,241,C
Old Sheep Done Know the Road
    arm,198,A
    det5,4,A
    fen,26,A
    joh1,160,A
    new,207,C
    pet,328,C
    rel,26,A
Old Ship Maria
    pet,186,C
Old Ship Marie
    bal,34,A
Old Ship of Zion (1)
"What ship is that a-sailing
Hallelujah..."
    new,156,C
    pet,185,C
    pet,186,C
    sew,35,A
Old Ship of Zion (2)
"Come along come along and
let's go home..."
    all,102,E
    bar,23,E
    cle,131,A
    cle,189,A
    det2,29,A
    fen,85,A
    rel,85,A

Old Ship of Zion (3)
"This ole ship is a reelin' an' a
rockin'..."
    odu,117,CH
Old Ship of Zion (4)
"Ole ship o' Zion ole ship o'
Zion..."
    ken1,126,CH
Old Time Religion
    blo,211,B
    cle,89,A
    det5,200,A
    joh,76,A
    ken1,15,E
    naa,22,D
    new,60,A
    odu,142,CH
    pet,62,C
    pet,101,C
    san,112,F
    sew,41,A
    worj1,65,CH
Old Zion's Children Marching
Along
    new,210,C
    pet,368,C
On My Journey
    cle,157,E
On My Knees - see -
Communion
On the Other Side of Jordan - see -
Going to Roll in My Jesus'
Arms
On to Glory
    all,66,E
    pet,242,C
One of These Days
    par,167,CH
One Sunday Morning
    afr,31,A
Only a Look
    cle,197,A
Onward Christian Soldiers
    naa,28,D

Open the Window Noah
    bry1,40,D
    new,161,C
    pet,329,C
Other World Is Not Like This
    odu,123,CH
Over My Head
    blo,211,B
    cle,167,D
Over the Crossing
    all,72,E
    pet,91,C
Over Yonder
    johg1,38,A

Paul and Silas
    odu,126,CH
    see also - All Night Long
Peter Go Ring Them Bells
    arm,174,A
    bry1,28,D
    bur2,198,A
    cha,68,A
    cle,97,A
    det5,204,A
    fen,2,AH
    joh,137,A
    pet,243,C
    rel,2,A
    san,100,F
    whi,28,A
    worj1,46,CH
    see also - I Heard from
        Heaven Today
Peter on the Sea
    bar,40,E
    det5,68,A
    fen,88,A
    pet,139,C
    rel,88,A
    whi,89,A
Pick and Shovel Song
    odu,255,CH
Pilgrim's Song
    det5,191,A

    lom2,438,AH
    new,170,C
    odu,137,CH
    pet,140,C
    rel,126,A
Plenty Good Room (1)
    "God's got plenty of room..."
    all,106,E
    pet,64,C
Plenty Good Room (2)
    "There's plenty good room plenty
    good room..."
    cle,99,A
    hay,64,AH
    pet,92,C
    pet,403,C
    worf,10,A
Poor Heathens Are Dying
    bal,15,A
    pet,330,C
Poor Little Jesus
    ken,78,AH
    lom2,446,AH
    new,56,C
    pet,35,C
Poor Me
    bar,24,E
    see also - Trouble Will
        Bury Me Down
Poor Moaner You Shall Be Free
    log,12,E
Poor Mourner
    nil,6,AH
Poor Mourner's Got a Home at
Last
    det1,22,A
    joh1,78,A
    johg1,56,A
    pet,92,C
Poor Pilgrim
    det5,169,E
    hay,77,AH
Poor Rosy
    all,7,E

Religion Is a Fortune
   arm,189,A
   det5,201,A
   fen,17,A
   joh1,53,A
   johg1,72,A
   pet,92,C
   rel,17,A
   worf,14,A
   worj1,48,CH
Religion So Sweet
   all,13,E
   lom,582,E
   pet,93,C
Religion That My Lord Gave Me
   pet,93,C
Remember Me
   pet,291,C
Remember the Dying Lamb
   mci,208,AH
   pet,245,C
Remon
   all,110,E
Restitution
   cha,99,A
Resurrection Morn
   all,54,E
   pet,246,C
Ride On
   det5,194,A
   pet,246,C
   rel,120,A
Ride on Conquering King
   dit,44,A
   par,182,AH
   pet,246,C
Ride on Jesus
   bal,92,E
   det5,148,A
   johg1,8,A
Ride on King Jesus
   bur2,147,A
   cha,111,A
   cle,77,A
   fis,138,AH

fis1,22,A
   new,52,E
   pet,141,C
   pet,247,C
   san,120,F
   sew,54,E
Ride on Moses
   joh,70,A
   pet,404,C
Ride the Chariot
   pet,405,C
Ring Jerusalem
   mci,210,AH
   pet,331,C
Ring the Bells
   dit,40,A
   pet,93,C
Rise and Shine
   arm,212,A
   cle,79,A
   det1,26,A
   det5,198,A
   fen,40,A
   johg,3,A
   new,104,C
   pet,405,C
   rel,40,A
Rise Mourners
   san,121,F
Rise Mourners Rise
   joh1,116,A
   pet,406,C
   sew,11,A
Rise Shine for Thy Light Is
  Coming
   pet,247,C
   worj1,49,CH
Rise Up Shepherd and Follow
   afr,33,A
   and,41,E
   bal,91,E
   blo,211,B
   det5,IV,A
   jac,31,A
   joh1,66,A

lom1,481,D
new,163,C
pet,188,C
rel,173,A
Road Is Rugged But I Must Go
dit,32,A
pet,141,C
Road to Heaven
log,19,E
Rock Chariot
cou,227,E
Rock Mount Sinai
hal,68,E
ken,46,AH
pet,248,C
Rock My Soul (1)
"Rock a my soul in the bosom of
Abraham..."
all,73,E
blo,212,B
lan,4,D
mci,196,AH
new,59,C
pet,406,C
Rock My Soul (2)
"Rocka my soul..."
pet,94,C
Rock of Ages
pet,94,C
Rock of Jubilee
all,25,E
pet,406,C
Rocking Jerusalem
bry,35,E
cle,103,E
pet,248,C
worj,226,A
Rocks and the Mountains
and,44,E
bry1,36,D
det5,161,A
pet,248,C
san,111,F
sew,24,A

Rocks Don't Fall on Me
bur2,55,A
joh,164,A
pet,290,C
worf,30,A
worj1,58,CH
Roll and Rock
mci,222,AH
pet,94,C
Roll Away That Stone
cha,116,A
Roll Him Out Again
bal,30,A
pet,332,C
Roll Jordan
log,18,E
Roll Jordan Roll (1)
"Roll Jordan roll I want to go to
heaven when I die..."
and,39,E
bal,77,A
bry,37,E
cha,70,A
cle,117,A
det3,16,AH
det5,52,A
det5,I,A
dit,51,A
joh,105,A
lom1,457,D
new,190,A
pet,141,C
rel,165,A
san,122,F
sew,32,A
Roll Jordan Roll (2)
"My brother sitting on the tree of
life..."
all,1,E
kre,165,A
pet,370,C
Roll Jordan Roll (3)
"Here He comes the Judge
severe..."
lom1,458,AH

Roll On
  pet,95,C
  worf,5,A
Roll the Old Chariot Along
  det5,192,A
  hal,22,A
  joh,110,A
  pet,370,C
  rel,106,A
Rolling in Jesus' Arms
  mci,224,AH
  new,62,C
  pet,95,C
Room Enough
  pet,95,C
  sew,30,A
Room Enough in the Heaven
  bal,85,A
  pet,407,C
Rough and Rolling Sea
  fen,90,A
  pet,37,C
  rel,90,A
Round About the Mountain
  pet,96,C
Round the Glory Manger
  afr,34,A
Rule Death in His Arms
  bar,22,E
Run Here Jeremiah
  mci,220,AH
  pet,142,C
Run Mary Run
  arm,188,A
  det5,18,A
  fen,16,A
  joh1,110,A
  new,105,C
  pet,142,C
  rel,16,A
Run Moaner Run
  mci,213,AH
  pet,249,C
  pet,332,C

Run Sinner Run
  johg,11,A
Run to Jesus
  det3,17,AH
  det5,15,E
  fis,142,AH
  new,98,E
  pet,143,C

Sabbath Has No End
  all,69,E
  bar,37,E
  par,172,E
  pet,371,C
Sail Oh Believer
  all,24,E
  pet,188,C
Sailing Over Yonder
  fis,148,AH
  mci,215,AH
  pet,96,C
Same Train
  bal,9,A
  dit,53,A
  joh1,60,A
  odu,112,CH
  pet,188,C
Samson
  lom1,478,D
  lom3,6,E
Samson's Wife Sat on His Knees
  log,24,E
Satan's Camp Fire
  all,27,E
  pet,292,C
Satisfied
  odu,249,CH
Save Me Jesus Save Me Now
  bal,60,A
  pet,189,C
Save Me Lord Save Me
  det2,18,A
  pet,189,C
  sew,46,A

Save Me Now Save Me
    bal,39,A
Scandalize My Name
    cle,159,E
    hal,65,A
    johg1,12,A
    new,212,C
    pet,37,C
Sea Is Going to Deliver Up Dry
  Bones
    bal,31,E
    pet,332,C
See Four and Twenty Elders - *see* -
  Four and Twenty Elders
See the Signs of Judgment
    pet,292,C
    worj,225,A
Seek and Ye Shall Find
    blo,212,B
    det5,20,A
    fen,101,A
    pet,333,C
    rel,101,A
Send One Angel Down
    ken,117,AH
    mci,207,AH
    pet,333,C
Send Them Angels Down
    mci,216,AH
    pet,190,C
Serving My God
    hal,40,A
    pet,250,C
Shall I Die
    all,41,E
    pet,37,C
Shepherd Shepherd
    pet,38,C
Shine Like a Star in the Morning
    jon,271,E
Shine Shine
    pet,250,C
Shine Shine I'll Meet You in the
  Morning
    gla,20,D

    pet,236,C
    sew,37,E
Shock Along John
    all,67,E
Shoot dat Buffey - *see* - Trip to
  Raleigh
Shout All Over God's Heaven
  - *see* - Going to Shout All Over
  God's Heaven
Shout Away
    all,71,E
Shout for Joy
    pet,251,C
Shout Jerusalem
    mci,228,AH
    pet,251,C
Shout on Children
    all,60,E
    pet,96,C
Show Me the Way (1)
  "Brother have you come to show
  me the way..."
    pet,333,C
Show Me the Way (2)
  "My good Lord show me the
  way..."
    joh1,33,A
    pet,184,C
    pet,334,C
    worf,22,A
Sin Sick Soul
    all,49,E
    pet,292,C
Sing Ho That I Had the Wings of a
  Dove
    fis,151,AH
    pet,407,C
    worf,16,A
Singing on the Old Church Ground
    hal,19,A
    pet,97,C
Singing With a Sword in My Hand
    joh,86,A
    pet,143,C

Sinner Die
    odu,75,CH
Sinner Man
    blo,212,B
    new,48,C
    pet,367,C
    sew,61,A
Sinner-Man So Hard to Believe
    johg1,48,A
Sinner Now Is the Time for to Pray
    ken1,19,E
Sinner Please Don't Let This
  Harvest Pass
    bur2,189,A
    cha,71,A
    fis,144,AH
    joh1,50,A
    pet,97,C
    whi,51,A
    worf,38,E
Sinner Won't Die No More
    all,85,E
    pet,251,C
Sinner You Better Get Ready
    arm,208,A
    bar,26,E
    det5,16,A
    fen,36,A
    pet,288,C
    rel,36,A
    san,105,F
Sinner You Know
    and,33,A
Sister Get Your Ticket Right
    bal,23,E
    pet,367,C
Sister Hannah
    hal,13,A
    pet,371,C
Sister Mary Had But One Child
    hay,98,AH
    pet,38,C
Sister Mary's Twelve Blessings
    lud,18,A

Sit Down Servant
    cle,160,A
    lom,584,E
    lom2,454,AH
    new,108,C
    pet,97,C
    pet,251,C
Sitting Down Beside the Lamb
    log,6,E
    pet,144,C
Sitting Down Side of My Jesus
    hal,59,E
    pet,98,C
Slavery's Chain
    det5,112,E
    new,109,C
    pet,252,C
So I Can Write My Name
    jes,60,AH
So Sad
    hal,61,E
    pet,293,C
Social Band
    all,105,E
    pet,39,C
Soldier for Jesus
    bar,27,E
    bar,9,E
Solid Rock
    naa,35,D
Some Come Cripple - see - Hail
  the Crown
Some Day
    cle,207,A
Some of These Days (1)
    "I'm gonna tell God how you
    treat me..."
        gri,20,E
        new,110,C
        pet,293,C
Some of These Days (2)
    "I'm going down to the river of
    Jordan..."
        johg,17,A
        pet,334,C

Some of These Mornings
    arm,190,A
    det5,46,A
    fen,18,A
    pet,98,C
    rel,18,A
    worj1,47,CH
Some Valiant Soldier
    all,50,E
Some Will Love You and Some
  Will Hate You
    bal,68,E
    pet,372,C
Somebody Got Lost in the Storm
    fis,154,AH
    pet,39,C
Somebody's Buried in the Graveyard
    pet,190,C
    worf,8,A
    worj1,34,AH
    worj1,60,CH
Somebody's Calling My Name
 - see - Hush Somebody's Calling
 My Name
Somebody's Knocking at Your
  Door
    and,34,A
    bap,480,A
    bry1,13,D
    cha,75,A
    cle,154,A
    det5,144,A
    fis,164,AH
    hal,12,A
    joh,85,A
    new,63,C
    pet,372,C
    rel,155,A
    whi,65,A
Sometimes I Feel
    pet,40,C
Sometimes I Feel Like a
  Motherless Child
    bar,18,E
    bur,26,A

bur2,64,A
cle,83,A
cle,155,A
det5,172,E
fis,157,AH
fis1,30,A
gri,72,E
joh1,30,A
lom2,460,AH
new,213,C
pet,40,C
rel,115,A
whi,48,A
worj1,54,CH
Sometimes I Feel Like I Wanna Go
Home
    pet,190,C
Sometimes I Feel Like I Want to
  Go Home
    fis,162,AH
Sometimes My Trouble - see -
  Were You There
Somewhere Around a Throne
    whi,121,A
Soon and Very Soon
    cle,198,D
Soon I Will Be Done
    cle,158,A
    det5,234,A
    lom1,472,D
    naa,43,D
    new,167,C
    pet,98,C
    pet,408,C
    san,123,F
    worj1,56,CH
Soon in the Morning
    bar,6,E
Soon One Morning
    gri,8,E
    lom2,450,AH
    lom3,30,E
    pet,41,C
Soon We Will be Done - see -
  Soon I Will Be Done

Soon Will I Be Done - *see* - Soon I
  Will Be Done
Sorry to Tell
    hal,61,E
    pet,41,C
Sound the Jubilee
    lud,12,A
Spirit of the Lord Done Fell on Me
    jes,10,AH
Stand By Me
    fis,166,AH
    pet,144,C
Stand on a Sea of Glass
    bar,28,E
Stand Steady
    jes,30,AH
Stand Still Jordan
    bur,18,A
    bur2,34,A
    joh,82,A
    johg1,62,A
    pet,145,C
Stand the Storm
    det5,189,A
    pet,146,C
Stand Up Like Soldiers
    ken1,32,CH
Stand Up Stand Up for Jesus
    naa,36,D
Standing in the Need of Prayer
    and,35,A
    blo,212,B
    bur2,201,A
    cha,78,A
    cle,110,A
    det5,183,A
    fis,168,AH
    joh,94,A
    johg1,40,A
    new,51,C
    pet,22,C
    pet,44,C
    san,61,F
    whi,35,A

Standing on the Sea of Glass
    dit,38,A
    mci,226,AH
    pet,145,C
Stars Begin to Fall
    all,25,E
Stars Begin to Fall - *see also* -
  Stars in the Elements
Stars in the Elements
    det5,162,A
    fen,84,A
    pet,294,C
    rel,84,A
Stars in the Elements - *see also* -
  Stars Begin to Fall
Stay in the Field
    bar,27,E
    det2,23,A
    det5,22,A
    fen,103,A
    lud,19,A
    pet,146,C
    rel,103,A
    worj1,71,CH
Steady Jesus Is Listening
    pet,334,C
Steal Away
    and,22,E
    blo,212,B
    bur2,14,A
    cha,80,A
    cle,134,A
    det1,10,A
    det5,111,A
    fis,170,AH
    fis1,26,A
    hay,75,AH
    jac,61,A
    joh,114,A
    new,106,A
    odu,139,CH
    pet,191,C
    rel,152,A
    san,124,F
    sew,28,A

whi,46,A
worf,20,A
worj1,89,AH
Steal Away and Pray
    pet,146,C
Steal Away to My Father's
    Kingdom
    gri,78,E
    pet,191,C
Steamboat Song
    fis,172,AH
Story of Noah
    nil,4,AH
Study War No More - *see* - I Ain't
    Going to Study War No More
Sun Don't Set in the Morning
    det5,23,A
    jon,77,E
    new,212,C
    pet,408,C
    rel,130,A
Sun Mows Down
    pet,99,C
    worj,229,A
Sun Shine Into My Soul
    hal,73,E
    pet,408,C
Sun Will Never Go Down
    cou,238,E
Sunday Morning Band (1)
    "What kind of band you going to
    join..."
    mci,230,AH
    pet,252,C
Sunday Morning Band (2)
    "What band that Sunday
    morning..."
    pet,253,C
Sunshine Into My Soul - *see* - Sun
    Shine Into My Soul
Surely God Is Able
    cle,193,A
Sweet Canaan
    arm,234,A
    det5,188,A

fen,62,A
pet,192,C
rel,62,A
Sweet Heaven
    bar,10,E
    mci,237,AH
    pet,409,C
Sweet Heaven Is a Handsome Place
    log,17,E
Sweet Home
    pet,41,C
Sweet Turtle Dove
    arm,240,A
    det5,164,A
    fen,68,A
    pet,294,C
    rel,68,A
    see also - Jerusalem
        Morning
Sweet Water Rolling
    bal,49,E
    pet,335,C
Sweetest Sound I Ever Heard
    det1,20,A
Swing Down Chariot
    pet,192,C
Swing Low Chariot
    det5,100,A
    pet,192,C
Swing Low Sweet Chariot (1)
    Swing low sweet chariot coming
    for to carry me home..."
    and,38,A
    arm,179,A
    blo,212,B
    bry,43,E
    bur2,10,A
    cha,82,A
    cle,104,A
    det1,12,A
    det5,102,A
    fis,174,AH
    fis1,28,A
    gla,26,D
    jac,24,A

joh,62,A
johg1,36,A
lom,608,E
new,164,A
pet,193,C
san,125,F
sew,29,A
tob,39,E
whi,128,A
worf,21,A
worj1,121,AH
worj1,59,CH

Swing Low Sweet Chariot (2)
"Swing low sweet chariot don't
you leave me behind..."
det5,V,A
det5,101,A
fen,7,A
pet,42,C
pet,170,C
rel,7,A
san,44,F

Swing Low Sweet Chariot (3)
"Swing low oh swing low..."
par,154,E

Take Me to the Water
jac,99,A
Take My Mother Home
log,4,E
Takes a Little Bit of Man to Rock
Dan
hal,24,A
pet,372,C
Talk About Me
odu,84,CH
Tall Angel at the Bar
hal,46,E
jes,70,AH
ken,7,E
pet,294,C
Tell All the World John
new,108,C
pet,99,C
worf,34,A

Tell Brother Elijah
bar,5,E
Tell It
hal,26,A
new,214,C
pet,99,C
Tell Jesus
pet,373,C
rel,129,A
san,126,F
Tell My Jesus Morning
all,15,E
odu,93,CH
pet,253,C
Tell Them I'm Gone
gri,6,E
pet,193,C
Thank God I'm in the Field
hal,15,A
pet,409,C
Thank God I'm on My Way to
Heaven
pet,253,C
That Lonesome Stream
lom,602,E
That Lonesome Valley - see -
Lonesome Valley
That Sabbath Has No End
odu,63,CH
That Same Train
mci,79,AH
pet,194,C
That Suits Me
hal,63,A
johg1,26,A
ken,129,AH
par,137,E
pet,374,C
That Sun Going Down
hal,38,A
pet,290,C
Them Bones
lom3,23,E
Them Charming Bells
bar,15,E

Then My Little Soul's Going
- *see* - I'm Going to Join the
Great Association
There is a Balm in Gilead
jac,14,A
There Is a Mighty Shouting
mci,225,AH
pet,254,C
There Is Rest for the Weary
Traveler
bal,31,A
pet,100,C
There Was a Babe
afr,47,A
There Were Ten Virgins
det5,72,A
fen,90,A
pet,295,C
rel,90,A
san,37,F
sew,44,A
There's a Great Camp Meeting
- *see* - Walk Together Children
There's a Handwriting on the Wall
bal,29,A
joh1,171,A
pet,295,C
There's a Heavenly Home Up
Yonder
san,131,F
There's a Little Wheel - *see* - Little
Wheel Turning in My Heart
There's a Man Going Around
Taking Names
bro,12,A
fis,28,AH
ken1,100,AH
lom,591,E
pet,42,C
whi,58,A
There's a Meeting Here Tonight (1)
"I take my text in Matthew..."
all,9,E
pet,100,C

There's a Meeting Here Tonight (2)
"Get you ready there's a meeting
here tonight..."
and,16,A
cle,91,A
det1,11,A
det5,182,A
fis,16,AH
new,198,A
pet,147,C
tob,24,E
worj,219,A
There's a Mighty War in Heaven
mci,86,AH
pet,296,C
There's No Hiding Place Down
There
bry,49,E
bry1,33,D
joh,74,A
johg,16,A
new,41,C
pet,296,C
There's No One Like Jesus
odu,93,CH
There's Room Enough
pet,194,C
There's Something on My Mind
pet,42,C
worj,222,A
These Are All My Father's
Children
all,101,E
mci,88,AH
pet,147,C
pet,254,C
pet,374,C
san,133,F
sew,54,E
These Bones Going to Rise Again
bar,32,E
lom,597,E
lom1,476,D
These Dry Bones of Mine
bar,11,E

They Led My Lord Away
    hay,119,AH
    pet,43,C
They Look Like Men of War - *see* - Enlisted Soldiers
They Nail Him to the Cross
    odu,125,CH
They Shall Receive a Blessing
    cle,209,A
This Is a Sin Trying World
    pet,410,C
    worf,44,A
    worj1,75,AH
This Is the Christmas Time
    afr,49,A
This Is the Healing Water
    johg1,52,A
This Is the Man
    dit,36,A
    pet,100,C
This Is the Trouble of the World
    all,99,E
    pet,43,C
This Is the Way I Pray
    new,168,C
    pet,335,C
This Little Light of Mine
    bry1,16,D
    cle,132,A
    jac,122,A
This May Be My Last Time
    fis,176,AH
    naa,44,D
    pet,43,C
This May Be Your Last Time
    cou,229,E
This Old Time Religion - *see* - Old Time Religion
This Old World's a Hell to Me
    odu,116,CH
This Old World's Rolling
    odu,118,CH
This Train
    lom,593,E
    lom1,484,D

    pet,194,C
This World Is Not My Home
    bar,9,E
Three Long Nights and Three Long Days
    bal,47,A
    pet,254,C
Time for Praying
    cle,133,A
Time Is Drawing Nigh
    gri,54,E
    pet,296,C
Tis Jordan's River
    pet,410,C
    san,134,F
Tis Me O Lord - *see* - Standing in the Need of Prayer
Tis the Old Ship of Zion - *see* - Old Ship of Zion
To See God's Bleeding Lamb - *see* - Want to Go to Heaven When I Die
Toll the Bell Angel
    ken,150,AH
    pet,255,C
Tomorrow You May Die
    fis,178,AH
    pet,298,C
Tone the Bell Easy
    lom,605,E
Too Late
    bal,32,A
    joh1,102,A
    pet,298,C
Towe the Bell
    mci,217,AH
    pet,255,C
Tramping
    and,46,E
    cle,111,A
Travel On
    all,31,E
    pet,147,C
Traveling Shoes
    cou,233,E

Trees
    cle,191,D
Trip to Raleigh
    nil,10,AH
Trouble
    cha,124,A
Trouble Done Bore Me Down
    mci,238,AH
    new,220,C
    pet,44,C
Trouble of the World
    all,8,E
    pet,45,C
Trouble Will Bury Me Down
    pet,36,C
    whi,42,A
    see also - Poor Me
Trouble's Going to Weigh Me
  Down
    fis,182,AH
    pet,46,C
Troubled in Mind
    bar,24,E
Troubles Was Hard
    ken,82,AH
True Religion
    odu,83,CH
Trying to Cross the Red Sea
    pet,255,C
Trying to Get Home
    cle,130,A
    pet,148,C
Turn Back Pharaoh's Army
    pet,148,C
    sew,10,A
Turn Sinner
    mci,232,AH
    new,63,C
    pet,375,C
Turn Sinner Turn
    all,36,E
    pet,375,C

Twas on One Sunday Morning
    pet,195,C
Two Wings
    gri,80,E
    hay,41,AH
    ken,121,AH
    mci,233,AH
    pet,101,C
    pet,196,C
    pet,399,C

Under the Rail
    odu,260,CH
Until I Found the Lord
    cle,177,A
Until I Reach My Home
    hal,39,A
    joh,177,A
    pet,149,C
Up on the Mountain
    joh,64,A
    pet,46,C
Upon the Rock
    kre,162,A

View the Land
    arm,182,A
    det5,138,A
    fen,10,A
    pet,256,C
    rel,10,A

Wade In the Water
    and,11,A
    bry1,32,D
    bur,44,A
    bur2,50,A
    cle,129,D
    cou,28,E
    fis,184,AH
    jac,100,A
    joh1,84,A

lom1,470,D
naa,23,D
new,82,C
par,171,E
pet,149,C
pet,311,C
worf,8,E

Wait a Little While
pet,102,C
worj1,69,CH

Wait Mr Mackright
all,43,E
pet,376,C

Wake Up Children
bar,13,E

Wake Up Jacob
all,65,E
pet,376,C
whi,72,A

Wake Up Jonah
cou,223,E
lan,18,D

Walk About Elders
gri,46,E
pet,102,C

Walk God's Heavenly Road
mci,244,AH
pet,103,C

Walk in Jerusalem Just Like
John (1)
"Last Sunday morning last
Sunday morning..."
dit,50,A
pet,196,C

Walk in Jerusalem Just Like
John (2)
"I want to be ready..."
bar,35,E
joh1,58,A
new,153,C
pet,256,C

Walk in Jerusalem Just Like
John (3)
"When I come to die I want t'
be ready..."

mci,147,AH
pet,397,C

Walk in Jerusalem Just Like
John (4)
"Jerusalem Lord..."
bal,46,A
see also - I Want to Be
Ready

Walk Mary Down the Lane
joh1,147,A
pet,149,C

Walk Through the Valley
worj1,55,CH

Walk Through the Valley in Peace
bar,7,E

Walk Together Children
arm,222,A
bry,28,E
cle,156,A
det5,26,A
fen,50,AH
fis,188,AH
joh1,180,A
naa,4,D
new,169,C
pet,66,C
pet,197,C
rel,50,A
worj1,45,CH

Walk You in the Light
arm,238,A
det5,24,A
en,66,A
pet,103,C
rel,66,A
san,135,F

Walking in God's Commandments
hal,71,E
pet,335,C

Walking in the Light
det5,116,A
fen,102,A
odu,137,CH
pet,336,C
rel,102,A

Want to Go to Heaven When I Die
   bal,33,A
   det5,53,A
   det5,II,A
   joh1,152,A
   pet,101,C
   pet,195,C
   pet,197,C
   rel,170,A
   worf,15,A
Wasn't That a Mighty Day
   ken1,33,CH
Wasn't That a Wide River
   arm,194,A
   bur2,141,A
   cha,66,A
   det5,98,A
   fen,22,A
   joh,152,A
   pet,185,C
   rel,22,A
   san,113,F
   worj1,47,CH
Wasn't That a Witness for My
  Lord
   hal,72,E
   pet,376,C
Wasn't That a Wonder
   par,139,E
Wasn't That Hard Trials
   ken1,65,AH
Watch the Stars
   bal,58,A
   pet,402,C
Way By and By
   bal,49,A
   cou,253,A
   pet,103,C
Way Bye and Bye - *see* - Way By
  and By
Way Down in Hell
   mci,241,AH
   pet,46,C

Way in the Heaven By and By
   dit,23,A
   pet,103,C
Way Over in de Promise' Land
   - *see* - Wonder Where Is Good
  Old Daniel
Way Over in the Egypt Land
   san,136,F
Way Over Jordan
   pet,411,C
Way Up on the Mountain
   hal,34,E
   pet,411,C
Wayfaring Stranger - *see* -
  Pilgrim's Song
We Are Almost Home
   det5,89,A
   pet,151,C
   san,137,F
We Are Building on a Rock
   det2,27,A
   det5,115,A
   pet,105,C
   rel,123,A
We Are Climbing Jacob's Ladder
   jac,123,A
   see also - Jacob's Ladder
We Are Climbing the Hills of
  Zion
   pet,150,C
   san,139,F
We Are Traveling to the Grave
   det3,25,A
We Are Walking Down the Valley
   ken1,56,E
We Are Walking in the Light
   - *see* - Walking in the Light
We Need More Reapers
   san,141,F
We Shall Overcome
   cle,127,A
   gla,55,D
   jac,113,A
   lit,72,A
   naa,24,D

We Shall Walk Through the
Valley
    all,73,E
    and,36,E
    bap,501,A
    pet,377,C
We Will March Through the Valley
- *see* - We Shall Walk Through
the Valley
Wear a Starry Crown
    bar,16,E
Weary Traveler - *see* - Let Us Cheer
the Weary Traveler
Weep No More for Baby
    dit,39,A
Weeping Mary (1)
  "Weeping Mary weeping
Mary..."
    bur2,77,A
    fis,192,AH
    pet,105,C
Weeping Mary (2)
  "If there's anybody here like a
weeping Mary..."
    bur,38,A
    kre,157,A
    pet,337,C
Welcome Table - *see* - I'm Going
to Sit at the Welcome Table
We'll Die in the Field
    pet,150,C
    sew,21,A
We'll March Down Jordan
    mci,243,AH
    pet,377,C
We'll Overtake the Army
    pet,151,C
    san,140,F
Well She Ask Me in the Parlor
    odu,258,CH
We'll Stand the Storm
    new,208,A
    pet,105,C
    sew,39,A

We'll Wait Til Jesus Comes
    san,115,F
We're Almost Home - *see* - We Are
Almost Home
We're Some of the Praying People
    bar,16,E
Were You There
    and,43,A
    bal,88,E
    bap,108,A
    bar,40,E
    blo,212,B
    bry,39,E
    bur,40,A
    bur2,46,A
    cha,87,A
    cle,126,A
    det5,106,A
    fis,195,AH
    hay,127,AH
    jac,38,A
    joh1,136,A
    johg1,60,A
    new,215,C
    pet,41,C
    pet,47,C
    rel,162,A
    san,143,F
    whi,100,A
    worf,46,A
    worj1,100,AH
    worj1,51,CH
    worj2,2,A
We've Come This Far By Fatih
    cle,192,A
What a Beautiful City
    blo,211,B
    bry,33,E
    cle,169,D
What a Hard Time
    odu,87,CH
What a Trying Time
    all,74,E
    fis,210,AH

pet,47,C
pet,298,C
What Do You Say
  san,114,F
What Harm Has Jesus Done
  mci,246,AH
  pet,47,C
What is the Matter With the
  Mourners - see - Jubilee
What Kind of Shoes You Going to
  Wear
    det,2,A
What Month Was Jesus Born In
  afr,42,A
  cou,245,E
What Shall I Do
  pet,257,C
What Shall I Render
  cle,190,D
What You Going to Do
  log,1,E
  odu,77,CH
What You Going to Do When the
  Lamp Burns Down
    det2,30,A
    det5,140,A
    hal,28,A
    joh,170,A
    pet,299,C
    pet,378,C
    rel,136,A
What You Going to Name that
  Pretty Little Baby
    new,216,C
    pet,257,C
Wheel in a Wheel
  bal,2,A
  det5,184,A
  pet,48,C
  pet,106,C
  rel,110,A
  san,24,F
Wheel in the Middle of the Wheel
  hal,23,A
  odu,81,CH

When Christ the Lord Was Here
  san,144,F
When Do We Meet Again
  all,41,E
When I Am Gone Gone Gone
  bal,38,A
When I Come to Die
  pet,257,C
  rel,144,A
  san,116,F
When I Die
  gri,4,E
  pet,197,C
When I Fall on My Knees - see -
  Let Us Break Bread Together
When I Get in Heaven in My
  Elbow Chair
    bal,74,A
    pet,258,C
When I Get to Heaven
  det5,128,A
  fis,134,AH
  pet,239,C
  rel,140,A
When I Lay My Burden Down
  - see - Glory Glory Hallelujah
When I Rise Crying Holy
  par,148,A
When I'm Dead
  new,64,C
  pet,106,C
  worf,9,E
When I'm Gone (1)
  "When I'm gone Lord somebody's
  goin' t' miss me..."
    mci,40,AH
    pet,48,C
When I'm Gone (2)
  "It'll be Lord Lord Lord when I'm
  gone..."
    fis,198,AH
    gri,16,E
    lom1,471,D
    pet,337,C

When Israel Was in Egypt's - *see* -
Go Down Moses
When Jesus Brought the Light
to Me
    ken,40,E
When Jesus Comes
    gri,94,E
    pet,258,C
When Moses Smote the Water
    gla,22,D
    jes,54,AH
    pet,198,C
    sew,60,A
When My Blood Runs Chilly and
Cold
    lom,610,E
    lom2,452,AH
When My Lord Calls Me I Must
Go
    par,157,CH
When Shall I Get There
    pet,151,C
When the Chariot Comes
    bar,44,E
When the Devil Comes Around
    bur1,8,A
When the General Roll Is Called
    bar,29,E
    new,147,C
    see also - General Roll
    Call
When the Lord Called Moses
    fis,200,AH
    pet,378,C
When the Saints Go Marching In
    blo,212,B
    bry1,21,D
    johg,4,A
    lom1,454,D
    new,171,C
    pet,259,C
When the Stars Begin to Fall - *see* -
My Lord What a Morning

When the Train Comes Along
    bal,12,A
    dit,4,A
    new,65,C
    odu,111,CH
    pet,199,C
    pet,412,C
When We Do Meet Again
    pet,107,C
When You Feel Like Moaning
    cou,238,E
When You Hear My Coffin Sound
    dit,41,A
    pet,49,C
Where Do You Think I Found My
Soul
    san,146,F
Where Is Mary Gone
    log,2,E
Where Shall I Be (1)
    "Where shall I be when the first
    trumpet sounds..."
    bry,47,E
    det5,173,A
    hal,8,A
    joh,136,A
    pet,299,C
    rel,172,A
Where Shall I Be (2)
    "Moses lived till he got old..."
    odu,134,CH
Where Shall I Go
    new,112,C
    pet,49,C
White Horse Pawing in the Valley
    ken1,149,AH
White Marble Stone
    all,42,E
    pet,338,C
Who Built the Ark
    fis,204,AH
    pet,199,C
Who Do You Call the King
Emanuel
    fen,25,A

Who Is on the Lord's Side
    all,56,E
    pet,412,C
Who Is This Coming
    san,117,F
Who Locks the Lion's Jaw
    bal,36,A
    pet,200,C
Who Love My Lord
    mci,247,AH
    pet,260,C
Who Shall Deliver Poor Me
    ken1,116,AH
Who Will Join the Union
    arm,220,A
    det5,142,A
    fen,48,A
    pet,200,C
    rel,48,A
Who'll Be a Witness For - see -
Witness for My Lord
Who's Been Here
    bro,6,A
Who's Going to Close My Dying
Eyes
    ken,69,AH
    pet,49,C
Who's That Coming Over Yonder
    bry1,12,D
    hal,20,A
    joh,104,A
    pet,243,C
Who's That Yonder
    bar,45,E
    jes,6,AH
    jon,4,E
Why Don't You Come Along
    mci,242,AH
    pet,338,C
Why Don't You Deliver Me
    mci,248,AH
    pet,200,C
Why Don't You Let God's People
Go
    mci,250,AH

    pet,201,C
Why He's the Lord of Lords - see -
He Is the Lord of Lords
Wide Deep Troubled Water
    nil,13,AH
Wide River - see - Wasn't That a
Wide River
Winter
    all,78,E
    pet,201,C
Winter Will Soon Be Over
    arm,244,A
    bar,14,E
    det2,32,A
    fen,72,A
    rel,72,A
Wish I Was in Heaven Setting
Down
    gri,74,E
    new,113,C
    pet,412,C
    pet,413,C
Witness - see - Witness for My
Lord
Witness for My Lord
    hay,47,AH
    joh,130,A
    johg,22,A
    odu,132,CH
    pet,107,C
    pet,108,C
    whi,68,A
Woe Be Unto You
    lom,604,E
Woke Up This Morning
    cle,146,D
Woman at the Well
    blo,212,B
    cou,252,A
Wonder Where Is Good Old Daniel
    det5,73,A
    jon,145,E
    pet,108,C
    rel,107,A
    whi,78,A

Wonder Where Is My Brother Gone
  cou,228,E
Wondrous Love
  lom2,440,AH
Won't You Sit Down
  bry1,41,D
Working on the Building
  odu,72,CH
Workmen's Jingles
  odu,251,CH
Wrestle on Jacob
  all,4,E
  new,216,C
  pet,152,C
Wrestling Jacob
  bal,62,A
  bal,86,A
  bal,87,E
  det5,70,A
  hal,41,A
  new,217,A
  pet,152,C
  pet,153,C
  rel,131,A
  san,148,F
Wretched Man That I Am
  pet,36,C
  worj1,53,CH

Yes God Is Real
  cle,201,A
Yes I'm Going Up
  log,5,E
  worj1,66,CH
Yes Yonder Comes My Lord
  det5,219,A
  pet,289,C
  rel,112,A
Yonder Comes Sister Mary
  fis,208,AH
  pet,260,C
You Better Get Religion Sinner
Man
  ken1,141,AH

You Better Get Your Ticket
  odu,112,CH
You Better Run to the City of
  Refuge
  bal,44,A
  pet,301,C
You Can Dig My Grave
  tob,38,E
You Can't Cross Here
  bar,32,E
You Can't Find a New Hiding
Place
  bal,35,E
  pet,301,C
You Can't Stay Away
  odu,117,CH
You Go I'll Go With You (1)
  "You go I'll go with you..."
  bal,81,A
  dit,46,A
  joh1,44,A
  pet,339,C
You Go I'll Go With You (2)
  "Lord when I go and tell them
  what you say..."
  pet,108,C
You Going to Reap Just What You
Sow
  det2,28,A
  det5,28,A
You Got a Right
  hal,40,A
  new,114,C
  pet,153,C
You Got a Robe
  odu,97,CH
You Got to Walk That Lonesome
  Valley - see - Lonesome Valley
You Hear the Lambs - see - Hear
  the Lamb's Crying
You May Bury Me in the East
  bur2,137,A
  det,6,A
  fis,82,AH
  hay,63,AH

joh,181,A
pet,109,C
pet,302,C
sew,15,E
sew,15,A
worj1,60,CH

You Must Be Pure and Holy
all,107,E
pet,339,C

You Must Come in By and
Through the Lamb - *see* -
My God Is So High

You Must Have That True
Religion
bal,4,A
joh1,100,A
pet,379,C
san,150,F

You Publican You Pharisee
bal,51,E
pet,260,C

You Shall Reap
new,103,C
pet,303,C

You Won't Find a Man Like Jesus
worf,23,A

You'd Better Mind
cle,125,A
pet,302,C

You'd Better Run
bal,45,A
pet,153,C
pet,302,C

Young Lamb Mus' Fin' de Way
- *see* - Old Sheep Done Know
the Road

Your Low Down Ways
pet,303,C

Your Sins Are Going to Find
You Out
gri,52,E
pet,300,C

You're My Brother So Give Me
Your Hand
pet,380,C

You're Tired Child
hay,58,AH
pet,109,C

Zion
par,158,AH

Zion Hallelujah
mci,199,AH
pet,241,C

Zion Weep Low
arm,232,A
det5,196,A
fen,60,A
pet,261,C

Zion's Children
gla,24,D
pet,154,C
san,118,F
sew,42,E

First Line Index

Adam in de garden Eve she disobeyed - *see* - Good Lord Done Been Here

Adam where are you - *see* - What a Trying Time

After 'while after 'while - *see* - After a While

Ain't dat a pity Lord ain't dat a shame - *see* - Sinner-Man So Hard to Believe

Ain't dat good news oh Lord - *see* - Ain't That Good News (1)

Ain't dat hard trials tribulation very great- *see* - Hard Trials

Ain't I glad I ain't going to die no more - *see* - I Ain't going to Die No More

Ain't I glad I've got out the wilderness - *see* - Ain't I Glad I've Got Out the Wilderness

Ain't I glad oh ain't I glad - *see* - I Ain't Going to Die No More

Ain't it dinner ho ho - *see* - Ho-Ho

Ain't no no' dodgin' in de bushes iner Gawd's army - *see* - Coming Again By and By

Ain't that good news - *see* - Ain't That Good News (1)

Ain't that hard trials - *see* - Hard Trials (2)

Ain't you glad ain't you glad you got good religion - *see* - Ain't You Glad You Got Good Religion

Alive a-humble humble yourself de bell's a done a rung - *see* - Live Humble

All dem bones in de mornin' - *see* - Dry Bones Going to Rise

All I do de church keep a-grumblin' - *see* - All I Do the Church Keep Grumbling

All I want is a little more faith in Jesus - *see* - A Little More Faith in Jesus

All my sins are taken away taken away - *see* - All My Sins Are Taken Away

All night all day angels watching over me - *see* - Angels Are Watching Over Me

All night all night de angels are watchin' obuh me - *see* - Angels Are Watching Over Me

All night wrastlin' Jacob's all night all night - *see* - Wrestling Jacob

All over this world - *see* - All Over This World

All the Mount Zion members - *see* - Hold Out to the End

All them bones - *see* - Dry Bones Going to Rise

All them Mount Zion member - *see* - Hold Out to the End (2)

All-a-my troubles will soon be over with - *see* - All Over This World

Alleluia Alleluia - *see* - Alleluia

Aller ma sins are taken away - *see* - All My Sins Are Taken Away

Am I a soldier of the cross - *see* - Soldier of the Cross

Am I a soldier - *see* - Am I a Soldier

Amazing grace how sweet the soun' - *see* - Amazing Grace

Amazing grace how sweet the sound I want to die a-shouting - *see* - I Want to Die Shouting

Amen Amen Amen Oh lawdy - *see* - Amen

Amen amen amen see the little baby - *see* - Amen

Amen amen see the baby lying in the manger - *see* - Amen

An' a howdy howdy brother - *see* - Howdy Howdy

An' he year-de when Jordan roll - *see* - Roll Jordan Roll

An' I couldn't hear nobody - *see* - I Couldn't Hear Nobody Pray

Anchor believer anchor anchor in the Lord - *see* - Anchor in the Lord

And can it be my souls thou hast they God - *see* - Hymn

And I ain't got weary yet - *see* - I Ain't Got Weary Yet

And I can't stay away Lord - *see* - I Can't Stay Away

And I couldn't hear nobody pray - *see* - I Couldn't Hear Nobody Pray

And I won't stop praying - *see* - I Won't Stop Praying

And the moon will turn to blood - *see* - Day of Judgment

And when I come to die - *see* - Fold My Hands and Tie My Feet

And when I found Him this is what He said - *see* - I Look for Jesus All My Days

Angel came from heaven - *see* - Get on the Boat Little Children

Angel done changed my name - *see* - Angel Done Changed My Name

Angel dun change-er ma name - *see* - Angel Done Changed My Name

Angel roll de stone away - *see* - Angel Roll the Stone Away

Angels done bowed down - *see* - Angels Done Bowed Down

Animals a-comin' - *see* - Animals a Coming

Anyhow anyhow anyhow my Lord - *see* - Anyhow My Lord

Anyhow anyhow anyhow my Lord - *see* - I'm Going Up to Heaven Anyhow

Anyhow my Lord - *see* - I'm Going Up to Heaven Anyhow

Are you ready fer de judgement day - *see* - Are You Ready

Ark's a-moverin a moverin - *see* - Old Ark Is Moving Along

As I went down in the valley to pray - *see* - As I Went down in the Valley to Pray

As I went down in the valley to pray - *see* - Good Old Way

Ask an' a you shall be given - *see* - Love Come Trickling Down

At de jedgment bar at de jedgement - *see* - At the Judgment Bar

Ay said de blackbird to de crow - *see* - Black Bird and the Crow

Baby born in Bethlehem - *see* - New Born Baby

Baby's in Memphis layin' around - *see* - Baby's in Memphis

Band of Gideon over in Jordan - *see* - Band of Gideon

Band of Gideon - *see* - Gideon's Band

Baptist Baptist unbeliever - *see* - Jesus Locked the Lion's Jaw

Baptizin' begin oh halleluiah - *see* - Baptizing

Baptizing begin baptizing begin - *see* - Baptizing

Be with me Lord Be with me - *see* - Be With Me

Beams of heaven as I go through this wilderness - *see* - Some Day

Bear yo' burden bear yo' burden - *see* - Bear Your Burden

Been a lis'nin' all de night long - *see* - Hard Trials (3)

Been a long time prayin' far diser way - *see* - Done Found the Way at Last

Been a long time praying for this-a way - *see* - Done Found the Way at Last

Been a-listening all the night long - *see* - I've Been Listening All Night Long

Before I'd be a slave I'd be buried in my grave - *see* - Before I'd Be a Slave

Before this time another year I may be gone - *see* - Before This Time Another Year

Behold that star up yonder - *see* - Behold That Star

Believer oh shall I die - *see* - Shall I Die

Belshazza' had a feas' 'n' dazza han'writin' on de wall - *see* - Belshazzah Had a Feast

Bending knees a-aching - *see* - Over the Crossing

Better walk steady Jesus a-listenin' - *see* - Better Walk Steady

Big camp meeting on the praying ground - *see* - Poor Sinner Fare You Well

Black sheep black sheep - *see* - Black Sheep Where You Left Your Lamb

Blessed hope that in Jesus is given - *see* - Blessed Hope

Blin' man lying at de pool - *see* - Blind Man Lying at the Pool

Blin' man stood on de road an' cried - *see* - Blind Man Stood on the Road and Cried

Blood oh de blood oh de blood - *see* - Blood Done Sign My Name

Blood that Jesus shed for me - *see* - Blood Will Never Lose Its Power

Blow Gab'l Gab'l Gab'l in dat day - *see* - Blow Gabriel

Blow Gable at the judgement - *see* - Blow Gabriel

Blow Gabriel Judgement - *see* - Blow Gabriel

Blow yo' Gospel trumpet - *see* - Blow Your Gospel Trumpet

Bood oh the blood - *see* - Blood Done Sign My Name

Book of Revelation God to us revealed - *see* - Going to Heaven

Bow low elder Jesus is a-list'nin' - *see* - Bow Low Elder

Bow low Elder - *see* - Bow Low Elder

Brethen my way's cloudy - *see* - My Way's Cloudy

Brethren rise and shine and give God the glory - *see* - Brethren Rise and Shine

Brethren rise and shine - *see* - Rise and Shine

Bright angels on the water - *see* - Social Band

Broken-hearted world broken-hearted children - *see* - Old Man Devil Gotta Go Some

Brothe' Andrew whey you bin when de dry weathe' come - *see* - Upon the Rock

Brother an' a hey hey ma Lord who's dat comin' - *see* - Prancing Horses

Brother didn't conscience come and tell you - *see* - Go Down in the Valley and Pray

Brother don't you want to go - *see* - Don't You Want to Go

Brother Goerge's gone to glory - *see* - Sin Sick Soul

Brother guide me home and I am glad - *see* - Brother Guide Me Home

Brother guide me home - *see* - Brother Guide Me Home

Brother have you come to show me the way - *see* - Brother Have You Come

Brother have you come to show me the way - *see* - Show Me the Way (1)

Brother I never know I comin' here tonight - *see* - Coming Here Tonight

Brother Joe you ought to know my name - *see* - Book of Life

Brother less go down less go down - *see* - Down in the Valley to Pray

Brother Moses gone - *see* - Brother Moses Gone

Brother Rabbit Brother Bear - *see* - Raise the Iron

Brother will you come - *see* - I Belong to the Union Band

Brother you'd better be a prayin' - *see* - Brother You'd Better Be a Praying

Brothern my way my way's cloudy - *see* - My Way's Cloudy

Brothers brothers - *see* - There's Room Enough

Brothers don't get weary - *see* - Brothers Don't Get Weary

Brothers don't stay away - *see* - Room Enough

Bruddah I nebbuh know I comin' here tonight - *see* - Coming Here Tonight

Burden down Lord Burden down Lord since I lay - *see* - Burden Down

But He ain't comin' here t' die no mo' - *see* - But He Ain't Coming Here to Die No More

But He ain't comin' here t' die no mo' - *see* - Jesus Ain't Coming Here to Die No More

By an' by by an' by I'm gwinter lay down my he - *see* - By and By (1)

By an' by I'm goin' to lay down dis heavy load - *see* - By and By (1)

By and by by and by good Lord - *see* - Every Day Will Be Sunday

By and by by and by - *see* - By and By (1)

By and by I'm going to see them - *see* - By and By (1)

By and by we all shall meet again - *see* - By and By (2)

By and by we'll all go down - *see* - Come Let Us All Go Down

Calvary calvary calvary - *see* - Calvary

Calvary is a mountain high - *see* - Calvary's Mountain

Can't hide sinner can't hide - *see* - Can't Hide Sinner

Can't you heah what my Lawd said - *see* - Come Unto Me

Can't you live humble - *see* - Can't You Live Humble

Captain where are you bound for - *see* - Steamboat Song

Carolers start their singing - *see* - This Is the Christmas Time

Charley went out huntin' on a noomshiney night - *see* - Poor Mourner

Chatter with the angels soon in the mornin' - *see* - Chatter With the Angels

Children did you hear when Jesus rose - *see* - Did You Hear When Jesus Rose

Children go and I will send thee - *see* - Holy Baby

Children go where I send thee - *see* - Children Go Where I Send Thee

Children hail hail hail - *see* - Hail Hail Hail

Children sound the jubilee - *see* - Sound the Jubilee

Children we all shall be free - *see* - Children We All Shall Be Free

Children you'll be called on to march - *see* - Children You'll Be Called on

Chilly water Hallelujah to dat Lam' - *see* - Chilly Water

Christians hold up your heads - *see* - Christians Hold Up Your Heads

Church of God dat sound so sweet - *see* - Church of God

Climb up ye little children climb up ye older people - *see* - Climb Up Ye Little Children

Climbin' up d'mountain children - *see* - Climbing Up the Mountain

Coffin de coffin to bind me down - *see* - Coffin to Bind Me Down

Come all of God's children in the field - *see* - Come All of God's Children

Come along and let's go home - *see* - Old Ship of Zion (2)

Come along come along and let's go home - *see* - Old Ship of Zion (2)

Come along I am sorry for to leave you - *see* - Come Along

Come along Moses - *see* - Come Along Moses

Come along my brothers come along - *see* - Them Charming Bells

Come an' go to that lan' where I'm boun' - *see* - Come and Go

Come by here Lord come by here - *see* - Kum Ba Yah

Come come come and go wid me - *see* - Come Come Come and Go With Me

Come down angel and trouble the water - *see* - Let God's Saints Come In

Come down angels trouble the water - *see* - Come Down Angels

Come down come down come down sinner yo' none - *see* - Come Down Sinner

Come down come down my Lord - *see* - Come Down My Lord

Come down come down - *see* - Come Down Sinner; My Lord's Writing All the Time

Come down my Lord come down - *see* - My Lord's Writing All the Time

Come down - *see* - Come Down

Come here Lord - *see* - Come Here Lord

Come my brethren one an' all - *see* - General Roll Call

Come my brothers and sisters too - *see* - On to Glory

Come on el-duh let's go 'roun de wall - *see* - That Suits Me

Come on Mauma le's go roun' the wall - *see* - That Suits Me

Come to me ye who are hard opprest - *see* - Come to Me

Come trembling down go shouting home - *see* - Come Trembling Down

Comin' down de line my Lord - *see* - Coming Down the Line

Cotton needs a-pickin' so bad - *see* - Cotton Needs Picking

Couldn't hear nobody pray - *see* - I Couldn't Hear Nobody Pray

Crosser me over my Lord - *see* - Cross Me Over

Cruel Jews just look at Jesus - *see* - Cruel Jews

Cryin' aye Lawd don't leave me - *see* - Aye Lord Don't Leave Me

Cryin' oh Lord cryin' - *see* - Death's Going to Lay His Cold Icy Hands on Me (1)

Crying aye Lord don't leave me - *see* - Aye Lord Don't Leave Me

Cyan' hide sinner cyan' hide - *see* - Can't Hide Sinner

Daniel in de lion's den - *see* - Daniel's in the Lion's Den

Daniel saw de stone hewn out of the mountain - *see* - Daniel Saw the Stone (2)

Daniel saw de stone rollin' - *see* - Daniel Saw the Stone (1)

Dark was de night an' col' de groun' - *see* - Am I Born to Die

Dat day when you'se weary fightin' wiv sin - *see* - When the Devil Comes Around

Dat same train goin' t' be back tommorrow - *see* - That Same Train

Dat sun gwine down - *see* - That Sun Going Down

Day I lef' huh my mother's hous' huh - *see* - Day I Left My Home

Dear brother don't you leave - *see* - This Old World's a Hell to Me

Death ain't nothin' but a robber don't you see - *see* - Death Ain't Nothing But a Robber

Death gwineter lay his cold icy hands on me - *see* - Death's Going to Lay His Cold Icy Hands on Me (3)

Death he is a little man - *see* - Lord Remember Me

Death is goin' to lay his cold icy han' on me - *see* - Death's Going to Lay His Cold Icy Hands on Me (3)

Death is in this land - *see* - Death Is in This Land

Death t'row thy sting away - *see* - Death's Going to Lay His Cold Icy Hands on Me (2)

Death went out to the sinner's house come and go - *see* - Traveling Shoes

Debbil was a busy ole man - *see* - Roll Him Out Again

Deep deep river my home is over Jordan - *see* - Deep River

Deep river Lord I want to pass over into camp ground - *see* - Deep River

Delilah was a woman fine and fair - *see* - Samson

Delilie was a woman fine an' fair - *see* - Samson

Dem bones dem bones dem bones - *see* - Them Bones

Dem bones dem dry bones I hear the word of the Lord - *see* - Dry Bones

Dere is rest fo' de weary trabbler - *see* - There Is Rest for the Weary Traveler

Dere's a balm in Gilead - *see* - Balm in Gilead

Dere's a han' writin' on de wall - *see* - There's a Handwriting on the Wall

Dere's a little wheel a turnin' in my heart - *see* - Little Wheel Turning in My Heart

Dere's a man goin' roun' takin' names - *see* - There's a Man Going Around Taking Names

Dere's a mighty war in de hebben I John saw - *see* - There's a Mighty War in Heaven

Dere's a star in de Eas' on Christmas morn - *see* - Rise Up Shepherd and Follow

Dere's no hidin' place down dere - *see* - No Hiding Place; There's No Hiding Place Down There

Dere's one little two little three little angels - *see* - Band of Angels

Dere's room enough - *see* - Room Enough in the Heaven

Dese all-er ma father's chillun - *see* - These Are All My Father's Children

Devil was a busy ole man - *see* - Roll Him Out Again

Dey turn 'way Mary an'a Joseph - *see* - Round the Glory Manger

Dey whupped him up de hill - *see* - He Never Said a Mumbling Word

Did you hear how dey crucified my Lord - *see* - Did You Hear How They Crucified My Lord

Didn't it rain oh didn't it rain - *see* - Didn't It Rain (2)

Didn't it rain some fo'ty nights an' days - *see* - Didn't It Rain (1)

Didn't my Lord deliver Daniel and why not every man - *see* - Didn't My Lord

Deliver Daniel

Didn't old Pharaoh get lost - *see* - Trying to Cross the Red Sea

Didn't yo know pilgrim - *see* - Hear Gabriel Blow in That Morn

Didn't you hear my Lord when he called - *see* - Didn't You Hear

Didn't you know pilgrim - *see* - Hear Gabriel Blow in That Morn

Dig deep children - *see* - Dig Deep Children

Dis day Lord dere is a mighty shoutin' in de hebbe - *see* - There Is a Mighty Shouting

Dis ole worl' is not ma home - *see* - Come and Go With Me

Dis union oh dis union band - *see* - Big Camp Meeting in the Promised Land

Dis union sing dis union - *see* - Stand on a Sea of Glass

Divers never gave nothing to the poor - *see* - Divers Never Gave Nothing to the Poor

Do doan' yer weep for de baby - *see* - Do Don't You Weep for the Baby

Do don't touch my garment Good Lawd - *see* - Do Don't Touch My Garment Good Lord

Do don't touch-a my garment - *see* - Do Don't Touch My Garment Good Lord

Do don't you weep for the baby - *see* - Do Don't You Weep for the Baby

Do Lawd do Lawd do remember me - *see* - Do Lord Remember Me

Do Lord come show me the way - *see* - King Jesus Sitting on the Water Side

Do Lord do Lord 'member me - *see* - Do Lord Remember Me

Do tell de worl' I love ma Jesus - *see* - Who Love My Lord

Do tell the world - *see* - Who Love My Lord

Doan you want to go to Heaven - *see* - Tall Angel at the Bar

Does you call dat religion no no no - *see* - Does You Call That Religion

Don't be weary traveller come along home to Jesus - *see* - Don't Be Weary Traveler

Don't call de roll till I get there - *see* - Don't Call the Roll

Don't call the roll John - *see* - Don't Call the Roll

Don't come oh Lord in the mawnin - *see* - Don't Come Oh Lord

Don't leave me Lord - *see* - Don't Leave Me Lord

Don't let de wind don't let de wind - *see* - Don't Let the Wind Blow Here No More

Don't ye view dat ship a come a sailin' - *see* - Don't You View That Ship Come Sailing

Don't yo' hab eb'rybody fo' yo' fr'en' - *see* - Don't You Have Everybody for Your Friend

Don't yo' hear de Lam's a cryin' - *see* - Hear the Lamb's Crying

Don't you be like the foolish virgin - *see* - Zion

Don't you have everybody for your friend - *see* - Don't You Have Everybody for Your Friend

Don't you hear God talking hammering - *see* - Hammering Judgment

Don't you hear the lambs a-cryin' - *see* - Hear the Lamb's Crying

Don't you let nobody turn you roun' - *see* - Don't You Let Nobody Turn You Around

Don't you remember one mornin' - *see* - Hint to the Wise

Don't you see that ship a-sailing - *see* - Old Ship of Zion

Don't you view dat ship a-come a-sailin' - *see* - Don't You View That Ship Come Sailing

Don't you wish you were in hebben today - *see* - Don't You Wish You Were in Heaven

Don't you worry 'bout me - *see* - Jesus Going to Make Up My Dying Bed

Doncher let nobody turn you roun' - *see* - Don't You Let Nobody Turn You Around

Done foun' my los' sheep - *see* - Done Found My Lost Sheep

Done made my vow to the Lord - *see* - Done Made My Vow to the Lord

Done made my vow to the Lord - *see* - Made My Vow to the Lord

Doubtin' Thomas doubt no mo' - *see* - Angel's Waiting at the Tomb

Down in a valley sing hallelu - *see* - Mary Had a Baby

Down in de valley de sperret spoke - *see* - Dry Bones

Down in hell - *see* - Down in Hell

Down on me down on me - *see* - Down on Me

Downward road is crowded with unbelievin' souls - *see* - Downward Road Is Crowded (1)

Downward road is crowded crowded the wind blows east - *see* - Downward Road Is Crowded (2)

Dus dust an' ashes - *see* - Dust and Ashes

Dust dust and ashes fly over on my grave - *see* - Dust and Ashes

Early in de mornin' honey I'm goin' rise - *see* - Early in the Morning

Eb'ry time I feels de Spirit - *see* - Every Time I Feel the Spirit

Eb'ry time I think about Jesus - *see* - Calvary

Eb'rybody wants to know jis how I die - *see* - Everybody Wants to Know Just How I Die

Ef de Lord calls you - *see* - If the Lord Calls You

Ef you want to get to hebben come along - *see* - Did You Hear My Jesus

Elder we will die in the field - *see* - Sister Mary's Twelve Blessings

Elder you say you love King Jesus - *see* - Love King Jesus

Elijah rock shout shout - *see* - Elijah Rock

Ennyhow ennyhow ennyhow muh Lawd - *see* - Anyhow My Lord

Ev'ry little step goes higher higher higher - *see* - Every Little Step Goes Higher

Ev'ry time I feel de Spirit - *see* - Every Time I Feel the Spirit

Ev'ry time I think about Jesus - *see* - Calvary

Eve where is Adam - *see* - Adam in the Garden Pinning Leaves

Every little step goes higher higher higher - *see* - Every Little Step Goes Higher

Every time I feel the spirit moving in my heart - *see* - Every time I Feel the Spirit

Every time I feel the Spirit - *see* - I Will Pray

Every time I think about Jesus - *see* - Calvary

Everybody wants to know just how I die - *see* - Everybody Wants to Know Just How I Die

Everybody who am living everybody got to die - *see* - Everybody Got to Die

Everywhere I go everywhere I go my Lord - *see* - Everywhere I Go My Lord

Ezek'el saw the wheel 'way up in de middle - *see* - Ezekiel Saw the Wheel (2)

Ezekiel's wheel oh my soul - *see* - Ezekiel's Wheel

Faint not at even tide - *see* - Faint Not

Fairest Lord Jesus ruler of all nature - *see* - Fairest Lord Jesus

Faith of our fathers - *see* - Faith of Our Fathers

Fare you well my brother - *see* - Fare Ye Well

Farewell farewell to my only child - *see* - Like a Rough and a Rolling Sea; Rough and Rolling Sea

Farewell my brother farewell forever - *see* - Farewell My Brother

Farewell my dear mother - *see* - Farewell My Dear Mother

Father Abraham sitteth beside - *see* - Father Abraham

Father Abraham sittin' down side ob de Holy Lam' - *see* - Father Abraham

Fer I John saw de Holy number - *see* - John Saw the Holy Number

Fighting on hallelujah we are almost down to shore - *see* - Fighting On

Fire my Savior fire - *see* - Satan's Camp Fire

Firs' time Gawd called Adam Adam 'fused to answer - *see* - Adam in the Garden Pinning Leaves

Fisherman Peter on the sea - *see* - Fisherman Peter

Five of them were wise when the bridegroom came - *see* - There Were Ten Virgins

Fix me Jesus fix me right - *see* - Fix Me Jesus

Fly away be at rest- *see* - Fly to My Jesus' Arms

Fo' de Lawd gwine take my stan' - *see* - Poor Moaner You Shall Be Free

Fo' de Lord - *see* - For the Lord

Fo'ty days fo'ty nights when de rain kept a-fallin - *see* - Didn't It Rain (1)

Footprints of Jesus leading the way - *see* - Footprints of Jesus

For I'll be there - *see* - I'll Be There

For my Lord for my Lord - *see* - I'm Going to Lay Down My Life for My Lord

For the Lord for the Lord - *see* - For the Lord

Fox hab hole in de groun' - *see* - Hard Trials (1)

Foxes have holes in the ground and the birds have nests in the air - *see* - Foxes Have Holes in the Ground

Free at las' I thank God I'm free at las' - *see* - Free at Last

Freely go marching along - *see* - Baptizing Hymn

From heaven - *see* - Praise Chant

Gabriel's trumpet going to blow - *see* - Gabriel's Trumpet Going to Blow

Galman Day and a one two dun k'am die - *see* - Galman Day

Gambler get up off o' yo' knees - *see* - End of That Morning; Gambler Get Up
   Off of Your Knees

Get in the union Jesus is a listening - *see* - Get in the Union

Get on board little chillun - *see* - Get on Board Little Children

Get yo' ticket - *see* - Get Your Ticket

Get you ready dar's a meetin' here tonight - *see* - There's a Meeting Here
   Tonight (2)

Getting ready to die - *see* - Getting Ready to Die

Gif' ob Gawd is eternal life - *see* - Gift of God Is Eternal Life

Gift of God is eternal life - *see* - Fix Me Jesus; Gift of God Is Eternal Life

Gim me dat ole-time religion - *see* - Old Time Religion

Gimme yo' han' - *see* - Give Me Your Hand

Git on board o' ship o' Zion - *see* - Get on Board Old Ship of Zion

Git yo' ticket - *see* - Get Your Ticket

Give a way Jordan - *see* - Give Way Jordan

Give me a clean heart so I may serve - *see* - Give Me a Clean Heart

Give me that old time religion - *see* - Old Time Religion

Give me the wings oh good Lord - *see* - Give Me the Wings

Give me this-a-old time religion - *see* - Old Time Religion

Give me your hand - *see* - Give Me Your Hand

Give way Jordan - *see* - Give Way Jordan

Give-er me Jesus You may have all-er dis worl' - *see* - Give Me Jesus

Glory and honor praise Jesus - *see* - Glory and Honor (1)

Glory glory Halelujah when I lay muh burden - *see* - Glory Glory Hallelujah

Go and I will go with you - *see* - Go and I Go With You

Go chain the lion down before the heaven doors close- *see* - Go Chain the Lion Down (1)

Go chain the lion down - *see* - Go Chain the Lion Down (2)

Go down Moses 'way down in Egypt's lan' - *see* - Go Down Moses

Go 'Lija and git yo' horses - *see* - Go Elijah

Go Mary an' toll de bell - *see* - Go Mary and Toll the Bell (2)

Go Mary an' toll de bell who's all them come dressed in white- *see* - Go Mary and Toll the Bell (1)

Go Mary go - *see* - Remember the Dying Lamb

Go Mary go stay Martha stay - *see* - Remember the Dying Lamb

Go on brother go on go on - *see* - Go on Brother

Go round go round look at de mornin' star - *see* - Go Round Go Round

Go tell it on the mountain over the hills and every where - *see* - Go Tell It On the Mountain (1)

God be with you - *see* - God Be With You

God called Ezekiel by his word - *see* - Dry Bones

God got plenty o' room - *see* - Plenty Good Room (1)

God has smiled on me He has set me free - *see* - God Has Smiled on Me

God He called John while he was a writin' - *see* - John Was Writing

God is a God God don't never change - *see* - God Is a God

God is sweeping this world today - *see* - Stand Up Like Soldiers

God knows it's time - *see* - God Knows It's Time

God knows 'tis a better day than this a-coming - *see* - In the Army

God moves on the water - *see* - God Moves on the Water

God tol' Hezekiah - *see* - Little Black Train Is Coming

God walked around - *see* - I'll Make Me a Man

God's gonna set this world on fire - *see* - God's Going to Set This World on Fire

God's got plenty of room - *see* - Plenty Good Room

Goin' away to see ma Savior - *see* - Going Away to See My Lord

Goin' to lay down my sword and shield - *see* - Down By the Riverside

Goin' to set down an' rest awhile - *see* - Going to Set Down and Rest Awhile

Goin' to wake up the dead - *see* - God's Going Wake Up the Dead

Goin' to weep goin' to mourn - *see* - My Soul's Going to Heaven

Going away to see my Savior - *see* - Going Away to See My Lord

Going home in the chariot in the morning - *see* - Going Home in the Chariot

Going to hold out to the end - *see* - Going to Hold Out to the End

Going to lay down my burden - *see* - Down By the Riverside

Going to lay down my sword and shield - *see* - I Ain't Going to Study War No More

Going to march away in the gold band - *see* - Gold Band

Going to pull my war clothes down - *see* - Going to Pull My War Clothes

Going to quit all of my worldly ways - *see* - Going to Quit All of My Worldly Ways

Going to ride up in the chariot - *see* - Going to Ride Up in the Chariot

Going to roll in my Jesus' arms - *see* - Going to Roll in My Jesus' Arms

Going to see my mother some of these mornings - *see* - Some of These Mornings

Going to set down and rest a while - *see* - Going to Set Down and Rest Awhile

Going to walk about Zion I really do believe - *see* - Sabbath Has No End

Going to write to Master Jeses to send some valiant soldiers - *see* - Going to Write to Master Jesus

Good bye brother good bye brother - *see* - Good Bye Brother

Good bye brothers good bye sisters - *see* - Good Bye Brothers

Good bye city o' Babylon - *see* - Good Bye City of Babylon

Good bye mother good bye - *see* - Good Bye Mother

Good bye my brother - *see* - Good Bye

Good Lord I done good - *see* - Good Lord I Done Good

Good Lord I wonder is there anybody here getting ready to die - *see* - Is There Any Body Here Getting Ready to Die

Good Lord in dat heab'm - *see* - Got a Home at Last

Good Lord in the mansions above - *see* - In the Mansions Above

Good Lord shall I ever be the one - *see* - Good Lord Shall I Ever Be the One; We Are Building on a Rock

Good Lord when I die - *see* - Good Lord When I Die

Good morning everybody - *see* - Good Morning Everybody

Good news de chariot's a-comin' - *see* - Good news

Good news de chariot's comin' - *see* - Good News the Chariot's Coming

Good news good news angel bring glad tidings down - *see* - Good News Angels Bring the Tidings

Good news good news - *see* - Good News

Good news in the kingdom an' I won't die no more - *see* - Good News in the Kingdom

Good news member - *see* - Good News Member

Good news the chariot's coming - *see* - Good News the Chariot's Coming

Good old chariot swing so low - *see* - Swing Low Sweet Chariot

Good-bye Mother - *see* - Lord Time Is Drawing Nigh

Goodby city o' Babylon yo kingdom must come - *see* - City of Babylon

Goodbye brother goodbye brother - *see* - Good Bye Brother

Goodbye brothers goodbye sisters - *see* - Good Bye Brothers

Goodbye I'm goin' home - *see* - Somewhere Around a Throne

Goodbye my brother goodbye - *see* - Good Bye

Goose quill's a scratchin' in de count book - *see* - My Lord's Writing Down Time

Gospel train a-comin' t'ru de sun - *see* - Gospel Train

Gospel train am a comin' - *see* - Gospel Train

Gospel train is a-comin' - *see* - Gospel Train

Gospel train is passing through - *see* - Last Call

Got a crown up in de Kingdom ain't dat good news - *see* - Ain't That Good News

Got glory an' honor praise Jesus - *see* - Glory and Honor (1); Got Glory and Honor; Praise the Lamb

Got my letter got my letter - *see* - Got My Letter

Got to go to judgememt stand your trial - *see* - Got to Go to Judgement

Got to go to the judgement my myself - *see* - So Sad

Got two wings to veil yo' face - *see* - Two Wings

Graveyard I'm walking through the graveyard - *see* - Lay This Body Down

Great big stars 'way up yonder - *see* - Great Big Stars

Great day de riteous marchin' - *see* - Great Day

Great day for me great day for me I am so happy - *see* - Great Day for Me

Great day great day de righteous marchin' - *see* - Great Day

Great Gawd He rules all 'roun' de mountain - *see* - Jesus Rolling in His Arms

Green trees a-bowin' - *see* - Steal Away

Green trees rocky road - *see* - Green Trees

Guide me oh thou great Jehovah - *see* - I Fold Up My Arms and I Wonder

Guide my head while I run this race - *see* - Guide My Head

Gwine to git on de evening train - *see* - Get on the Evening Train

Gwine to lay down my burden down by the riverside - *see* - I Ain't Going to Study War No More

Gwine to quit all o' my worldly ways - *see* - Going to Quit All of My Worldly Ways

Gwine to ride up in the chariot - *see* - Going to Ride Up in the Chariot

Gwine to roll in my Jesus' arms - *see* - Going to Roll in My Jesus' Arms

Gwine to see my mother some o'dese mornin's - *see* - Some of These Mornings

Gwine to write to Massa Jesus - *see* - Turn Back Pharaoh's Army

Gwine-a lay down mah burden - *see* - I Ain't Going to Study War No More

Gwineter ride up in de chariot - *see* - Going to Ride Up in the Chariot

Hail de King of Babylon - *see* - Hail the King of Babylon

Hail Hail I belong to the bloodwashed army - *see* - My Name's Written on High

Hail hail Put John on de islan' - *see* - Put John on the Island

Hail John's army ben' down an' die - *see* - Hail John's Army Bend Down and Died

Hallelu O my Lord I'm gwineter see my mother again - *see* - Death Come to My House He Didn't Stay Long

Hallelu - *see* - Hallelu

Halleluiah to de Lamb ob Gawd - *see* - Halleluiah to the Lamb

Halleluja Halleluja my God - *see* - Walking in God's Commandments

Hallelujah an' a hallelujah - *see* - Hallelujah (2)

Hallelujah glory hallelujah truly I'm going - *see* - I Don't Care What the World May Do

Hallelujah good Lord - *see* - I Am the Light of the World

Hallelujah hallelujah - *see* - Hallelujah (1)

Hallelujah hallelujah new born again - *see* - New Born Again

Hallelujah kind Savior - *see* - Kind Savior

Hallelujah King Jesus - *see* - Hallelujah King Jesus

Hallelujah Lord I've been down into the sea - *see* - Been Down Into the Sea

Hallelujah Lord who'll jine de union - *see* - Who Will Join the Union

Hallelujah my God walking God's commandments - *see* - Walking in God's Commandments

Hallelujah o hallelujah Lord who'll jine de Union - *see* - Who Will Join the Union

Hallelujah oh hallelujah - *see* - Who Will Join the Union

Hallelujah to the Lamb - *see* - Hallelujah to the Lamb

Halleluyer to the Lam' - *see* - Going Down to Jordan

Hammer keeps ringing - *see* - Hammer Keeps Ringing

Han' me down Yo' silvah trumpet - *see* - Hand Me Down My Silver Trumpet

Hark listen to the trumpeters - *see* - Enlisted Soldiers

Has anybody here seen my Jesus - *see* - Has Anybody Here Seen My Lord

Have you got good religion - *see* - Certainly Lord

Have you got religion cert'nly Lord - *see* - Have You Got Good Religion

He carried his cross he carried his cross - *see* - They Nail Him to the Cross

He is King of kings he is Lord of lords - *see* - He Is King of Kings

He is King of Kings - *see* - He Is King of Kings

He is King of Kings - *see* - King of Kings

He is the Lord of lords - *see* - He's the Lord of Lords

He raise a poor Lazarus - *see* - He Raised Poor Lazarus

He rose he rose he rose from the dead - *see* - He Rose From the Dead

He sees all you do and He hears all you say - *see* - My Lord's Riding All the Time

He sees all you do and hears all you say - *see* - My Lord Is Riding All the Time

He sees all you do - *see* - My Lord's Riding All the Time

He'll lift you up if you ask Him - *see* - If You Ask Him

He's a dyin' bed-maker - *see* - Jesus Going to Make Up My Dying Bed

He's got His eyes on you - *see* - He's Got His Eyes on You

He's got the whole world in His hands - *see* - He's Got the Whole World in His Hands

He's the lily of the valley oh my Lord - *see* - He's the Lily of the Valley

He's the Lord of lords - *see* - He's the Lord of Lords

Heab'm I'm heab'm bound - *see* - Ain't Got Long to Stay Here

Healin' waters done move - *see* - Healing Waters

Hear that-a freedom train a-coming - *see* - Freedom Train Coming

Hearse keep a-rollin' somebody to de graveyard - *see* - I Feel Like My Time Ain't Long

Heav'n bell a-ring I know de road - *see* - Jesus Sitting on the Waterside

Heav'n bells a-ringin' and I'm a-goin' home - *see* - Heaven Bells Ringing and I'm Going Home

Heave away heave away - *see* - Heave Away

Heaven bell a ring I know the road - *see* - Jesus on the Waterside

Heaven heaven eb'rybody talking 'bout heaven - *see* - Going to Shout All Over God's Heaven

Heaven is a beautiful place I believe- *see* - Heaven Is a Beautiful Place (1)

Heaven is a beautiful place I know - *see* - Heaven Is a Beautiful Place (2)

Heaven is shining shining - *see* - Heaven Is Shining

Heaven sweet heaven - *see* - Sweet Heaven

Heaven's bell a-ringing - *see* - Jesus on the Waterside

Hebben is shinin' - *see* - Heaven Is Shining

Hebben sweet hebben oh Lord I want to go to hebben - *see* - Sweet Heaven

Heben is a beautiful place - *see* - Heaven Is a Beautiful Place

Helleluja kind Saviour let dis warfare be ended - *see* - Kind Savior

Here He comes the Judge severe - *see* - Roll Jordan Roll (3)

Hey slip de him slip slide him - *see* - Heave-A-Hora

Hey why don't you come along - *see* - Why Don't You Come Along

Hit's a mighty rocky road an' I'm mos' done trabbelin' - *see* - Mighty Rocky Road

Ho everyone that thirsts - *see* - Ho Every One That Thirsts

Hol' de win' don't let it blow - *see* - Hold the Wind Don't Let It Blow

Hold out yo' light you heav'n boun' so'dier - *see* - Hold Out Your Light

Hold out yo' light you Heav'n boun' soldier - *see* - Heaven-Bound Soldier

Hold the wind don't let it blow - *see* - Hold the Wind Don't Let It Blow

Holy Bible book divine - *see* - Holy Bible

Holy holy holy is my God - *see* - Holy Is My God

Holy Holy yo' promise to answer prayer - *see* - Holy Holy You Promised to Answer Prayer

How can I pray how can I pray - *see* - How Can I Pray

How I got over how I got over - *see* - How I Got Over

How long de train been gone - *see* - How Long Has the Train Been Gone

How long watchman - *see* - How Long Watchman

How many members gone - *see* - How Long Has the Train Been Gone

How yo' do believer how yo' do today - *see* - How You Do Believer

How's you know written down - *see* - My Name's Been Written Down

Humble humble humble - *see* - Humble

Humble humble humble yourselves - *see* - Going to Live Humble to the Lord

Humble humble I've been trying to live humble - *see* - I've Been Trying to Live Humble

Humm Lordy chained in hell an' can't come out - *see* - Lord Answer My Prayer

Hunt till you find him - *see* - Hunting for the Lord

Hunt until you find Him - *see* - Hunting for the Lord

Hurry mourner hurry mourner - *see* - Sun Mows Down

Hurry on my weary soul - *see* - I Heard From Heaven Today

Hush hush somebody's callin' mah name - *see* - Hush Somebody's Calling My Name

Hush oh hush sombody's callin' me - *see* - My Lord What Shall I Do

Hypocrite and the concubine - *see* - Hypocrite and the Concubine

I ain't going to grief my Lord no mo' - *see* - I Ain't Going to Grieve My Lord No More

I ain't going to trust nobody - *see* - I Ain't Going to Trust Nobody

I ain't got time to tarry - *see* - Poor Sinner Fare You Well

I ain't gwine grief muh Lawd no mo' - *see* - I Ain't Going to Grieve My Lord No More

I aint gwine er trus' nobody dat day - *see* - I Ain't Going to Trust Nobody

I am a Baptist Preacher and scorned on every hand - *see* - Missionary Baptist Song

I am a po' pilgrim of sorrow - *see* - Poor Pilgrim

I am a poor pilgrim of sorrow - *see* - City Called Heaven

I am a poor wayfaring stranger - *see* - Pilgrim's Song; Poor Pilgrim

I am a trouble in the mind - *see* - I'm Troubled in Mind

I am boun' for the Promised Lan' - *see* - I Am Bound for the Promised Land

I am free ma Lord - *see* - I Am Free

I am goin' obuh dere In muh father's house - *see* - I Am Going Over There

I am goin' to join in this army of the Lord - *see* - I Am Going to Join in this Army

I am goin' to walk with Jesus by myself - *see* - I'm Going to Walk With Jesus By Myself

I am huntin' for a city for to stay a while - *see* - I Am Hunting for a City

I am not afraid to die - *see* - I Am Not Afraid to Die

I am on my mission - *see* - Gospel Train

I am seekin' for a city Hallelujah - *see* - I Am Seeking for a City

I am so glad I've been in the grave and rose again - *see* - I'm So Glad (4)

I am talkin' 'bout the same train - *see* - Same Train

I am the true vine - *see* - I Am the True Vine

I am trampin' I am trampin' - *see* - Heaven Is Going to Be My Home

I and Satan had a race - *see* - I and Satan Had a Race

I ask all them brothers around - *see* - Archangel Open the Door

I asked Father Georgy for religion - *see* - This Is the Trouble of the World

I been a-listening all the night time - *see* - I've Been Listening All Night Long

I been 'buked an' I been scorned - *see* - Hell and Heaven; I've Been Rebuked

I been in de storm so long - *see* - I've Been in the Storm So Long

I been in some strange lan' so far from home - *see* - I Heard a Voice Couldn't Tell Where

I believe I'll go back home - *see* - I Believe I'll Go Back Home

I believe in the God of Elijah - *see* - God of Elijah

I believe this is Jesus - *see* - I Believe This Is Jesus

I build my house upon the rock - *see* - Bound to Go

I called to my Father - *see* - Save Me Lord Save Me

I can't stand the fire - *see* - I Can't Stand the Fire

I can't stay away - *see* - I Wish I Had Died in Egypt Land

I can't stay behind the roses bloom- *see* - I Can't Stay Behind (2)

I can't stay behind there's room enough in the heaven - *see* - I Can't Stay Behind (1)

I cannot stay away - *see* - I Never Intend to Die in Egypt Land

I come dis hight to sing an' pray - *see* - Oh Yes

I come empty to Thee Lord - *see* - I Am Coming to a King

I come this night for to sing and pray - *see* - I Come This Night

I come this night for to sing and pray - *see* - Oh Yes (2)

I couldn't hear nobody pray I was way down yonder by myself - *see* - I Couldn't Hear Nobody Pray

I do know Gawd don't lie - *see* - I Do Know God Don't Lie

I don' wan' be buried in de stawm - *see* - Who's Going to Close My Dying Eyes

I don't care for riches - *see* - I Don't Care for Riches

I don't care where you bury my body - *see* - My Little Soul; Shine Shine

I don't feel know ways tired I come too far from - *see* - I Don't Feel No-Ways Tired

I don't feel weary and noways tired - *see* - I Don't Feel Weary

I don't know I don't know I don't know - *see* - May Be the Last Time

I don't possess houses or lands - *see* - Christ Is All

I done been home I done try on my robe - *see* - I Done Been Home

I done been home - *see* - I Done Been Home

I feel all all right no condemnation - *see* - No Condemnation in My Soul

I feel all right no condemnation - *see* - No Condemnation in My Soul

I feel like dying in the service of my Lord - *see* - I Feel Like Dying in This Army

I feel like I feel like Lord - *see* - I Feel Like My Time Ain't Long

I feel like I feel like my time ain't long - *see* - I Feel Like My Time Ain't Long

I found free grace and dying love - *see* - New Born Again

I found Jesus over in Ziyun - *see* - I Found Jesus Over in Zion

I got a cross you got a cross - *see* - Going to Shout All Over God's Heaven

I got a hidun place in de Word of God - *see* - I Got a Hiding Place

I got a home in de rock don't yuh see - *see* - I Got a Home in That Rock

I got a home where liars can't go - *see* - I Got a Home

I got a key to thuh kingdom - *see* - I Got a Key to the Kingdom

I got a letter dis mornin' aye Lawd - *see* - I Got a Letter This Morning

I got a light the light that shineth - *see* - I Got a Light

I got a mother in de bright shinin' world - *see* - I Got a Mother in the Bright Shining World

I got a new name over in Zion - *see* - I Got a New Name

I got a robe an' you got a robe - *see* - Going to Shout All Over God's Heaven

I got a robe you got a robe all God's chillun got a robe - *see* - Going to Shout All Over God's Heaven

I got a sister over yonder - *see* - Over Yonder

I got mah swoad in mah han' - *see* - I Got My Sword in My Hand

I got on my shoes like John - *see* - My Sister Ain't You Mighty Glad

I got shoes - *see* - I Got Shoes

I got to lay in yonder graveyard - *see* - I Got to Lay in Yonder Graveyard

I hab a leader obuh dere - *see* - I Have a Leader Over There

I had so many many sins - *see* - All the Way to Calvary

I have a Leader Over There - *see* - I Have a Leader Over There

I have been tempted oh yes - *see* - In the Morning

I have been tryin' a great long while - *see* - Lord I Just Got Over

I have bin a-istenin' all de night long - *see* - I've Been Listening All Night Long

I hear' a mighty moanin' - *see* - In Some Lonesome Graveyard

I heard de preachin' of de elder - *see* - I Heard the Preaching of the Elder

I heard my mother say Give me Jesus - *see* - Give Me Jesus

I hold my brother with a trembling hand - *see* - Wrestle on Jacob

I hope my mother will be there in that beautiful world on high - *see* - I Hope My Mother Will Be There

I know a man that was here before Christ - *see* - My Trouble Is Hard

I know a wide river 'taint no Mississippi - *see* - Wide Deep Troubled Water

I know dat de bell dun ring - *see* - Bell Done Ring

I know de Lord's laid His hands on me - *see* - I Know the Lord's Laid His Hands on Me

I know I have another buildin' children - *see* - I Know I Have Another Building

I know I know Lord believer I know - *see* - Believer I Know

I know I know my Lord - *see* - I Know That My Redeemer Lives

I know I would like to read like to read - *see* - I Know I Would Like to Read

I know member know Lord - *see* - Bell Done Rung (1)

I know my Jesus loves me O my Lord - *see* - I Know My Jesus Loves Me

I know my Lord I know these bones gwineter rise again - *see* - These Bones Going to Rise Again

I know my road is rough an' rocky - *see* - I Know My Road Is Rough and Rocky

I know that the bell done rung - *see* - Bell Done Rung (2)

I know the Lord ha' laid his hands on me - *see* - I Know the Lord's Laid His Hands on Me

I knows I's a witeness for my Lord - *see* - Samson's Wife Sat on His Knees

I look away yonder what do I see - *see* - John's Gone Down on the Island

I love everybody I love everybody in my heart - *see* - I Love Everybody

I love myu blessed Savior - *see* - I Love My Blessed Savior

I love the Lord - *see* - I Love the Lord

I love to hear my bass-o - *see* - Band of Music

I lub muh blessed Savior - *see* - I Love My Blessed Savior

I mean to lift up a standard for my King - *see* - I Mean to Lift Up the Standard for My King

I meet little Rosa early in the morning - *see* - Early in the Morning

I met my mother the other day - *see* - Scandalize My Name

I must walk my lonesome valley - *see* - Lonesome Valley

I never felt such love in my soul before - *see* - I Never Felt Such Love in My Soul Before

I promised my Lord I would deny Him not - *see* - Pray on the Way

I saw de light - *see* - I Saw the Light

I saw the beam in my sister's eye - *see* - I Saw the Beam in My Sister's Eye

I sought my Lord in the wilderness - *see* - I'm Going Home

I stood on de ribber ob Jerdon - *see* - I Stood on the River of Jordan

I stood outside the gate - *see* - I Stood Outside the Gate

I t'ank Gawd fer I got religion - *see* - I Got My Religion on the Way

I take my text in Matthew - *see* - There's a Meeting Here Tonight (1)

I thank God for I got religion - *see* - I Got My Religion on the Way

I think I hear my brother say - *see* - Stars Begin to Fall

I think I heard a rumbling in the sky - *see* - There's No One Like Jesus

I think I heard him say while he was dy'in on de Cross - *see* - Take My Mother Home

I thought I had a friend was true - *see* - I Thought I Had a Friend

I wait upon the Lord - *see* - Go in the Wilderness

I want dat house what's built wit'out han's - *see* - House That's Built Without Hands

I want Jesus to walk with me - *see* - I want Jesus to Walk With me

I want some valiant soldier here - *see* - Hail Mary

I want to be my Father's children - *see* - Trouble of the World

I want to be ready my Lord to walk in Jerusalem - *see* - I Want to Be Ready

I want to be ready - *see* - Walk in Jerusalem Just Like John (2)

I want to climb up Jacob's ladder - *see* - Jacob's Ladder (2)

I want to die easy when I die - *see* - I Want to Die Easy When I Die

I want to die like-a Lazarus die - *see* - I Want to Die Like Lazarus

I want to go where Jesus is to play upon the golden harp - *see* - I Want to Go Where Jesus Is

I wanta live so God can use me - *see* - I Want to Live So God Can Use Me

I wants to climb up Jacob's ladder - *see* - Jacob's Ladder

I was but young but I recall - *see* - God's Amazing Grace

I was lost in sin and sorrow - *see* - Old Ship of Zion

I was walking along the other day - *see* - Other World Is Not Like This

I was way down a yonder a by myself - *see* - Dum-A-Lum

I went down in the valley - *see* - That Sabbath Has No End

I went to de hillside I went to pray - *see* - Angels Done Changed My Name

I went to the hillside I went to pray - *see* - I Went to the Hillside

I will overcome - *see* - I Will Overcome

I wish I have had an eagle's wings - *see* - I Wish I Have Had an Eagle's Wings

I wish I was in Heaven sittin' down sittin' down - *see* - Wish I Was in Heaven Sitting Down

I woke up dis mornin' wid mah min' an' it was stayed - *see* - Woke Up This Morning

I woke up this morning with my mind - *see* - My Mind Stayed on Freedom

I wonder where is my sister she is gone away - *see* - Israelites Shouting

I'll be there I'll be there - *see* - General Roll

I'll be there in the morning - *see* - When the General Roll Is Called

I'll be there in the morning when he gen'ral roll is called - *see* - I'll Be There in the Morning

I'll meet you way up yonder in a few day - *see* - I'll Meet You Way Up Yonder

I'm a child of grace - *see* - I'm a Child of Grace

I'm a goin' in Zion - *see* - Sabbath Has No End

I'm -a goin' to tell you 'bout de comin' of de Saviour - *see* - In That Great Getting Up Morning (2)

I'm a going to eat at the welcome table - *see* - I'm Going to Eat at the Welcome Table

I'm a going to travel - *see* - L'Envoi

I'm a gwinter sing gwinter sing all along de way - *see* - Going to Sing All Along the Way

I'm a po' lil' orphan in dis worl' - *see* - I'm a Poor Little Orphan

I'm a poor wayfarin' stranger - *see* - Pilgrim's Song

I'm a rolling I'm a rolling - *see* - I'm Rolling (1)

I'm a rolling thro' an unfriendly world - *see* - I'm Rolling (2)

I'm a soldier for Jesus - *see* - Soldier for Jesus

I'm a soldier in the army of the Lord - *see* - I'm a Soldier in the Army of the Lord

I'm a soldier of de cross in de ahmy o' my Lawd - *see* - I'm a Soldier of the Cross

I'm a solger in de army ob de lord - *see* - I'm a Soldier in the Army of the Lord

I'm a soljuh in the Army of thuh Lawd - *see* - I'm a Soldier in the Army of the Lord

I'm a trabblin' to de land - *see* - I'm Traveling to the Land

I'm a trav'ling to the grave - *see* - I'm Traveling to the Grave

I'm a travelin' to the land - *see* - I'm Going Down to the River of Jordan; I'm Traveling to the Land

I'm a traveling to the grave - *see* - I'm Traveling to the Grave

I'm a witness faw mah Lawd - *see* - I'm an Everyday Witness

I'm a-going to eat at the welcome table - *see* - I'm Going to Eat at the Welcome Table

I'm a-going to join the band Hallelujah - *see* - I'm Going to Join the Band

I'm a-gwine to tell you 'bout de comin' ob de Saviour - *see* - In That Great Getting Up Morning

I'm a-rollin thro an unfriendly world - *see* - I'm Rolling

I'm a-rolling in Jesus' arms - *see* - Rolling in Jesus' Arms

I'm a-runnin' fo' muh life - *see* - I'm Running for My Life

I'm a-trampin' trampin' tryin' to make heaven my - *see* - Tramping

I'm a-trav'ling - *see* - I'm Traveling to the Grave

I'm agoing to eat at the welcome table - *see* - I'm Going to Eat at the Welcome Table

I'm all wore out a-toilin' fo' de Lawd - *see* - I'm All Wore Out Toiling for the Lord

I'm comin' yes Lord I'm comin' - *see* - I Don't Want You Go on and Leave Me

I'm go'n'ter set down at de welcome table - *see* - Some of These Days (2)

I'm goin' down to de ribbuh of Jerdan, Oh yes - *see* - I'm Going Down to the River of Jordan

I'm goin' t' hol' out to de en' - *see* - Hold Out to the End (1)

I'm goin' t' stay in de battle fiel' - *see* - I'm Going to Stay in the Battlefield

I'm goin' to climb up Jacob's ladder - *see* - Save Me Jesus Save Me Now

I'm goin' to cross that ocean by mysel' - *see* - When My Lord Calls Me I Must Go

I'm goin' to lay dowm my burdens - *see* - I Ain't Going to Study War No More

I'm goin' to see my lovin' Father when I get home - *see* - I'm Going to See My Loving Father When I Get Home

I'm goin' to sing - *see* - I'm Going to Sing

I'm goin' to wait I'm goin' to wait - *see* - I'm Going to Wait Until the Holy Ghost Comes

I'm goin' up home soon in de morning - *see* - Soon in the Morning

I'm going back with Jesus when He comes - *see* - I'm Going Back with Jesus

I'm going down to the river of Jordan - *see* - Some of These Days (2)

I'm going home children - *see* - I'm Going Home Children

I'm going to be a Christian if I keep praying on - *see* - If I Keep Praying On

I'm going to do all I can for my Lord - *see* - I'm Going to Do All I Can

I'm going to heaven and I don't want to stop - *see* - All My Sins Done Taken Away

I'm going to hold out to the end - *see* - Hold Out to the End

I'm going to join the band Hallelujah - *see* - I'm Going to Join the Band

I'm going to join the great 'sociation - *see* - I'm Going to Join the Great Association

I'm going to lay down my sword and shield - *see* - I Ain't Going to Study War No More

I'm going to live with Jesus - *see* - I'm Going to Live With Jesus

I'm going to sing all along the way - *see* - I'm Going to Sing

I'm going to sing - *see* - Going to Sing All Along the Way

I'm going to sing when the spirit says sing - *see* - I'm Going to Sing

I'm going to sit at the welcome table - *see* - I'm Going to Sit at the Welcome Table

I'm going to stay in the battlefield - *see* - I'm Going to Stay in the Battlefield

I'm going to tell God all my troubles - *see* - I'm Going to Tell God All My Troubles

I'm going to tell you about the coming of the Saviour - *see* - In That Great Getting Up Morning (2)

I'm gonna tell God how you treat me - *see* - Some of These Days (1)

I'm gwine to jine de great 'sociation - *see* - I'm Going to Join the Great Association

I'm gwine to tell you bout de comin' ob de Savior - *see* - In That Great Getting Up Morning

I'm in trouble Lord - *see* - I'm in Trouble

I'm jes' a-goin' over on de other side of Jordan - *see* - Going Over on the Other Side of Jordan

I'm just a poor wayfaring stranger - *see* - Pilgrim's Song

I'm just a-goin' over Jordan - *see* - I'm Just Going Over Jordan

I'm just a-goin' over there - *see* - I'm Just Going Over There

I'm no ways weary I'm no way tired - *see* - Old Ship of Zion

I'm not weary yet - *see* - Not Weary Yet

I'm runnin' on I'm runnin' on - *see* - I'm Running On

I'm running for my life - *see* - I'm Running for My Life

I'm so glad dere aint no devil in our lan' - *see* - No Devil in Our Land

I'm so glad dun jes got out ob dat Egypt lan' - *see* - I'm So Glad (2)

I'm so glad I'm so glad - *see* - I'm So Glad (3); No Devil in Our Land

I'm so glad Jesus lifted me - *see* - I'm so Glad Jesus Lifted Me

I'm so glad - *see* - Glad I Got Religion

I'm so glad the angels brough the tidings down - *see* - I'm So Glad (1)

I'm so glad trouble don't last alway - *see* - I'm So Glad Troubles Don't Last Always; What Shall I Do

I'm so glad troubles don't last always - *see* - I'm So Glad Troubles Don't Last Always

I'm sometimes up I'm sometimes down - *see* - Trouble Will Bury Me Down

I'm trampin' trampin' try'n' to make heaven ma home - *see* - Tramping

I'm traveling to the grave - *see* - I'm Traveling to the Grave

I'm troubled I'm troubled I'm troubled in mind - *see* - I'm Troubled in Mind (2)

I'm troubled in mind - *see* - I'm Troubled in Mind (1)

I'm working on the building for my Lord - *see* - I'm Working on the Building

I'se gwine to bear Lord - *see* - Bear Your Burden

I'se mighty tired - *see* - I'm Mighty Tired

I've a crown up in the kingdom - *see* - Ain't That Good News (2)

I've a message f'om ma Lord Halleluiah - *see* - I've a Message From My Lord

I've been a list'ing all de night long - *see* - I've Been Listening All Night Long

I've been 'buked an' I've been scorned - *see* - I've Been Rebuked

I've been in de storm so long children - *see* - I've Been in the Storm So Long

I've been listening all the night long - *see* - I've Been Listening All Night Long

I've been redeemed - *see* - I've Been Redeemed

I've been tempted - *see* - Ride on Conquering King

I've been toiling at the mill so long - *see* - I've Been Toiling at the Hill

I've been travelin' all de day ride on Moses - *see* - Ride on Moses

I've got a home in the rock don't you see - *see* - I Got a Home in That Rock

I've got a mother in de heaven - *see* - I've Got a Mother in the Heaven

I've got a robe you've got a robe - *see* - Going to Shout All Over God's Heaven

I've got shoes - *see* - I Got Shoes

I've got to go to judgement I don't know how soon - *see* - Lord Bless the Name

I've got to walk my lonesome valley - *see* - Lonesome Valley

I've just come from the fountain Lord - *see* - I've Just Come From the Fountain

If anybody ask you who I am - *see* - If Anybody Ask You Who I Am

If God was to call me I would not care - *see* - Gospel Train

If I had a hammer - *see* - If I Had a Hammer

If I had died when I was a babe - *see* - If I Had Died When I was a Babe

If I had it you could get it - *see* - Baby Mine

If I have my ticket Lord can I ride - *see* - If I Have My Ticket Lord

If I was a mourner just like you - *see* - If I Was a Mourner

If I wus a sinner man tell you what I'd do - *see* - Working on the Building

If my mother ask you for me - *see* - Drinking of the Wine

If there's anybody here like weeping Mary - *see* - Weeping Mary (2)

If when you give the best of your service - *see* - He'll Understand and Say Well Done

If ye love God serve Him - *see* - If You Love God Serve him

If ye want to see Jesus go in the wilderness - *see* - If You Want to See Jesus

If you can't come Lawd send a one angel down - *see* - Send One Angel Down

If you don't like the way I work jus' pay me off - *see* - If You Don't Like the Way I Work

If you look up the road - *see* - Join the Angel Band

If you love God serve Him - *see* - If You Love God Serve Him

If you see my mother - *see* - Ride on Conquering King

If you wanna know where I'm going - *see* - Going Up

If you want to get to heaven come along come along - *see* - Did You Hear My Jesus

If you want to get to hebben come along come alo - *see* - If You Want to Get to Heaven

If you want to go to heaven - *see* - Blood-Strained Banders

If you want to see Jesus - *see* - Leaning on the Lord

If you want to see Jesus go in the wilderness - *see* - If You Want to See Jesus

If you want to go to Heaven you must be new-born again - *see* - New Born Again

Imer rollin' in Jesus' arms - *see* - Rolling in Jesus' Arms

In bright mansions above in bright mansions above - *see* - In Bright Mansions Above

In de Lord in de Lord my soul's been anchored in de Lord - *see* - My Soul's Been Anchored in the Lord (2)

In de mornin' by de bright light - *see* - In the Morning

In de mornin' O in de mornin' - *see* - I Want to See Jesus in the Morning

In God we trust with all our heart and soul - *see* - In God We Trust

In that great gittin' up mornin' - *see* - In That Great Getting Up Morning (1)

In the Lord my soul's been anchored in the Lord - *see* - My Soul's Been Anchored in the Lord (2)

In the morning - *see* - I Going Put on My Golden Shoes; In the Morning

In the morning oh in the morning I want to see Jesus - *see* - I Want to See Jesus in the Morning

In the morning when I rise - *see* - Tell My Jesus Morning

In the morning when I rise give me Jesus - *see* - Give Me Jesus

In the river of Jordan John baptized - *see* - In the River of Jordan

In the River uv Jurdun - *see* - Sabbath Has No End

In the valley on my knees - *see* - I Couldn't Hear Nobody Pray

In-a this-a band we have sweet music - *see* - Jesus Is Risen From the Dead

Is there anybody here that loves my Jesus - *see* - Is There Anybody Here

Isaac a-ransom while he lay upon an altar bound - *see* - Didn't Old Pharaoh Get Lost

Ise a gwine ter jine de band - *see* - I'm Going to Join the Band

It breaks my heart to see my baby part - *see* - It's Moving Day

It makes no difference what church you may belong to - *see* - You're My Brother So Give Me Your Hand

It may be the last time - *see* - It May Be the Last Time

It was all ober dis worl' - *see* - All Over This World

It was on one Sunday morning - *see* - One Sunday Morning

It was po' little Jesus - *see* - Poor Little Jesus

It'll be Lord Lord Lord when I'm gone - *see* - When I'm Gone

It's a Mighty Rocky Road - *see* - Mighty Rocky Road

It's a-me it's a-me oh Lord - *see* - Standing in the Need of Prayer

It's always midnight 'way down in Hell - *see* - Way Down in Hell

It's down into the water - *see* - Baptism

It's Going to be a Mighty Day - *see* - It's Going to be a Mighty Day

It's me it's me O Lord standing in need of prayer - *see* - Standing in the Need of Prayer

Jacob's ladder long an' tall - *see* - Jacob's Ladder Long and Tall

Jay Gooze said-a befo' he died - *see* - Jay Gooze

Jedus blood sone mek me whole - *see* - Jesus's Blood Done Make Me Whole

Jedus done just what he said - *see* - Jesus Done Just What He Said

Jehovah hallelujah - *see* - Jehovah Hallelujah

Jerusalem Lawd - *see* - Walk in Jerusalem Just Like John (4)

Jerusalem my happy home - *see* - Ring Jerusalem

Jes' wait a little while - *see* - Old Ark Is Moving Along

Jes you git on de boat little chillun - *see* - Get on the Boat Little Children

Jesus Blood done Make Me Whole - *see* - Jesus Blood done Make Me Whole

Jesus done just what he said - *see* - Jesus Done Just What He Said

Jesus locked the lion's jaw - *see* - Jesus Locked the Lion's Jaw

Jesus He wore the starry crown - *see* - Jesus Wore the Crown

Jesus heal' de sick, give sight to de blin' - *see* - Jesus Healed the Sick

Jesus is litening all day long - *see* - Jesus Is Listening

Jesus met the woman at the well - *see* - Woman at the Well

Jesus rides that milk-white horse - *see* - Jesus Rides That Milk-White Horse

Jesus was a sittin' at the last Passover - *see* - Last Supper

Jesus was settin' at the last Passover - *see* - My Time Is Come

Jews dey took our savior - *see* - Jews They Took Our Savior

Jews killed poor Jesus - *see* - Jews Killed Poor Jesus

Job Job good Lord tell me how you feel - *see* - Job Job

Job Job what you reckin' - *see* - Job

John Brown's body lies a-mould'ring in the grave - *see* - John Brown's Body

John de Bunyan O Lord - *see* - John the Bunyan

John hallelujah oh John spirit of the Lord done fell on me - *see* - Spirit of the Lord Done Fell on Me

John John with the holy order - *see* - John John of the Holy Order

John John you will see John - *see* - John John

John sae de holy numbah - *see* - John Saw the Holy Number

John saw de number dat no man could number - *see* - John Saw the Number No Man Could Number

John saw the holy number sitting on the golden - *see* - Golden Altar

John saw the number that no man could number - *see* - John Saw the Number No Man Could Number

John the bunyan oh Lord - *see* - John the Bunyan

John wrote a letter and he wrote it in haste - *see* - It Just Suits Me

John's on de island on his knees - *see* - John's on the Island on His Knees

Join on join my Lord - *see* - Join the Heaven With the Angels

Jonah was a lad he was Amittai son - *see* - According to My Lord's Command

Jordan's mill's a-grinding - *see* - Jordan's Mills

Joshua fight de battle ob Jericho an de walls come tumblin' down - *see* - Joshua Fought the Battle of Jericho

Joshua fought the battle 'round Jericho's wall - *see* - I'm Going Where There Ain't No More Dying

Joys are flowing like a river - *see* - Blessed Quietness

Jubalee Jubalee oh my Lord - *see* - Jubilee

Jubalee what is the matter wid de mourners - *see* - Jubilee

Judgement Judgement Judgement day is a-rollin' - *see* - Judgment Day Is Rolling Around

Judgement Judgement Oh how I long to go - *see* - Judgment

Juniors ride aller roun' Gawd's alter - *see* - No Liar Can Stand

Just above my head - *see* - Just Above my Head

Just as you live just as you die - *see* - Judgment Will Find You So

Just as you live - *see* - Judgment Will Find You So

Just behold how many dangers - *see* - Appolyon and the Pilgrim

Just behold that number - *see* - From Every Graveyard; Just Behold That Number

Just let me get up in the house of God - *see* - Let Me Get Up

Just wait a little while - *see* - Didn't It Rain; Old Ark Is Moving Along (2)

Keep a-inchin' along keep a-inchin' along - *see* - Keep Inching Along

Keep in the middle of the road - *see* - Keep in the Middle of the Road

Keep yo' han' on de plow - *see* - Hold On

Keep your lamps trimmed and a-burning - *see* - Keep Your Lamps Trimmed

King cried - *see* - Daniel Daniel Servant of the Lord

King David was good - *see* - King David

King Jedus is muh only Fr'en - *see* - King Jesus Is My Only Friend

King Jesus built me a house above - *see* - King Jesus Built Me a House Above

King Jesus is a-listenin' all day long - *see* - King Jesus Is Listening

King Jesus is my only friend - *see* - King Jesus Is My Only Friend

Kum ba yah my Lord Kum ba yah - *see* - Kum Ba Yah

Lamb beautiful lamb - *see* - Lamb Beautiful Lamb

Lamb done been down here and died - *see* - Sinner Won't Die No More

Lamb of God just as I am oh Lamb of God I come - *see* - Just As I Am

Lamb sitting down side ob my Jesus - *see* - Sitting Down Side of My Jesus

Land I am bound for - *see* - Sweet Canaan

Land I am bound for sweet Canaan's happy land - *see* - Land I Am Bound For

Last Sunday morning last Sunday morning - *see* - Walk in Jerusalem Just Like John (1)

Lawd dese bones ob mine - *see* - Lord These Bones of Mine

Lawd He thought He'd make a man - *see* - These Bones Going to Rise Again

Lawd I got two wings fo' to veil mah face - *see* - Two Wings

Lawd I jes come from de fountain - *see* - His Name So Sweet

Lawd I want two wings to veil my face - *see* - Two Wings

Lawd I wish I had an Eagle's wings - *see* - Eagle's Wings

Lawd if I got my ticket can I ride - *see* - If I Got My Ticket Lord

Laz'reth is dead oh bless Gawd - *see* - I Am the Truth and the Light

Le's go down to Jurdon - *see* - Religion So Sweet

Lead me lead me my Lord - *see* - Lead Me to the Rock

Lead me to the Rock lead me to the Rock - *see* - King Jesus Is the Rock

Lead on O King Eternal - *see* - Lead on O King Eternal

Let de church roll on Lord - *see* - Let the Church Roll On

Let de Heb'n-light shine on me - *see* - Let the Heaven Light Shine on Me

Let me ride oh let me ride - *see* - Let Me Ride

Let me shine - *see* - Let Me Shine

Let me tell you 'bout Lord Lord Lord - *see* - Lamb's Blood Done Washed Me Clean

Let me tell you what is naturally the fact - *see* - Who Is on the Lord's Side

Let the church roll on Lord - *see* - Let the Church Roll On

Let the heaven light shine on me - *see* - Let the Heaven Light Shine on Me

Let us break bread together - *see* - Communion

Let us break bread together on our knees - *see* - Let Us Break Bread Together

Let us cheer the weary traveller - *see* - Let Us Cheer the Weary Traveler

Let us move along move along - *see* - Move Along

Let us praise Him - *see* - Let Us Praise Him

Let yo' light shine all over the world - *see* - Walking in the Light

Let yo' light shine judgment day is tryin' time - *see* - Judgment Day Is Trying Time

Let's keep de ark a movin' fer to hear what Jesus - *see* - Keep the Ark Moving

Let-n me ride oh low down the chariot - *see* - Low Down Chariot

Li'l boy name David shepherd on de mountain - *see* - Little Boy Named David

Li'l David play on yo' hawp - *see* - Little David (3)

Lie on me lie on all lie on everybody - *see* - Road to Heaven

Lift ev'ry voice and sing 'til earth and heaven - *see* - Lift Every Voice and Sing

Light bugs glimmer down de lane - *see* - My Merlindy Brown

Lightnin' flashin' and the thunder rollin' - *see* - I Know My Time Ain't Long

Like Jesus like Jesus and you won't find a man like Jesus - *see* - You Won't Find a Man Like Jesus

Listen to de lambs all a-cryin' - *see* - Listen to the Lambs

Lit' David play on yo' harp - *see* - Little David (2)

Little Boy how old are you - *see* - Conviction of the Wise Men in Jerusalem

Little children then won't you be glad - *see* - Little Children Then Won't You Be Glad

Little children you better believe - *see* - Little Children You Better Believe

Little chillun I believe - *see* - LIttle Children

Little Lamb - *see* - Little Innocent Lamb

Little talk wid Jesus makes it right - *see* - Little Talk With Jesus Makes It Right

Little talk with Jesus makes it right all right - *see* - Little Talk With Jesus Makes It Right

Live a-humble humble - *see* - Live Humble

Live humble humble humble your soul - *see* - Bell Done Ring

Live humble humble humble yourselves - *see* - Glory and Honor (2)

Live humble humble Lord - *see* - Humble Yourself the Bell Done Rung

Live-a humble Lord Humble yo'self de bell done ring - *see* - Humble Yourself the Bell Done Ring

Long time mo'ner - *see* - Leaning on That Lamb

Look away in-a-heaven - *see* - Look Away in the Heaven

Look what a wonder Jedus done - *see* - Look What a Wonder Jesus Done

Look-a death look-a death - *see* - Never a Man Speak Like This Man

Look-a how dey done muh Lawd - *see* - Look at How They Done My Lord

Lord called David an He called three times - *see* - Little David

Lord called David - *see* - Little David (1)

Lord Daniel's in de lion's den - *see* - Daniel's in the Lion's Den

Lord don't move this mountain but give me strength - *see* - Lord Don't Move This Mountain

Lord giv' me mer trumpet an' tole me ter blow - *see* - Going Lay Down My Life for My Lord

Lord have mercy - *see* - Lord Have Mercy

Lord he though he'd make a man - *see* - These Bones Going to Rise Again

Lord help me to hold out - *see* - Lord Help Me to Hold Out

Lord help the poor and needy - *see* - In This Land

Lord I can not stay here by mase'f - *see* - Lord I Can Not Stay Here By Myself

Lord I can't stay away - *see* - I Can't Stay Away

Lord I cannot stay here by myself - *see* - I Cannot Stay Here By Myself

Lord I couldn't hear nobody pray oh Lord - *see* - I Couldn't Hear Nobody Pray

Lord I cried I cried - *see* - Until I found the Lord

Lord I done done O Lord I done done - *see* - Lord I Done Done

Lord I hear show'rs of blessing - *see* - Even Me

Lord I keep so busy praising my Jesus - *see* - Ain't Got Time to Die

Lord I neber knowed de battle was so hard - *see* - Thank God I'm in the Field

Lord I want some valiant soldier - *see* - Some Valiant Soldier

Lord I want to be a Christian in a my heart - *see* - Lord I Want to Be a Christian

Lord I want to go to heaven fer to stan'my trials - *see* - Great Judgment Day

Lord I want two wings to veil my face - *see* - Two Wings

Lord I want you to touch me - *see* - Lord Touch Me

Lord I wish I had an eagle's wings - *see* - Eagle's Wings

Lord I wish I had come when you called me - *see* - Lord I Wish I Had Come

Lord I wonder by an' by - *see* - Bye and Bye

Lord I wonder - *see* - Bye and Bye

Lord I'm bearing heavy burdens - *see* - Trying to Get Home

Lord I'm hungry I want to be fed - *see* - Lord I'm Hungry

Lord I'm sick an' I want to be healed - *see* - Heal Me Jesus

Lord I've done what you told me to do - *see* - I Done What You Told Me to Do

Lord if I got my ticket - *see* - If I Got My Ticket Lord

Lord is dis hebben - *see* - Lord Is This Heaven

Lord is listening all day long - *see* - Bear Your Burden

Lord is on the givin ghand trouble will bury me down - *see* - Poor Me

Lord is this heaven - *see* - Lord Is This Heaven

Lord it's gettin' late over in the evenin' - *see* - It's Getting Late in the Evening

Lord Lord Lord you've sure been good to me - *see* - Lord Lord Lord

Lord make me more patient - *see* - Lord Make Me More Patient

Lord oh hear me praying Lord - *see* - Hear Me Praying

Lord oh Lord Keep me f'om sinkin' down - *see* - Keep Me From Sinking Down

Lord oh Lord - *see* - Trouble Done Bore Me Down

Lord oh my good Lord keep me from sinkin' down - *see* - Keep Me From Sinking Down

Lord sen'er one angel down - *see* - Send One Angel Down

Lord Shout for joy - *see* - Shout for Joy

Lord the big fish swallow ole Jonah whole - *see* - Big Fish

Lord the Lord the Lord is my shepherd - *see* - Lord Is My Shepherd

Lord these bones of mine - *see* - Lord These Bones of Mine

Lord until I reach my home - *see* - Lord Until I Reach My Home

Lord w'at shall I do trubble dun bore me down - *see* - Trouble Done Bore Me Down

Lord when I go and tell them what you say - *see* - You Go I'll Go With You (2)

Lord will preserve him if he will only pray - *see* - Lord Heal Him

Lord write my name - *see* - Lord Write My Name

Lord you must have that pure religion - *see* - Pure Religion

Lord's been here and blessed my soul - *see* - Lord's Been Here

Lordy jes' give me a lone white robe - *see* - Choose You a Seat and Set Down

Lordy won't you he's me - *see* - In This Field

Love come twinkling down - *see* - Love Come Twinkling Down

Ma little soul's determin' - *see* - My Soul's Determined

Ma Lord 'liver Daniel - *see* - Why Don't You Deliver Me

Ma soul is a witness for my Lord - *see* - Witness for My Lord

Mah brudder's died an' gone to hebben - *see* - My Brother's Died and Gone to Heaven

Mammy is massa going to sell us tomorrow - *see* - Mother Is Master Going to Sell Us Tomorrow

Mammy's baby go ter sleep - *see* - Negro Lullaby

March along march along I will see Him again - *see* - March Along

March along oh Canaan land - *see* - Walk God's Heavenly Road

March on and we shall gain the victory - *see* - March On

Marching up the heavenly road - *see* - Marching up the Heavenly Road

Mary an' Martha jes' gone 'long - *see* - Mary and Martha

Mary don' yer weep don' yer moan - *see* - Mary Don't You Weep

Mary had a baby aye Lawd - *see* - Mary Had a Baby

Mary oh Martha - *see* - Rocking Jerusalem

Mary oh Martha oh Mary ring dem bells - *see* - Rocking Jerusalem

Mary set her table in spite of all her foes - *see* - Did You Hear When Jesus Rose

Mary wat yuh weepin' about - *see* - Mary What You Weeping About

Mary wept an'-a Marthy moaned - *see* - Mary Wept and Marthy Moaned

Mary what you going to name that pretty little baby - *see* - What You Going to Name that Pretty Little Baby

Mary wo' three links of chain every link was Jesus' name - *see* - Keep Your Hand on the Plow

Massa take dat new bran coat - *see* - Away Down in Sunbury

May de Lord He will be glad of me - *see* - Bright Sparkles in the Churchyard

Me and God goin' to de graveyard field - *see* - Sitting Down Beside the Lamb

Me 'n' my pahdner an' two'r three mo' - *see* - Lordy Lordy Lordy

Me no weary yet - *see* - Not Weary Yet

Meet oh Lord on the milk-white horse - *see* - Meet Oh Lord

Member you will linger - *see* - Children Do Linger

Members don't get weary - *see* - Don't Get Weary; Members Don't Get Weary

Michael row the boat ashore - *see* - Michael Row the Boat Ashore

Michie Preval li donin gran bal - *see* - Calinda

Mighty fortress is our God - *see* - Mighty Fortress in Our God

Mine eyes have seen the glory of the coming of the Lord - *see* - Battle Hymn of the Republic

Mmmm - *see* - Funeral Chant

Mo parle Remon - *see* - Remon

Mo'ner why don't you pray - *see* - I Can't Stay Away

Moon come down like a piper's stem - *see* - Free Free My Lord

Mos' done toilin' here - *see* - Almost Done Toiling Here

Moses lived till he got old - *see* - Where Shall I Be (2)

Moses smote de water and de chillun - *see* - Moses Smote the Water

Most done toiling here oh bretheren - *see* - Almost Done Toiling Here

Mother I believe that Christ was crucified - *see* - Heaven Bells

Mother is massa gwine to sell us tomorrow - *see* - Mother Is Master Going to Sell Us Tomorrow

Motherless children have a hard time - *see* - Motherless Children Have a Hard Time

Mourner look at the people at the bar of God - *see* - At the Bar of God

Move me move me move me to do thy will - *see* - Move Me

Move members move Daniel - *see* - Move Members Move

My baby is lak' a little black star - *see* - My Little Black Star

My blessed Lord gimme the lil' book now Daniel - *see* - So I Can Write My Name

My bretheren don't get weary - *see* - My Brethren Don't Get Weary

My brethuh want to get religion - *see* - Lonesome Valley

My brother built a house in Paradise - *see* - Built a House in Paradise

My brother I do wonder - *see* - My Brother I Do Wonder

My brother sitting on the tree of life - *see* - Roll Jordan Roll (2)

My brother take care of Satan - *see* - My Army's Crossing Over

My brother want to get religion - *see* - Lonesome Valley

My brother wont you give up the world - *see* - Give Up the World (2)

My brother's died and gone to heaven - *see* - My Brother's Died and Gone to Heaven

My faith looks up to Thee - *see* - My Faith Looks Up to Thee

My father how long - *see* - My Father How Long; My Ship Is on the Ocean

My father took a light and went to Heaven - *see* - My Father Took a Light

My God He is a man a man of war - *see* - My God He Is a Man of War

My God is a rock in a weary land - *see* - My God Is a Rock

My God is so high you can't get over Him - *see* - My God Is So High

My good Lawd done been heah - *see* - Bless My Soul And Gone

My good Lord keep me from sinking down - *see* - Keep Me From Sinking Down

My good Lord show me de way - *see* - My Good Lord Show Me the Way; Show Me the Way (2)

My good Lord's done been here - *see* - My Good Lord Done Been Here

My good old auntie's gone along - *see* - Gone Along

My head wet wid de mid night dew - *see* - My Head Wet With the Midnight Dew

My hope is built on nothing less than Jesus' blood - *see* - Solid Rock

My King Emanuel my Emanuel above sing Glory to my King Emanuel - *see* - King Emanuel (2)

My little soul soul's determined - *see* - My Soul's Determined

My little soul's going to shine shine - *see* - My Little Soul's Going to Shine

My Lord called John while he was a-writin' - *see* - John the Revelator

My Lord command me to go in de wilderness - *see* - White Horse Pawing in the Valley

My Lord delibered Daniel - *see* - My Lord Delivered Daniel

My Lord delivered Daniel - *see* - Why Don't You Deliver Me

My Lord good and kind take the little babe - *see* - New Burying Ground

My Lord my Lord - *see* - Heaven Bell Ring

My Lord my Lord what shall I do - *see* - Heaven Bell Ring

My Lord says he's gwineter rain down fire - *see* - My Lord Says He's Going to Rain Down Fire

My Lord this is a needed time - *see* - When I Rise Crying Holy

My Lord what a mornin' when the stars begin - *see* - My Lord What a Morning

My Lord's comin' again - *see* - My Lord's Coming Again

My Lord's done just what He said - *see* - My Sin's Been Taken Away

My Lord's goin' move this wicked race - *see* - My Lord's Going to Move This Wicked Race

My lovin' brother - *see* - My Loving Brother

My loving brother - *see* - Rock of Ages

My mother and my father both are dead - *see* - I Cannot Stay Here By Myself

My mother has gone to journey away - *see* - In the Kingdom

My mother has reached the bright glory - *see* - I Heard of a City Called Heaven

My mother 'n' yo' mother both daid an' gone - *see* - Poor Sinner Man

My mother you follow Jesus - *see* - I Wish I Been Theree

My mother's in heaven - *see* - My Mother's in Heaven

My mudder's in de road most done trabelling - *see* - Almost Done Traveling

My ship is on the ocean poor sinner fare you well - *see* - My Ship Is on the Ocean

My sister's took her flight - *see* - Angel's Waiting at the Door

My soul in a witness for my Lord - *see* - Witness for My Lord

My soul is a witness for my Lord - *see* - Jesus Got His Business Fix; My Soul

Is a Witness for My Lord; Witness for My Lord

My soul's been anchored in the Lord - *see* - My Soul's Been Anchored in the Lord (1)

My time is come O my time is come - *see* - My Time Is Come

My way's cloudy - *see* - My Way's Cloudy

Never leave me alone alone - *see* - Never Leave Me Alone

Never saw such a man before - *see* - Never Saw Such a Man

New Jerusalem new Jerusalem - *see* - Sitting Down Beside the Lamb

No harm have I done you on my knees - *see* - Come Here Jesus If You Please

No harm no harm no harm - *see* - Poor Mourner's Got a Home at Last

No hidin' place - *see* - No Hiding Place

No I ain't ashame - *see* - No I Ain't Ashamed

No mo' muh dear brudduh - *see* - No More My Dear Brother

No more auction block for me - *see* - Many Thousand Gone

No more peck of corn for me - *see* - Many Thousand Go

No more rain fall for wet you - *see* - No More Rain Fall to Wet You

Noah Noah who built this ark - *see* - Noah Noah

Nobody knows de trouble I see Lord - *see* - Nobody Knows the Trouble I See

Nobody knows de trouble I've seen - *see* - Nobody Knows the Trouble I've Seen

Nobody knows the trouble I feel - *see* - Nobody Knows the Trouble I Feel

Nobody knows the trouble I've had - *see* - Nobody Knows the Trouble I've Had

Nobody knows who I am - *see* - Heaven Bells Ringing in My Soul; Nobody Knows Who I Am

Norah hist the windah let the dove come in - *see* - Noah Hoist the Window

Norah Norah lem-me come in - *see* - Hold On

Not just to kneel with the angels nor to see love - *see* - Just to Behold His Face

Not my brother nor my sister but it's me oh Lord - *see* - Standing in the Need of Prayer

Now didn't it rain chil'ren - *see* - Didn't It Rain (3)

Now didn't ole Norah build himself an ark - *see* - Story of Noah

Now I went down to Raleigh - *see* - Trip to Raleigh

Now I'm troubled in mind - *see* - Troubled in Mind

Now let me fly way in the middle of the air - *see* - Now Let Me Fly

Now we take this feeble body - *see* - Now We Take This Feeble Body

Nummer me one - *see* - Number Me One

O I know the Lord laid His hands on me - *see* - I Know the Lord Has Laid His Hands on Me

Oh de robe de robe my Lord - *see* - Oh the Robe

Oh freedom oh freedom after a while - *see* - Oh Freedom

Oh freedom over me and before i'd be a slave - *see* - Oh Freedom

Oh glory oh glory - *see* - Oh Glory

Oh graveyard oh graveyard - *see* - Oh Graveyard

Oh Holy Lord done with the sin and sorrow - *see* - Oh Holy Lord

Oh Holy Lord - *see* - Oh Holy Lord

Oh Holy savior - *see* - Oh Holy Savior

Oh Jerusalem oh my Lord - *see* - Oh Jerusalem

Oh Mary oh Martha go tell my disciples - *see* - Oh Mary Oh Martha

Oh Mary what you gonna name that pretty little baby - *see* - Oh Mary

Oh oh ah ah oh ah - *see* - Dark Was the Night

Oh shout oh shout - *see* - Oh Shout Away

Oh sinner yo' bed's too short - *see* - Oh Sinner

Oh the sunshine - *see* - Oh the Sunshine

Oh yes oh yes - *see* - Oh Yes (1)

Ol' ark's a-moverin' - *see* - Old Ark Is Moving Along (1)

Ol' sheep done know de road - *see* - Old Sheep Done Know the Road

Old Satan is a busy old man - *see* - Come Go With Me

Old Satan is one busy ole man - *see* - Old Satan

Old Satan told me to my face - *see* - I Know When I'm Going Home

Old time religion is good enough for me - *see* - Old Time Religion

Old Zion's children marching along - *see* - Old Zion's Children Marching Along

Ole Satan is a busy old man - *see* - Come and Go With Me

Ole sheep done know de road - *see* - Old Sheep Done Know the Road

Ole ship o' Zion ole ship o' Zion - *see* - Old Ship of Zion (4)

On Jordan's stormy banks I stand - *see* - Bound for the Promised Land

On mah journey now Mount Zion - *see* - On My Journey

On my hourney now - *see* - Mount Zion

On Sunday morning I seek my Lord - *see* - Join Them

One cold freezing morning I lay this body down - *see* - Every Hour in the Day

One day as another hallelu hallelu - *see* - Hallelu Hallelu

One day I'se a-walking along - *see* - Done Been Sanctified

One day one day while walking along - *see* - Jesus Done Bless My Soul

One dese fine mawnin's at break of day - *see* - I'm Going Home on a Cloud

One mornin' soon ah heard the angels singin' - *see* - I Heard the Angels Singing

One morning soon my Lord - *see* - I Going Try the Air

One of these mornings at the rising of the sun - *see* - I Got a Home in This Rock

One'a these days - *see* - One of These Days

Only a look at Jesus Oh so bowed down with care - *see* - Only a Look

Onward Christian soldiers - *see* - Onward Christian Soldiers

Open the window Noah - *see* - Open the Window Noah

Our Father which art in heaven hallowed a-be Thy name - *see* - The Lord's Prayer

Over my head I hear music in the air - *see* - Over My Head

Over my head there's trouble in the air - *see* - Over My Head

Paul an' Silas laid in jail all night long - *see* - Who Shall Deliver Poor Me

Paul and Silas bound in jail - *see* - All Night Long; Paul and Silas

Peter an' John stood on de sho' - *see* - Send Them Angels Down

Peter go ring the bells - *see* - Peter Go Ring Them Bells

Peter on the sea sea sea - *see* - Peter on the Sea

Phar'oh Why don't you let Gawd's people go - *see* - Why Don't You Let God's People Go

Plenty good room in my Father's kingdom - *see* - Plenty Good Room

Po' heathens are dyin' - *see* - Poor Heathens Are Dying

Po' li'l Jesus hail Lawd child o' Mary - *see* - Poor Little Jesus

Po' moanuh won't chew jus' believe - *see* - Living Humble

Po' mourner's got a home at las' - *see* - Poor Mourner's Got a Home at Last

Po' sinner now is yo time - *see* - What You Going to Do When the Lamp Burns Down

Poor Daniel he lean on the Lord's side - *see* - Lean on the Lord's Side

Poor heathens are dyin' - *see* - Poor Heathens Are Dying

Poor mourner's got a home at last - *see* - Poor Mourner's Got a Home at Last

Poor Rosy poor gal - *see* - Poor Rosy

Poor sinner now is your time - *see* - Poor Sinner

Praise God from whom all blessings flow - *see* - Praise God From Whom All Blessings Flow

Praise member praise God - *see* - Praise Member

Pray all the members - *see* - Pray All the Members

Pray is the key to the kingdom - *see* - Praying Is the Key to the Kingdom

Pray on brothers pray all night - *see* - Pray All Night

Pray on my brudder don't you get tired - *see* - Enlisted in the Field of Battle

Pray on pray on - *see* - Pray On

Prayer is the key to heaven - *see* - Prayer Is the Key of Heaven

Praying in de lan' - *see* - Praying in the Land

Preacher you oughta been there - *see* - Roll Jordan Roll

Prepare me one body - *see* - Prepare Me One Body

Prepare me prepare me Lord - *see* - Prepare Us

Pure city Babylon's fallin to rise no more - *see* - Babylon's Falling

Rain fall and wet Becca Lawton - *see* - Rain Fall and Wet Becca Lawton

Read in de gospel o' Mathayew - *see* - Mary Where Is Your Baby

Read in Genesis you understand - *see* - Witness for My Lord

Redeem redeem been wash in de blood ob de Lamb - *see* - Been Washed in the Blood

Redeem' redeem' been washed in de blood - *see* - Oh Redeemed Redeemed

Reign my saviour reign Master Jesus - *see* - Reign My Savior

Reign oh reign oh reign my Savior - *see* - Join the Army of the Lord

Reign oh Reign oh Reign my Saviour - *see* - Reign Master Jesus

Reign oh reign oh reign my Saviour - *see* - Reign Oh Reign

Religion is a fortune I raly do believe - *see* - Religion Is a Fortune

Religion that my Lord gave me - *see* - Religion That My Lord Gave Me

Repent sinner hammer ring - *see* - Christians' Hymn of the Crucifixion

Restitution it's a great great doctrine - *see* - Restitution

Rich folks worries' 'bout trouble - *see* - Satisfied

Ride on Jedus ride on Jedus - *see* - Ride on Jesus

Ride on King Jesus no man can a-hinder me - *see* - Ride on King Jesus

Ride on ride on - *see* - Ride On

Ride the chariot in the morning Lord - *see* - Ride the Chariot

Ride up in the chariot - *see* - I Hope I'll Join the Band

Ring the bells all God's children - *see* - Ring the Bells

Rise an' shine an' give God de glory glory - *see* - Rise and Shine

Rise mourner rise mourner - *see* - Rise Mourners Rise

Rise mourners can't you rise - *see* - Rise Mourners

Rise shine for thy light is-a-coming - *see* - Rise Shine for Thy Light IsComing

Road is rugged but I must go - *see* - Road Is Rugged But I Must Go

Rock a my soul in the bosom of Abraham - *see* - Rock My Soul

Rock chariot I told you to rock Judgement goin' - *see* - Rock Chariot

Rock Mount Sinai in de mawnin - *see* - Rock Mount Sinai

Rock my soul - *see* - Rock My Soul (2)

Rock of jubilee poor fallen soul - *see* - Rock of Jubilee

Rock-er ma soul in de bosom ob Abraham - *see* - Rock My Soul (1)

Rocks and mountains shall all flee away - *see* - Rocks and the Mountains

Rocks don't fall on me - *see* - Rocks Don't Fall on Me

Rocks on the mountains - *see* - Rocks and the Mountains

Roll an' rock can't you come along - *see* - Roll and Rock

Roll awy that stone brother and let Lord Jesus out - *see* - Roll Away That Stone

Roll de ol' chariot along yes roll de ol' chariot - *see* - Roll the Old Chariot Along

Roll Jordan roll I want to go to heaven when I die - *see* - Roll Jordan Roll (1)

Roll on roll on sweet moments roll on - *see* - Roll On

Roll the old chariot along - *see* - Roll the Old Chariot Along

Roun' about de mountain - *see* - Around About the Mountain

Run here Jeremiah - *see* - Run Here Jeremiah

Run here mama run here mama - *see* - Pick and Shovel Song

Run Mary run hallelu hallelu - *see* - Resurrection Morn

Run Mary run I know de udder worl' is not like dis' - *see* - Run Mary Run

Run mo'ner run heaven is a shinin' - *see* - Run Moaner Run

Run mo'ner run Hebben is a shinin' - *see* - Heaven Is Shining

Run moaner run - *see* - Heaven Is Shining

Run sinner run - *see* - Run Sinner Run

Run to Jesus shun de danger - *see* - Run to Jesus

Rune here Jeremiah ho ma Lord - *see* - Run Here Jeremiah

Sail oh believer sail - *see* - Sail Oh Believer

Sail Ooh sail sail oh brudder - *see* - Sailing Over Yonder

Same train same train same train carry my mother - *see* - Same Train

Sanctify me sanctify me - *see* - Just Now

Satan comes like a busy old man - *see* - Hard to Rise Again

Saw the beam in my sister's eye - *see* - I Saw the Beam in my Sister's Eye

Sea gwine deliver up dry bones - *see* - Sea Is Going to Deliver Up Dry Bones

See four and twenty elders on their knees - *see* - Four and Twenty Elders

See how they done my Lord - *see* - He Never Said a Mumbling Word

See the signs of the judgement - *see* - Satan's Camp Fire; See the Signs of Judgment

See the signs of the Judgement yes - *see* - Time Is Drawing Nigh

Seek and ye shall find knock and de door shall be opened - *see* - Seek and Ye Shall Find

Serving my God - *see* - Serving My God

Set down servant I cain' set down - *see* - Sit Down Servant

Shepherd shepherd where'd you lose your sheep - *see* - Shepherd Shepherd

Shine shine I'll meet you in the morning - *see* - Shine Shine I'll Meet You in the Morning

Shine shine shine - *see* - Shine Like a Star in the Morning

Shock along John shock along - *see* - Shock Along John

Shout Jerusalem preach Jerusalem in de mornin' - *see* - Shout Jerusalem

Shout oh shout oh shout away - *see* - Shout Away

Shout on children you never die - *see* - Shout on Children

Sing a ho that I had the wings of a dove - *see* - Sing Ho That I Had the Wings of a Dove

Sing all the way - *see* - Hear the Angels Singing

Singin' 'way in de hebben I won't die no mo' - *see* - I Won't Die No More

Singin' wid a sword in ma hand Lord - *see* - Singing With a Sword in My Hand

Singing with a sword in my hand - *see* - Singing With a Sword in My Hand

Sinnah ain you tired of sinnin' - *see* - Tell Brother Elijah

Sinner die sinner die - *see* - Sinner Die

Sinner going to sing around - *see* - Hope I Join the Band

Sinner man how can it be - *see* - Wheel in Middle of Wheel

Sinner man where you gonna run to - *see* - Sinner Man

Sinner now is de time for to pray - *see* - Sinner Now Is the Time for to Pray

Sinner oh sinner man - *see* - Sinner Man

Sinner please doan let dis harves' pass - *see* - Sinner Please Don't Let This Harvest Pass

Sinner sinner you better pray - *see* - Cold Icy Hand; Death's Going to Lay His Cold Icy Hands on Me (1)

Sinner today you better repent - *see* - Tomorrow You May Die

Sinner what you goin' to do - *see* - What You Going to Do

Sinner you know you're bound to die - *see* - Sinner You Know

Sinner you'd better get ready ready my Lord - *see* - Sinner You Better Get Ready

Sister Dolly light the lamp - *see* - White Marble Stone

Sister git yo' ticket right - *see* - Sister Get Your Ticket Right

Sister Mary Aunt Jane - *see* - Workmen's Jingles

Sister Mary had-a but one child - *see* - Sister Mary Had But One Child

Sister Mary y'ought to been there - *see* - Roll Jordan

Sister Rosy you get to heaven before I go - *see* - Travel On

Sister when you pray you must pray to the Lord - *see* - I'm on My Journey Home

Sister you can't stay away - *see* - You Can't Stay Away

Sit down servant sit down - *see* - Sit Down Servant

Sit down sister sit down I know you're tired - *see* - You're Tired Child

Slavery's chain done broke at last - *see* - Slavery's Chain

So glad I done done - *see* - I Done What You Told Me to Do

Some come cripple an' some come lame - *see* - Hail the Crown

Some glad morning when this life is o'er - *see* - I'll Fly Away

Some go to meeting to sing and shour - *see* - Dry Bones Going to Rise

Some have crippled and some come lame - *see* - Hail the Crown

Some o' dese mornin's bright an' fair - *see* - Away in the Middle of the Air

Some seek the Lord and they don't seek him right - *see* - Almost Over

Some will lub yo' and some will hate yo' - *see* - Some Will Love You and Some Will Hate You

Somebody got lost in de storm - *see* - Somebody Got Lost in the Storm

Somebody knockin' at yo' door - *see* - Somebody's Knocking at Your Door

Somebody's buried in the graveyard - *see* - Somebody's Buried in the Graveyard

Somebody's knockin' at your door O sinner why don't you answer - *see* - Somebody's Knocking at Your Door

Sometime I feel lak I nevah been bawn again - *see* - And I Cry

Sometimes I feel like a moanin' dove - *see* - Sometimes I Feel; Sometimes I Feel Like a Motherless Child

Sometimes I feel like a motherless child - *see* - Sometimes I Feel Like a Motherless Child

Sometimes I feel like I wanna go home - *see* - Sometimes I Feel Like I Wanna Go Home

Sometimes I feel so lonely sometimes I feel so blue - *see* - Be Still and Listen

Song-a ho that I had the wings of a dove - *see* - Sing Ho That I Had the Wings of a Dove

Soon and very soon we are going to see the King - *see* - Soon and Very Soon

Soon I'll be done with the trouble of this world - *see* - Soon I Will Be Done

Soon in de mornin' give me Jesus when I die - *see* - Give Me Jesus When I Die

Soon one mawnin' Death come creepin' in yo' room - *see* - Soon One Morning

Soon-a-will be done-a-with the troubles of the world - *see* - Soon I Will Be Done

Sorry to tell you - *see* - Sorry to Tell

Sperrit say I want yuh fo' to Go down death - *see* - Go Down Death

Stan' steady bretheren - *see* - Stand Steady

Stan' still Jordan Lord I can't stan' still - *see* - Stand Still Jordan

Stand on the sea of glass - *see* - Standing on the Sea of Glass

Stand the storm - *see* - We'll Stand the Storm

Stand the storm it won't be long - *see* - Stand the Storm

Stand up stand up for Jesus - *see* - Stand Up Stand Up for Jesus

Standin' on de sea ob glass wit' de gospel - *see* - Standing on the Sea of Glass

Stars in the elements are falling - *see* - Stars in the Elements

Stay in de field 'til de war is ended - *see* - Stay in the Field

Stay in the field childeren ah stay in the field - *see* - Stay in the Field

Steady Jesus is listening - *see* - Steady Jesus Is Listening

Steal away and pray - *see* - Steal Away and Pray

Steal away steal away - *see* - Steal Away to My Father's Kingdom

Steal away steal away steal away Jesus - *see* - Steal Away

Sun don't set in the morning - *see* - Sun Don't Set in the Morning

Sun give a light in the heaven all around - *see* - Give Up the World (1)

Sun shine sun shine sun shine into my soul - *see* - Sun Shine Into My Soul

Sun will never go down go down - *see* - Sun Will Never Go Down

Surely surely He's able to carry you thro' - *see* - Surely God Is Able

Sweep it clean ain't goin er tarry here - *see* - Ain't Going to Tarry Here

Sweet heaven but how I long to be there - *see* - Sweet Heaven

Sweet heaven is a handsome place - *see* - Sweet Heaven Is a Handsome Place

Sweet home - *see* - Sweet Home

Sweet turtle dove - *see* - Jerusalem Morning

Sweet turtle dove she sing-a so sweet Muddy wate - *see* - Sweet Turtle Dove

Sweet watuh rollin' sweet watuh rollin' - *see* - Sweet Water Rolling

Sweetest sound I ever heard - *see* - Sweetest Sound I Ever Heard

Swing down chariot and let me ride - *see* - Swing Down Chariot

Swing low chariot low in the Eas' let God's people - *see* - Swing Low Chariot

Swing low oh swing low - *see* - Swing Low Sweet Chariot (3)

Swing low sweet chariot - *see* - Swing Low Sweet Chariot (1)

Swing low sweet chariot Comin' for to carry me home - *see* - Swing Low Sweet Chariot (1)

Swing low sweet chariot don't you leave me behind - *see* - Swing Low Sweet Chariot (2)

Swing low sweet chariot pray let me enter in - *see* - Danville Chariot; I Don't Want to Stay Here No Longer

T'ree long nights and t'ree long days - *see* - Three Long Nights and Three Long Days

Take me to the water to be baptized - *see* - Take Me to the Water

Takes a little bit ob man to rock Dan - *see* - Takes a Little Bit of Man to Rock Dan

Takes a pu'e in heart to drive Satan away - *see* - Drive Satan Away

Tallest tree in Paradise - *see* - Blow Your Trumpet Gabriel

Tell all the world John tell all the world John - *see* - Tell All the World John

Tell how He came from nation to nation - *see* - Jehovah Has Triumph Messiah Is King

Tell it tell it sittin' down side o' de Holy - *see* - When I Get to Heaven

Tell Jesus done all I can - *see* - Tell Jesus

Tell Jesus done done all I can - *see* - For My Lord

Tell me how did you feel whem you come out of the wilderness - *see* - Come Out the Wilderness

Tell me my sistuh - *see* - My Soul Wants to Go Home to Glory

Tell me sinner and tell me true - *see* - Sister Hannah

Tell me who do you call de Wonderful Counsellor - *see* - Glory Hallelujah to the New-Born King

Tell yuh 'bout a man wat live befo' Chris' - *see* - Troubles Was Hard

Tell-a me who dat had a rod - *see* - Moan Member Moan

That same train's going to be back tomorrow - *see* - That Same Train

That Sun Going Down - *see* - That Sun Going Down

That was a mighty day - *see* - Wasn't That a Mighty Day

Then God walked around and God looked around on all that he had made - *see* - I'll Make Me a Man

Then let us go down to Jordan - *see* - Let Us Go Down to Jordan

There are four and twenty elders on their knees - *see* - Four and Twenty Elders

There are some things I may not know - *see* - Yes God Is Real

There is a balm in Gilead - *see* - Balm in Gilead

There is rest for the weary traveler - *see* - There Is Rest for the Weary Traveler

There was a babe in manger lay - *see* - There Was a Babe

There was one there was two there was three little angels - *see* - Band of Angels

There were ten virgins when the bridegroom came - *see* - There Were Ten Virgins

There's a bold little preacher in my heart - *see* - In My Heart

There's a handwriting on the wall - *see* - There's a Handwriting on the Wall

There's a heavenly home up yonder - *see* - There's a Heavenly Home Up Yonder; When Shall I Get There

There's a little wheel turning in my heart - *see* - Little Wheel Turning in My Heart

There's a love feast in heaven - *see* - Love Feast in Heaven

There's a man goin' 'roun' takin' names - *see* - There's a Man Going Around Taking Names

There's a Mighty War In Heaven - *see* - There's a Mighty War in Heaven

There's a sick man at the pool - *see* - Lord Heal Him

There's a Star in the East on Christmas Morn - *see* - Rise up Shepherd and Follow

There's comfort in heaven and I feel it in my soul - *see* - Comfort in Heaven

There's no hiding place down there - *see* - There's No Hiding Place Down There

There's no rain to wet you - *see* - I Want to Go Home

There's plenty good room plenty good room - *see* - Plenty Good Room (2)

There's plenty-uh room - *see* - Away in the Kingdom

There's room enough in the heaven - *see* - Room Enough in the Heaven

There's singing here - *see* - Run Mourner Run

There's somethin' on my mind - *see* - There's Something on My Mind

There's something on my mind that's worrying me - *see* - There's Something on My Mind

These all of my Father's children - *see* - These Are All My Father's Children

They call Bro' Noah a foolish man - *see* - Forty Days and Nights

They crucified my Lord and he never said a mumblin' word - *see* - He Never Said a Mumbling Word

They crucified my Savior and nailed him to the cross - *see* - He Rose From the Dead

They crucified my Savior and nailed Him to the cross - *see* - He Arose

They led him to Pilate's bar - *see* - He Never Said a Mumbling Word

They led my Lord away away - *see* - They Led My Lord Away

They took my blessed Lawd - *see* - He Never Said a Mumbling Word

They whipped Him up the hill - *see* - He Never Said a Mumbling Word

This day Lord - *see* - There Is a Mighty Shouting

This is a sin-trying world - *see* - This Is a Sin Trying World

This is de healin' water water - *see* - This Is the Healing Water

This is the Man who made the earth - *see* - This Is the Man

This is the way I pray in my home - *see* - This Is the Way I Pray

This little light of mine I'm gonna let it shine - *see* - This little Light of Mine

This may be your last time - *see* - This May Be Your Last Time

This old time religion - *see* - Old Time Religion

This old world is not my home - *see* - Come and Go With Me

This ole ship is a reelin' an' a rockin' - *see* - Old Ship of Zion (3)

This train is bound for glory this train - *see* - This Train

This world is not my home - *see* - This World Is Not My Home

Those cruel people those cruel people - *see* - Hammering

Thou art great and Thou art good - *see* - Grace Before Meat at Hampton

Three long nights an' three long days - *see* - Walk Mary Down the Lane

Three long nights and three long days - *see* - Three Long Nights and Three Long Days

Throw me any way - *see* - In That Old Field

Til I reach my home - *see* - Lord Until I Reach My Home

Time for praying won't be long - *see* - Time for Praying

Tis de ole ship Maria, Don't yo' want to go - *see* - Old Ship Marie

Tis Jordan's river and I must go 'cross - *see* - Tis Jordan's River

Tis me oh Lord standing in the need of pray'r - *see* - Standing in the Need of Prayer

Tis that ole-time religion - *see* - Old Time Religion

Tis the old Ship of Zion - *see* - Old Ship of Zion

Tis the ole ship Maria - *see* - Old Ship Marie

Titty Mary you know I'm going to follow - *see* - Going to Follow

To lands in the shadow of darkness - *see* - Hour is Come

Tol' Jesus it would be all right if He changed - *see* - Changed My Name

Tone de bell dun got over at las' - *see* - Towe the Bell

Too late too late sinner - *see* - Too Late

Towe the bell done got over - *see* - Towe the Bell

Traveling traveling we are traveling - *see* - We Are Traveling to the Grave

Trees don't want to be mountains they just praise - *see* - Trees

Trouble trouble all Ah see - *see* - Trouble

Trouble's gwine ter weigh me down - *see* - Trouble's Going to Weigh Me Down

Trumpet sounds it in my soul - *see* - Moaning

Truth that frees is from above - *see* - Half Has Never Been Told

Turn sinner turn while yo' maker axer yo' to turn - *see* - Turn Sinner

Twas dahk as midnight wen Jesus brought the light - *see* - When Jesus Brought the Light to Me

Twas on one Sunday morning - *see* - Twas on One Sunday Morning

Under the rail under the tie - *see* - Under the Rail

Until I reach my home - *see* - Lord Until I Reach My Home

Until I reach my home - *see* - Until I Reach My Home

Virgin Mary had a little baby - *see* - Pretty Little Baby

Virgin Mary had one son - *see* - Jesus Ain't Coming Here to Die No More

W'at harm Jesus dun-er yo' - *see* - What Harm Has Jesus Done

W'ener dis war fare is ended - *see* - My Sister You'll Be Called On

Wade in nuh watuh childun - *see* - Wade in the Water

Wait a little while - *see* - Wait a Little While

Wait Mr Mackright - *see* - Wait Mr Mackright

Wait my brother better true believe - *see* - My Body Rocked a Long Fever

Wait poor Daniel - *see* - Lean on the Lord's Side

Wake up children - *see* - Wake Up Children

Wake up Jacob day is breaking - *see* - Wake Up Jacob

Walk about elders Jesus a listenin' - *see* - Walk About Elders

Walk in kind Saviour - *see* - No Man Can Hinder Me

Walk Jerusalem jes' like John - *see* - Walk in Jerusalem Just Like John (2)

Walk Jordan's long road - *see* - Religion So Sweet

Walk together children don't you get weary - *see* - Walk Together Children

Walk you in de light Walkin' in de light o'God - *see* - Walk You in the Light

Want to go to heaven when I die - *see* - Want to Go to Heaven When I Die

Wasn' that a witness fo' my Lord - *see* - Wasn't That a Witness for My Lord

Wasn' that a wonder in the Heaven - *see* - Wasn't That a Wonder

Wasn't dat a wide river dat river of Jordan - *see* - Wasn't That a Wide River

Wasn't it a pitty an' a shame - *see* - He Never Said a Mumbling Word

Wasn't that a wide river of Jordan Lord - *see* - Wasn't That a Wide River

Wasn't that a witness for my Lord - *see* - Wasn't That a Witness for My Lord

Wasn't that hard trials great tribulation - *see* - Wasn't That Hard Trials

Watch de stars see how dey run - *see* - Watch the Stars

Watch the stars see how they run - *see* - Watch the Stars

Way bye and bye oh way bye and bye - *see* - Way By and By

Way down yonder in the middle of the field - *see* - Let Me Fly

Way in the heaven by and by - *see* - Way in the Heaven By and By

Way out yondah in de ocean - *see* - My Lord God Rocking in the Weary Land

Way over in de Egyp'lan' - *see* - March On

Way over in the Egypt land you shall gain the victory - *see* - Way Over in the Egypt Land

Way over Jordan - *see* - Way Over Jordan

Way over Jordan view de land view de land - *see* - View the Land

Way up on de mountain Lord - *see* - Up on the Mountain

Way up on the mountain Lord - *see* - Way Up on the Mountain

We am clim'in' Jacob's ladder - *see* - Jacob's Ladder

We are almost home to ring those charming bells - *see* - We Are Almost Home

We are building on a Rock on high - *see* - We Are Building on a Rock

We are climbing Jacob's ladder soldiers of the cross - *see* - Jacob's Ladder (1)

We are climbing the hills of Zion - *see* - We Are Climbing the Hills of Zion

We are going to wear a crown - *see* - Wear a Starry Crown

We are our heavenly Father's children - *see* - He Knows Just How Much We Can Bear

We are sailin' over yonder on de udder side de sho - *see* - Sailing Over Yonder

We are standing in the shadow of a parting soon to come - *see* - Ode

We are walkin' down the valley Our Savior so low - *see* - We Are Walking Down the Valley

We are walking in de light of God - *see* - Walking in the Light

We going to do what the spirit say - *see* - Do What the Spirit Say Do

We got deacons in de church - *see* - God's Going to Straighten Them

We need more reapers in the harvest field - *see* - We Need More Reapers

We shall overcome some day - *see* - We Shall Overcome

We shall walk thro' the valley in peace - *see* - We Shall Walk Through the Valley

We shall walk through the valley and the shadow of death - *see* - Walk Through the Valley

We will crownd him Lord of all - *see* - Crowned Him Lord of All

We will walk thro' the valley in peace - *see* - Walk Through the Valley in Peace

We'll march down Jerden hallelu - *see* - We'll March Down Jordan

We'll overtake the army - *see* - We'll Overtake the Army

We'll sail away to Heaven like a feather in the wind - *see* - Like a Feather in the Wind

We'll wait till Jesus comes - *see* - Down By the River (1)

We'll wait till Jesus comes down by the river - *see* - We'll Wait Til Jesus Comes

We're almost home - *see* - We Are Almost Home

We're singing singing tonight - *see* - Singing on the Old Church Ground

We're some of the praying people - *see* - We're Some of the Praying People

We've come this far by faith - *see* - We've Come This Far By Fatih

Weep no more for baby my heart - *see* - Weep No More for Baby

Weep no more Marta - *see* - Happy Morning

Weep no more Mother - *see* - Happy Morning

Weepin' Mary weepin' Mary - *see* - Weeping Mary (1)

Weeping Mary tall angel at de bar - *see* - Tall Angel at the Bar

Well brother the downward road is crowded - *see* - Downward Road

Well did you say that you love Jesus - *see* - Love the Lord

Well God don't like it - *see* - God Don't Like It

Well I may be sick an' cannot rise - *see* - When the Train Comes Along

Well I met my sister de other day - *see* - Scandalize My Name

Well I tole my captain my feet wus cold - *see* - Grade Song

Well I'm crossing Jordan river - *see* - I'm Crossing Jordan River

Well in that new Jerusalem - *see* - In the New Jerusalem

Well my mother got a letter oh yes - *see* - My Mother Got a Letter

Well my mother's goin' to heaven - *see* - Going to Outshine the Sun

Well one Monday mornin' - *see* - Grey Goose

Well she ask me whuk in de parlor whuk - *see* - Well She Ask Me in the Parlor

Well the blind man stood by the way and cried - *see* - Blind Man Stood on the Road and Cried

Well the horse wheel rolling - *see* - Every Day

Well the ole worl' is a rollin' rollin' rollin' - *see* - This Old World's Rolling

Well there are sinners here and sinners there - *see* - Heaven

Well there's going to be a big camp meeting - *see* - I Ain't Going to Study War No More

Well you better git yo' ticket - *see* - You Better Get Your Ticket

Well you must have that true religion - *see* - True Religion

Wen I lay my body down aye Lawd in de graveyahd - *see* - Toll the Bell Angel

Went to the graveyard the other day - *see* - I Feel Like My Time Ain't Long (1)

Were you there when they crucified my Lord - *see* - Were You There

Whah you runnin' sinner - *see* - In That Great Day

What a beautiful city - *see* - What a Beautiful City

What a happy new year - *see* - Happy New Year

What a hard time - *see* - What a Hard Time

What a you say seekers About dat Gospel war - *see* - Die in the Field

What band that Sunday morning - *see* - Sunday Morning Band

What do you say seekers - *see* - We'll Die in the Field; What Do You Say

What harm Jesus done you - *see* - What Harm Has Jesus Done

What is that up yonder I see - *see* - I Want to Join the Band

What kind of band you going to join - *see* - Sunday Morning Band

What kind of shoes is dem you wear - *see* - These Dry Bones of Mine

What kind of shoes you going to wear - *see* - What Kind of Shoes You Going to Wear

What make old Satan to follow me - *see* - Hold Your Light

What makes my sister shout so blod - *see* - I Do Love the Lamb

What month was Jesus born in - *see* - What Month Was Jesus Born In

What shall I render into God for all His mercies - *see* - What Shall I Render

What ship is that a sailing - *see* - Old Ship of Zion (1)

What ship is that a-sailing Hallelujah - *see* - Old Ship of Zion (1)

What ship is that you're enisted upon - *see* - Old Ship of Zion (1)

What wondrous love is this oh my soul - *see* - Wondrous Love

What you goin' to do wen death comes creeping in - *see* - My Lord What Shall I Do

What you gwine to do when de world's on fire - *see* - What You Going to Do

What you say seekers - *see* - Die in the Field

Wheel in a wheel oh my Lord - *see* - Wheel in a Wheel

Wheel oh wheel - *see* - Ezekiel Saw the Wheel (1)

Wheel wheel in de middle ob de wheel - *see* - Wheel in the Middle of the Wheel

Wheel wheel wheel oh wheel my Lord - *see* - Ezekiel Said Here Was a Wheel in a Wheel

When a my blood runs chilly an' col' I've got to go - *see* - When My Blood Runs Chilly and Cold

When Christ the Lord was here below - *see* - Down By the River (2); When Christ the Lord Was Here

When de clouds hang heavy an' it look like rain - *see* - Lord How Long

When de Saints come marchin' in - *see* - When the Saints Go Marching In

When de storm of life is ragin' stan' by me - *see* - Stand By Me

When de train comes along - *see* - When the Train Comes Along

When do we meet again - *see* - When do we Meet Again

When God commanded Michael in the morning to stretch at dividing line - *see* - Rule Death in His Arms

When He calls me I will answer - *see* - I'll Be Sleeping in My Grave

When I come to die - *see* - When I Come to Die

When I come to die give me Jesus - *see* - Give Me Jesus

When I come to die I want to be ready - *see* - Walk in Jerusalem Just Like John (3)

When I die I will sleep away - *see* - I Will Sleep Away

When I get in heaven in my elbow chair - *see* - When I Get in Heaven in My Elbow Chair

When I get to heav'n goin' to set right down - *see* - When I Get to Heaven

When I lay my body down - *see* - Toll the Bell Angel

When I was a learner I sought both night and day - *see* - Go Tell It on the Mountain (2)

When I was a seeker I sought both night and day - *see* - Go Tell It on the Mountain (2)

When I was wicked an' a prone to sin - *see* - You Must Be Pure and Holy

When I wus hangin' over hell - *see* - Hanging Over Hell

When I'm dead and buried don't you grieve after me - *see* - Don't You Grieve After Me (2)

When I'm dead and buried don't you weep after me - *see* - Don't You Weep After Me

When I'm dead don't you grieve after me - *see* - When I'm Dead

When I'm gone doan' yer grieve after me - *see* - When I'm Gone

When I'm gone gone gone - *see* - When I Am Gone Gone Gone

When I'm gone Lord somebody's goin' t' miss me - *see* - When I'm Gone

When I'm gone O mother don't you weep - *see* - Mother Don't You Weep

When I'm on my sick bed nobody visit me - *see* - For I Ain't Going to Die No More

When Israel was in Egypt's land - *see* - Go Down Moses

When Jesus comes - *see* - When Jesus Comes

When Jesus died upon the cross - *see* - His Love Comes Trickling Down

When Jesus met the woman at the well oh - *see* - Woman at the Well

When Moses an' his soldiers form Egypt's land did - *see* - He's Just the Same Today

When Moses and his soldiers form Egypt's land did flee - *see* - He's Just the Same Today

When Moses smote de water de chillun all crossed over - *see* - When Moses Smote the Water

When muh mother done gone - *see* - Never Me One

When my cross is heavy I shall not be moved - *see* - I Shall Not Be Moved

When the clouds hang heavy and it looks like rain - *see* - How Long

When the Lord called Moses - *see* - When the Lord Called Moses

When the saints go marching in - *see* - When the Saints Go Marching In

When the storm of life is raging - *see* - Stand By Me

When the train comes along - *see* - When the Train Comes Along

When the world is all on fiyuh - *see* - Hide Me

When this warfare is ended - *see* - My Sister You'll Be Called On

When we do meet again - *see* - When We Do Meet Again

When you feel like moanin' it ain't nothin' but l - *see* - When You Feel Like Moaning

When you hear dat Ise a-dyin' - *see* - Tone the Bell Easy

When you hear my coffin sound - *see* - When You Hear My Coffin Sound

When you hear the thunder rolling - *see* - In That Day

When you look way 'cross dat lonesome stream - *see* - That Lonesome Stream

When you miss me from round the fiahside - *see* - Tell Them I'm Gone

When you walk-a that lonesome valley - *see* - Lonesome Valley

When-a my blood runs chilily an' col' - *see* - When My Blood Runs Chilly and Cold

Where do you think I found my soul - *see* - Listen to the Angels

Where do you think I found my soul - *see* - Where Do You Think I Found My Soul

Where is Mary gone - *see* - Where Is Mary Gone

Where shall I be when the first trumpet sounds - *see* - Where Shall I Be (1)

Where shall I go - *see* - Where Shall I Go

Where you boun' boun' fer Canaan land - *see* - Bound for Canaan Land

Where you going sinner - *see* - You Can't Cross Here

Who built de Ark Noah Noah - *see* - Who Built the Ark

Who dat a-comin' ovah yondah Hallelujah - *see* - Who's That Coming Over Yonder

Who dat comin tall angel at de bar - *see* - Tall Angel at the Bar

Who do you call de King Emanuel - *see* - King Emanuel (1)

Who do you call the King Emanuel - *see* - Who Do You Call the King Emanuel

Who is dat yondah - *see* - Who's That Yonder

Who is de ruler Arkangel - *see* - Archangel

Who is going to lay this body - *see* - Graveyard

Who is that a-coming - *see* - Don't You Grieve After Me (1)

Who is that yonder all dressed in red - *see* - I Heard the Angels Singing

Who is this a-coming don't you grieve after me - *see* - Who Is This Coming

Who lock who lock de lion who lock - *see* - Who Locks the Lion's Jaw

Who shall ascend into the hill of the Lord - *see* - They Shall Receive a Blessing

Who will drive the chariot when she comes - *see* - When the Chariot Comes

Who's been here since I've been gone - *see* - Who's Been Here

Who's dat yandah - *see* - Who's That Yonder

Who's going to close my dying eyes - *see* - Who's Going to Close My Dying

Eyes

Who's going to lay this body - *see* - Graveyard

Who's gonna make up muh dyin' bed - *see* - When I Die

Whom is the ruler Arkangel - *see* - Archangel

Why does you tarry sinner - *see* - He Is Waiting

Why dont you cum along - *see* - Why Don't You Come Along

Why He's the Lord of lords and the King of kings - *see* - He Is the Lord of Lords

Why should I feel discouraged - *see* - His Eye Is on theSparrow

Winter oh the winter - *see* - Winter

Winter'll soon be ober children - *see* - Winter Will Soon Be Over

Wish I was in heaven sitting down - *see* - Wish I Was in Heaven Sitting Down

Wo' his purple an' linen too - *see* - Dives and Lazarus

Woe be unto you - *see* - Woe Be Unto You

Won't you come won't you come - *see* - Come Sinner Come

Won't you sit down - *see* - Won't You Sit Down

Wonder where is good ole Daniel - *see* - Wonder Where Is Good Old Daniel

Wonder where is my brother gone - *see* - Wonder Where Is My Brother Gone

World is full of forms and changes - *see* - After a While

World of form and changes is just now so confusing - *see* - Is It True

Wrastlin' Jacob Jacob day is breaking - *see* - Wrestling Jacob

Wrastlin' Jacob let me go - *see* - Wrestling Jacob

Wretched man that I am - *see* - Wretched Man That I Am

Write my name de angels in de heab'n - *see* - Angels in Heaven Going to Write My Name

Yes I know you goin' talk 'bout me - *see* - Talk About Me

Yes I want God's heab'n to be mine - *see* - I Want God's Heaven to Be Mine

Yes I'm bound to carry my soul to my Jesus - *see* - I'm Almost Done Traveling

Yes I'm going up - *see* - Yes I'm Going Up

Yes I'm gwine tu march down - *see* - March Down to Jordan

Yes I'm gwine up gwine all the way - *see* - Going Up

Yes the book of Revolution's to be bro't forth - *see* - Mighty Day

Yes we'll all fall on our knees - *see* - Lord Have Mercy

Yes we'll gain this world - *see* - Down By the River (3)

Yes yonder comes my Lord - *see* - Yes Yonder Comes My Lord

Yo' better run run run - *see* - You'd Better Run

Yo' better run, yo' better run - *see* - You Better Run to the City of Refuge

Yo' cyan' find a new hidin' place - *see* - You Can't Find a New Hiding Place

Yo' go I'll go wid yo' - *see* - You Go I'll Go With You (1)

Yo' mus' hab dat true religion - *see* - You Must Have That True Religion

Yo' publican yo' pharisee - *see* - You Publican You Pharisee

Yo' religion nebbuh mek yo' shame - *see* - Hold Out

Yo' save muh brudduh save me now - *see* - Save Me Now Save Me

Yonder come er sister all dressed in black - *see* - Cross Me Over

Yonder come sister Mary - *see* - Yonder Comes Sister Mary

You are not higher than your lowest thought - *see* - Hymn to Parnassus

You better git religion sinner man - *see* - You Better Get Religion Sinner Man

You better run run run - *see* - You'd Better Run

You better run you better run - *see* - You Better Run to the City of Refuge

You call yourself a church member - *see* - Oh Daniel

You can dig my grave with a silver spade - *see* - You Can Dig My Grave

You can hinder me here - *see* - Just Going Over in the Heavenly Land

You can run a long time - *see* - Your Sins Are Going to Find You Out

You can't find a new hiding place - *see* - You Can't Find a New Hiding Place

You go I'll go wid you - *see* - You Go I'll Go With You (1)

You goin' to reap jus' what you sow - *see* - You Going to Reap Just What You Sow

You got a right I got a right - *see* - You Got a Right

You got a robe I got a robe - *see* - You Got a Robe

You got to walk a that lonesome valley - *see* - Lonesome Valley

You hear de lambs a-cryin' - *see* - Hear the Lambs Crying

You may bury me in de Eas' - *see* - You May Bury Me in the East

You may run to the rock - *see* - Can't Hide Sinner

You may talk about me just as much as you please - *see* - Thank God I'm on My Way to Heaven

You mus' hab dat true religion - *see* - You Must Have That True Religion

You needn't mind my dying - *see* - Jesus Going to Make Up My Dying Bed

You publican you pharisee - *see* - You Publican You Pharisee

You ride that horse - *see* - Jesus Won't You Come By and By

You shall reap just what you sow - *see* - You Shall Reap

You will wish you had religion in dat army by and by - *see* - Hail Sinners Hail-lo

You'd better mind how you talk - *see* - You'd Better Mind

You'd better run run run-a-run - *see* - You'd Better Run

You're going to reap just what you sow - *see* - You Going to Reap Just What You Sow

You've gotta get a glory in the work you do - *see* - Glow Within

Young people who delight in sin - *see* - Downward Road Is Crowded (1)

Your low down ways - *see* - Your Low Down Ways

Your religion never make you shame - *see* - Hold Out

Zekus wheel oh my soul - *see* - Ezekiel's Wheel

Zion halleluiah - *see* - Zion Hallelujah

Zion weep-a low Zion weep-a low - *see* - Zion Weep Low

Zion's children comin along - *see* - Zion's Children

Alternate Title Index

A Witness - *see* - Witness for My Lord

Adam in de Garden Pinnin' Leaves - *see* - Adam in the Garden Pinning Leaves

After 'While - *see* - After a While

Ain't Dat Good News - *see* - Ain't That Good News

Ain't Goin' Er Tarry Here - *see* - Ain't Going to Tarry Here

Ain't Goin' to Study War No Mo' - *see* - I Ain't Going to Study War No More

Ain't Goin' to Study War No More - *see* - I Ain't Going to Study War No More

Ain't I Glad - *see* - I Ain't Going to Die No More

All God's Chillun Got Wings - *see* - Going to Shout All Over God's Heaven

All I Do de Church Keep A-Grumblin' - *see* - All I Do the Church Keep Grumbling

All I Do the People Keep A-Grumbeling - *see* - All I Do the People Keep Grumbling

All I Want - *see* - A Little More Faith in Jesus

All I Want Is a Little More Faith - *see* - A Little More Faith in Jesus

All Muh Sins Done Taken Away - *see* - All My Sins Are Taken Away

All My Sins Are Taken Away - *see* - All My Sins Been Taken Away

All Night All Day - *see* - Angels Are Watching Over Me

All Ober Dis Worl' - *see* - All Over This World

All-er Ma Sins Are Taken Away - *see* - All My Sins Are Taken Away

An' He Never Said a Mumblin' Word - *see* - He Never Said a Mumbling Word

An' I Cry - *see* - And I Cry

Anchor Believer Anchor - *see* - Anchor in the Lord

Angel Band - *see* - Band of Angels

Angel Dun Change-er Ma Name - *see* - Angel Done Changed My Name

Angel Roll de Stone Away - *see* - Angel Roll the Stone Away

Angels in Heab'n Gwineter Write My Name - *see* - Angels in Heaven Going to Write My Name

Angel's Waitin' At de Tomb - *see* - Angel's Waiting at the Tomb

Ante-Bellum Sermon - *see* - Joshua Fought the Battle of Jericho

Anybody Here - *see* - Is There Anybody Here

Arkangel - *see* - Archangel

At de Jedgement Bar - *see* - At the Judgment Bar

Auction Block - *see* - Many Thousand Gone

Aye Lawd Don't Leave Me - *see* - Aye Lord Don't Leave Me

Aye Lord Time Is Drawin' Nigh - *see* - Lord Time Is Drawing Nigh

Babylon's Fallin' - *see* - Babylon's Falling

Band o' Gideon - *see* - Band of Gideon

Band ob Music - *see* - Band of Music

Baptizin' - *see* - Baptizing

Bear de Burden - *see* - Bear Your Burden

Bear Yo' Burden - *see* - Bear Your Burden

Been A-Listening - *see* - I've Been Listening All Night Long

Been A-Listening All the Night Long - *see* - I've Been Listening All Night Long

Been Wash in de Blood ob de Lamb - *see* - Been Washed in the Blood

Bell Da Ring - *see* - Bell Done Rung

Belshazza' Had a Feas' - *see* - Belshazzah Had a Feast

Bin A-Listenin' - *see* - I've Been Listening All Night Long

Black-Bird an' de Crow - *see* - Black Bird and the Crow

Bles' My Soul an' Gone - *see* - Bless My Soul and Gone

Blin' Man Lying at de Pool - *see* - Blind Man Lying at the Pool

Blin' Man Stood on de Road an' Cried - *see* - Blind Man Stood on the Road and Cried

Blin' Man Stood on de Way an' Cried - *see* - Blind Man Stood on the Road and Cried

Blood Has Signed My Name - *see* - Blood Done Sign My Name

Blow Gab'l - *see* - Blow Gabriel

Blow Gable Blow - *see* - Blow Gabriel

Blow Yo' Gospel Trumpet - *see* - Blow Your Gospel Trumpet

Boun' fer Canaan Lan' - *see* - Bound for Canaan Land

Bright Sparkles in de Churchyard - *see* - Bright Sparkles in the Churchyard

Brother You'd Better Be a Prayin' - *see* - Brother You'd Better Be a Praying

But He Ain't Comin' Here t' Die No Mo' - *see* - But He Ain't Coming Here to Die No More

By an' By - *see* - By and By

By and By I'm Goin' to See Them - *see* - By and By

Bye and Bye - *see* - By and By

Cert'n'y Lord - *see* - Certainly Lord

Changed Mah Name - *see* - Changed My Name

Children Did You Hear When Jesus Rose - *see* - Did You Hear When Jesus Rose

Choose You a Seat 'n' Set Down - *see* - Choose You a Seat and Set Down

City o' Babylon - *see* - City of Babylon

Climbin' Up d'Mountain - *see* - Climbing Up the Mountain

Come an' Go Wit Me - *see* - Come and Go With Me

Come By Here - *see* - Kum Ba Yah

Come By Here My Lord - see - Kum Ba Yah

Come Come Come and Go Wid Me - see - Come and Go With Me

Come Let Us All Go Down - see - Good Old Way

Come On Sinner - see - I'm All Wore Out Toiling for the Lord

Come Out de Wilderness - see - Come Out the Wilderness

Comin' Ag'in By an' By - see - Coming Again By and By

Comin' Down de Line - see - Coming Down the Line

Comin' Here Tonight - see - Coming Here Tonight

Cotton Needs A-Pickin' - see - Cotton Needs Picking

Couldn't Hear Nobody Pray - see - I Couldn't Hear Nobody Pray

Cross-er Me Over - see - Cross Me Over

Crownd Him Lord of All - see - Crowned Him Lord of All

Crucified - see - Were You There

Crucifixion - see - He Never Said a Mumbling Word

Cyan' Hide Sinner Cyan' Hide - see - Can't Hide Sinner

Daniel - see - Didn't My Lord Deliver Daniel

Daniel in de Lion's Den - see - Daniel's in the Lion's Den

Daniel Saw de Stone - see - Daniel Saw the Stone

Daniel Saw the Stone Rolling - see - Daniel Saw the Stone

Dar's a Meetin' Here Tonight - see - There's a Meeting Here Tonight

Dat Lonesome Stream - see - That Lonesome Stream

Dat Sabbath Hath No End - see - That Sabbath Has No End

Dat Same Train - see - That Same Train

Dat Suits Me - see - That Suits Me

Day I Lef' My Home - see - Day I Left My Home

De Angel in Heben Gwine to Write Muh Name - see - Angels in Heaven
    Going to Write My Name

De Angel Roll de Stone Away - see - Angel Roll the Stone Away

De Angels Are Watchin' Obuh Me - see - Angels Are Watching Over Me

De Bell Dun Ring - *see* - Bell Done Ring

De Blin' Man - *see* - Blind Man Stood on the Road and Cried

De Blin' Man Stood On De Road An' Cried - *see* - Blind Man Stood on the Road and Cried

De Blood Done Sign My Name - *see* - Blood Done Sign My Name

De Church ob God - *see* - Church of God

De Downward Road Is Crowded - *see* - Downward Road Is Crowded

De Gif' ob Gawd Is Eternal Life - *see* - Gift of God Is Eternal Life

De Gospel Train - *see* - Get on Board Little Children

De Gospel Train - *see* - Gospel Train

De Hebben Is Shinin' - *see* - Heaven Is Shining

De Jews Dey Took Our Savior - *see* - Jews They Took Our Savior

De Milk-White Horses - *see* - Band of Gideon

De New Born Baby - *see* - New Born Baby

De Ol' Ark's A-Moverin' - *see* - Old Ark Is Moving Along

De Ol' Ark's A-Moving an' I'm Goin' Home - *see* - Old Ark Is Moving Along

De Old Ark A-Moverin' Along - *see* - Old Ark Is Moving Along

De Old Sheep Done Know de Road - *see* - Old Sheep Done Know the Road

De Ole Ark A-Moverin' Along - *see* - Old Ark Is Moving Along

De Ole Ship Marie - *see* - Old Ship Maria

De Po' Heathens Are Dyin' - *see* - Poor Heathens Are Dying

De Sea Gwine Deliver Up de Dry Bones - *see* - Sea Is Going to Deliver Up Dry Bones

De Udder Worl' Is Not Lak Dis - *see* - Other World Is Not Like This

De Winter'll Soon Be Ober - *see* - Winter Will Soon Be Over

Death Goin' t' Lay His Col' Icy Han' on Me - *see* - Death's Going to Lay His Cold Icy Hands on Me

Death Is Goin' to Lay His Cold Icy Han' on Me - *see* - Death's Going to Lay His Cold Icy Hands on Me

Death is in Dis Land - *see* - Death Is in This Land

Death's Go'n'ter Lay His Col' Icy Hands on Me - *see* - Death's Going to Lay His Cold Icy Hands on Me

Dem Bones - *see* - Them Bones

Dere Is a Mighty Shoutin' - *see* - There Is a Mighty Shouting

Dere Is Rest fo' de Weary Trabbler - *see* - There Is Rest for the Weary Traveler

Dere's a Han' Writin' on de Wall - *see* - There's a Handwriting on the Wall

Dere's a Little Wheel A-Turnin' - *see* - Little Wheel Turning in My Heart

Dere's a Little Wheel A-Turnin' in My Heart - *see* - Little Wheel Turning in My Heart

Dere's a Man Goin' 'Roun' Takin' Names - *see* - There's a Man Going Around Taking Names

Dere's a Mighty War in de Hebben - *see* - There's a Mighty War in Heaven

Dere's No Hidin' Place Down Dere - *see* - There's No Hiding Place Down There

Dere's No One Lak Jesus - *see* - There's No One Like Jesus

Dese All-er Ma Father's Chillun - *see* - These Are All My Father's Children

Dese Bones Gwine Rise Again - *see* - These Bones Going to Rise Again

Dese Bones Gwine to Rise Again - *see* - These Bones Going to Rise Again

Dese Dry Bones of Mine - *see* - These Dry Bones of Mine

Did You Hear How Dey Crucified My Lord - *see* - Did You Hear How They Crucified My Lord

Didn't Old Pharoah Get Los' - *see* - Didn't Old Pharaoh Get Lost

Die in de Fiel' - *see* - Die in the Field

Dives and Laz'us - *see* - Dives and Lazarus

Do Doan' Yer Weep for de Baby - *see* - Do Don't You Weep for the Baby

Do Don't Touch-a My Garment Good Lord - *see* - Do Don't Touch My Garment Good Lord

Does Yo' Call Dat Religion - *see* - Does You Call That Religion

Done Carry de Key an' Gone Home - *see* - Too Late

Done Foun' My Los' Sheep - *see* - Done Found My Lost Sheep

Done Made My Vow - *see* - Done Made My Vow To the Lord

Don't Call de Roll - *see* - Don't Call the Roll

Don't Let de Wind Blow Me Here No More - *see* - Don't Let the Wind Blow
Here No More

Don't Ye View Dat Ship A-Come A-Sailing - *see* - Don't You View That
Ship Come Sailing

Don't Yo' Hab Eberybody fo' Yo' Fr'en' - *see* - Don't You Have Everybody
for Your Friend

Don't Yo' Hear de Lam's A-Cryin' - *see* - Hear the Lamb's Crying

Don't You Grieve for Me - *see* - Angel's Waiting at the Door

Don't You Hear the Lambs - *see* - Hear the Lamb's Crying

Don't You Hear the Lamb's A-Cryin' - *see* - Hear the Lamb's Crying

Don't You Let Nobody Turn You Roun' - *see* - Don't You Let Nobody Turn
You Around

Don't You See - *see* - I Got a Home in That Rock

Don't you View Dat Ship A-Come A-Sailin' - *see* - Don't You View That
Ship Come Sailing

Don't You Weep After Me - *see* - Mother Don't You Weep

Don't You Weep When I'm Gone - *see* - Mother Don't You Weep

Don't You Wish Were in Hebben - *see* - Don't You Wish You Were in Heaven

Down By the River - *see* - Down By the Riverside

Drinkin' of the Wine - *see* - Drinking of the Wine

Dry Bones Goin' Rise - *see* - Dry Bones Going to Rise

Dry Bones Goin' t' Rise Ag'in - *see* - Dry Bones Going to Rise

Dun Found de Way at Las' - *see* - Done Found the Way at Last

Dust an' Ashes - *see* - Dust and Ashes

Early in de Mornin' - *see* - Early in the Morning

Eb'rybody Wants to Know Jis How I Die - *see* - Everybody Wants to Know
Just How I Die

Ebery Time I Feels de Spirit - *see* - Every Time I Feel the Spirit

Ef de Lord Calls You - *see* - If the Lord Calls You

Ef Ye Want to See Jesus - *see* - If You Want to See Jesus

Ef You Want to Get to Hebben - see - If You Want to Get to Heaven

Elder You Say You Love King Jesus - see - Love King Jesus

End o' Dat Morning - see - End of That Morning

Ennyhow Muh Lawd - see - Anyhow My Lord

Ev'ry Time I Feel the Spirit - see - Every Time I Feel the Spirit

Ev'rybody Got to Die - see - Everybody Got to Die

Every Day'll Be Sunday - see - Every Day Will Be Sunday

Ezek'el Saw the Wheel - see - Ezekiel Saw the Wheel

Ezekiel Said Dere Was a Wheel in a Wheel - see - Ezekiel Said Here Was a
    Wheel in a Wheel

Ezekiel Saw de Wheel - see - Ezekiel Saw the Wheel

Five of Them Were Wise - see - There Were Ten Virgins

Fix Me Jedus - see - Fix Me Jesus

Fo' De Lord - see - For the Lord

Fohty Days an' Nights - see - Forty Days and Nights

For I Ain' Goin' T' Die No Mo' - see - For I Ain't Going to Die No More

Free at Las' - see - Free at Last

Freedom Train A-Comin' - see - Freedom Train Coming

Get on Board - see - Gospel Train

Get on Board Little Children - see - Gospel Train

Get Yo' Ticket - see - Get Your Ticket

Gimme Dat Ol'-Time Religion - see - Old Time Religion

Gimme Yo' Han' - see - Give Me Your Hand

Gimmie That Ole Time Religion - see - Old Time Religion

Git on Board Little Chillen - see - Get on Board Little Children

Git on Board o' Ship o' Zion - see - Get on Board Old Ship of Zion

Git on Bo'd Lit'l' Children - see - Gospel Train

Git on de Boat Little Chillun - see - Get on the Boat Little Children

Git on the Evening Train - *see* - Get on the Evening Train

Git Yo' Ticket - *see* - Get Your Ticket

Give A-Way Jordan - *see* - Give Way Jordan

Give-er Me Jesus - *see* - Give Me Jesus

Give-er Me Jesus W'en I Die - *see* - Give Me Jesus When I Die

Give Me That Old Time Religion - *see* - Old Time Religion

Glory an' Honor - *see* - Glory and Honor

Glory and Honor - *see* - Live Humble

Glory Hallelujah to de New-Born King - *see* - Glory Hallelujah to the
    New-Born King

Go and I Go Wid You - *see* - Go and I Go With You

Go Down in de Lonesome Valley - *see* - Lonesome Valley

Go 'Lija - *see* - Go Elijah

Go Mary an' Toll de Bell - *see* - Go Mary and Toll the Bell

Go Tell It on de Mountain - *see* - Go Tell It on the Mountain

God Got Plenty O' Room - *see* - Plenty Good Room

God's a-Gwineter Trouble de Water - *see* - Wade in the Water

God's Goin' to Straighten Them - *see* - God's Going to Straighten Them

God's Goin' Wake Up the Dead - *see* - God's Going Wake Up the Dead

God's Going to Trouble the Water - *see* - Wade in the Water

God's Gonna Set This World on Fire - *see* - God's Going to Set This World
    on Fire

God's Got Plenty of Room - *see* - Plenty Good Room

Goin' Away to See-er Ma Lord - *see* - Going Away to See My Lord

Goin' Down to Jordan - *see* - Going Down to Jordan

Goin' Over on de Uddah Side of Jordan - *see* - Going Over on the Other Side
    of Jordan

Goin' to Outshine the Sun - *see* - Going to Outshine the Sun

Goin' to Set Down and Rest Awhile - *see* - Going to Set Down and Rest
    Awhile

Goin' to Shout - *see* - Going to Shout All Over God's Heaven

Goin' to Shout All Over God's Heav'n - see - Going to Shout All Over God's Heaven

Goin' Up Yonder - see - Going Up

Going to Study War No More - see - I Ain't Going to Study War No More

Good By City o' Babylon - see - Good Bye City of Babylon

Good Lord Dun Been Here - see - Good Lord Done Been Here

Good Lord, Shall I Be de One - see - Good Lord Shall I Be the One

Good Lord Shall I Ever Be de One - see - Good Lord Shall I Ever Be the One

Good News - see - Good News Angels Bring the Tidings

Good News - see - Good News the Chariot's Coming

Good News de Chariot's Comin' - see - Good News the Chariot's Coming

Good Old Chariot - see - Swing Low Sweet Chariot

Good Old Chariot - see - Tell My Jesus Morning

Good Old Chariot Swing So Low - see - Swing Low Sweet Chariot

Gospel Train - see - Get on Board Little Children

Got a Home at Las' - see - Got a Home at Last

Got Glory an' Honor - see - Got Glory and Honor

Got Religion All Around the World - see - Christians Hold Up Your Heads

Graveyard - see - Oh Graveyard

Great Camp Meeting - see - Walk Together Children

Great Camp Meeting in the Promised Land - see - Walk Together Children

Great Gittin' Up Mornin' - see - In That Great Getting Up Morning

Gwine-a Study War No Mo' - see - I Ain't Going to Study War No More

Gwine Lay Down My Life for My Lord - see - Going Lay Down My Life for My Lord

Gwine ter Jine de Band - see - I'm Going to Join the Band

Gwine to Live Humble to de Lord - see - Going to Live Humble to the Lord

Gwine to Quit All O' My Worldly Ways - see - Going to Quit All of My Worldly Ways

Gwine to Ride Up in the Chariot - see - Going to Ride Up in the Chariot

Gwine To Roll in My Jesus' Arms - see - Going to Roll in My Jesus' Arms

Gwine to Shout All Over God's Heaven - *see* - Going to Shout All Over God's Heaven

Gwine Up - *see* - Going Up

Gwineter Ride Up in de Chariot Soon-a in de Mornin' - *see* - Going to Ride Up in the Chariot

Gwinter Sing All Along de Way - *see* - Going to Sing All Along the Way

Hail de King of Babylon - *see* - Hail the King of Babylon

Hail John's Army Ben' Down an' Die - *see* - Hail John's Army Bend Down and Died

Halleluiah to de Lamb - *see* - Halleluiah to the Lamb

Han' Me Down - *see* - Hand Me Down My Silver Trumpet

Handwritin' on de Wall - *see* - There's a Handwriting on the Wall

Hangin' Over Hell - *see* - Hanging Over Hell

He Arose - *see* - Jews Killed Poor Jesus

He Nevuh Said a Mumbalin' Word - *see* - He Never Said a Mumbling Word

He Raise a Poor Lazarus - *see* - He Raised Poor Lazarus

He Understands He'll Say Well Done - *see* - He'll Understand and Say Well Done

Healin' Waters - *see* - Healing Waters

Hear de Angels Singin' - *see* - Hear the Angels Singing

Hear de Lambs A-Cryin' - *see* - Hear the Lamb's Crying

Hear Gabriel Blow in Dat Morn - *see* - Hear Gabriel Blow in That Morn

Hear the Lambs A-Crying - *see* - Hear the Lamb's Crying

Heaven Bell A-Ring - *see* - Heaven Bell Ring

Heaven Bells A-Ringing - *see* - Heaven Bells Ringing in My Soul

Heaven Bells Ringin' and I'm A-Goin' Home - *see* - Heaven Bells Ringing and I'm Going Home

Heaven Goin' to Be My Home - *see* - Heaven Is Going to Be My Home

Heav'n Bells A-Ringin' in Mah Soul - *see* - Heaven Bells Ringing in My Soul

Heav'n-Boun' Soldier - *see* - Heaven-Bound Soldier

Heav'n Heav'n - *see* - Going to Shout All Over God's Heaven

Hebben Is A-Shinin' - *see* - Heaven Is Shining

Heben Goin' to Be Muh Home - *see* - Heaven Is Going to Be My Home

Heben Is a Beautiful Place - *see* - Heaven Is a Beautiful Place

He's Jus' de Same Today - *see* - He's Just the Same Today

He's the Lord of Lords - *see* - He Is the Lord of Lords

Hide-A-Me - *see* - Hide Me

His Love Comes A-Tricklin' Down - *see* - His Love Comes Trickling Down

Hol' de Win' Don't Let It Blow - *see* - Hold the Wind Don't Let It Blow

Hol' Out to de En' - *see* - Hold Out to the End

Hold Out Yo' Light - *see* - Hold Out Your Light

Holy Holy Yo' Promise to Answer Prayer - *see* - Holy Holy You Promised to Answer Prayer

Holy Lord - *see* - Oh Holy Lord

Holy Savior - *see* - Oh Holy Savior

Hope I Jine de Ban' - *see* - Hope I Join the Band

House What's Built Wit'out Han's - *see* - House That's Built Without Hands

How Long de Train Been Gone - *see* - How Long Has the Train Been Gone

How Yo' Do Believer How Yo Do Today - *see* - How You Do Believer

Humble Yo'self de Bell Done Ring - *see* - Humble Yourself the Bell Done Ring

Hush Hush Somebody's Callin' Mah Name - *see* - Hush Somebody's Calling My Name

I Aint Gwine er Trus' Nobody - *see* - I Ain't Going to Trust Nobody

I Ain't Gwine Grief Muh Lawd No Mo' - *see* - I Ain't Going to Grieve My Lord No More

I Am Bound fo' de Promised Lan' - *see* - I Am Bound for the Promised Land

I Am de Light uv de Worl' - *see* - I Am the Light of the World

I Am de Truth an' de Light - *see* - I Am the Truth and the Light

I Am Goin' Obuh Dere - *see* - I Am Going Over There

I Am Goin' to Join in This Army - *see* - I Am Going to Join in This Army

I Am Huntin' fo' a City - *see* - I Am Hunting for a City

I Been A-Listening - *see* - I've Been Listening All Night Long

I Been 'Buked An' I Been Scorned - *see* - I've Been Rebuked

I Been in the Storm So Long - *see* - I've Been in the Storm So Long

I Couldn' Hear Nobody Pray - *see* - I Couldn't Hear Nobody Pray

I Do Know Gawd Don't Lie - *see* - I Do Know God Don't Lie

I Do Love de Lamb - *see* - I Do Love the Lamb

I Doan' Want Fu' t' Stay Hyeah No Longah - *see* - I Don't Want to Stay Here No Longer

I Done Done - *see* - I Done What You Told Me to Do

I Done Done What Ya' Tol' Me to Do - *see* - I Done What You Told Me to Do

I Don't Feel No-Ways Tired - *see* - I Am Seeking for a City

I Don't Want to Stay Here - *see* - Swing Low Sweet Chariot

I Feel Like Dyin' in Dis Army - *see* - I Feel Like Dying in This Army

I Goin' Put on my Golden Shoes - *see* - I Going Put on My Golden Shoes

I Goin' Try the Air - *see* - I Going Try the Air

I Got a Hidin' Place - *see* - I Got a Hiding Place

I Got a Home in-a Dat Rock - *see* - I Got a Home in That Rock

I Got a Home in de Rock - *see* - I Got a Home in That Rock

I Got a Letter Dis Mornin' - *see* - I Got a Letter This Morning

I Got a Mother in de Bright Shinin' World - *see* - I Got a Mother in the Bright Shining World

I Got a Robe - *see* - Going to Shout All Over God's Heaven

I Got Ma 'Ligion on de Way - *see* - I Got My Religion on the Way

I Got Mah Swoad in Mah Han' - *see* - I Got My Sword in My Hand

I Got Two Wings - *see* - Two Wings

I Hab a Leader Obuh Dere - *see* - I Have a Leader Over There

I Have Another Building - *see* - I Know I Have Another Building

I Heard de Preachin' of de Word o' God - *see* - I Heard the Preaching of the

Elder

I Heard From Heaven Today - *see* - Peter Go Ring Them Bells

I Heard the Angels Singin' - *see* - I Heard the Angels Singing

I Heard the Preaching of the Word of God - *see* - I Heard the Preaching of the Elder

I Know de Lord's Laid His Hands on Me - *see* - I Know the Lord's Laid His Hands on Me

I Know de Udder Worl' Is Not Like Dis' - *see* - Run Mary Run

I Lub Mih Blessed Savior - *see* - I Love My Blessed Savior

I Must Walk My Lonesome Valley - *see* - Lonesome Valley

I Saw de Light - *see* - I Saw the Light

I Stood on de Ribber ob Jerdon - *see* - I Stood on the River of Jordan

I Thank God I'm Free at Las' - *see* - Free at Last

I Want God's Heab'n to Be Mine - *see* - I Want God's Heaven to Be Mine

I Want to Be a Christian in My Heart - *see* - Lord I Want to Be a Christian

I Want to Be Ready - *see* - Walk in Jerusalem Just Like John

I Want to Climb Up Jacob's Ladder - *see* - Jacob's Ladder

I Want to Die A-Shouting - *see* - I Want to Die Shouting

I Want to See Jesus in de Mornin' - *see* - I Want to See Jesus in the Morning

I Wanta Live So God Can Use Me - *see* - I Want to Live So God Can Use Me

I Wants to Climb Up Jacob's Ladder - *see* - Jacob's Ladder

I Will Be There in the Morning - *see* - I'll Be There in the Morning

I Wish I Had Been There - *see* - I Wish I Been There

I Won't Die No Mo' - *see* - I Won't Die No More

I Would Like to Read - *see* - I Know I Would Like to Read

If I Got My Ticket Can I Ride - *see* - If I Got My Ticket Lord

If I Have Mah Tickit Lawd - *see* - If I Have My Ticket Lord

If I Keep Prayin' on - *see* - If I Keep Praying on

If You Can't Come Send One Angel Down - *see* - Send One Angel Down

I'll Be Sleepin' in Mah Grave - *see* - I'll Be Sleeping in My Grave

I'll Hear de Trumpet Soun' - *see* - You May Bury Me in the East

I'm A-Going to Eat at the Welcome Table - *see* - I'm Going to Eat at the Welcome Table

I'm A-Going to Join the Band - *see* - I'm Going to Join the Band

I'm A-Going to Sing - *see* - I'm Going to Sing

I'm a Po' Lil' Orphan - *see* - I'm a Poor Little Orphan

I'm A-Rollin' - *see* - I'm Rolling

I'm A-Rolling Through an Unfriendly World - *see* - I'm Rolling

I'm A-Runnin' Fo' Muh Life - *see* - I'm Running for My Life

I'm a Soldier of de Cross - *see* - I'm a Soldier of the Cross

I'm a Solger in de Army ob de Lord - *see* - I'm a Soldier in the Army of the Lord

I'm a Trabblin' to de Land - *see* - I'm Traveling to the Land

I'm A-Trav'ling to the Grave - *see* - I'm Traveling to the Grave

I'm A-Travelin' to the Land - *see* - I'm Traveling to the Land

I'm A-Trouble in the Mind - *see* - I'm Troubled in Mind

I'm All Wore Out A-Toiling for the Lord - *see* - I'm All Wore Out Toiling for the Lord

I'm Goin' Down to de Ribbuh ob Jerdan - *see* - I'm Going Down to the River of Jordan

I'm Goin' Home on a Cloud - *see* - I'm Going Home on a Cloud

I'm Goin' t' Stay in de Battle Fiel' - *see* - I'm Going to Stay in the Battlefield

I'm Goin' to See Muh Lovin' Father When I Git Home - *see* - I'm Going to See My Loving Father When I Get Home

I'm Goin' to Sing - *see* - I'm Going to Sing

I'm Goin' to Wait Till de Holy Ghost Come - *see* - I'm Going to Wait Until the Holy Ghost Comes

I'm Goin' to Walk With Jesus by Myself - *see* - I'm Going to Walk With Jesus By Myself

I'm Goin' Where Dere Ain't No Mo' Dyin' - *see* - I'm Going Where There Ain't No More Dying

I'm Going Over There - *see* - I Am Going Over There

I'm Going to Join the Great 'Sociation - see - I'm Going to Join the Great Association

I'm Going to Join this Army - see - I Am Going to Join in this Army

I'm Gonna Sing - see - I'm Going to Sing

I'm Gwine to Jine de Great 'Sociation - see - I'm Going to Join the Great Association

I'm Gwine Up to Heab'n Anyhow - see - I'm Going Up to Heaven Anyhow

I'm Just A-Goin' Over Jordan - see - I'm Just Going Over Jordan

I'm Just A-Goin' Over There - see - I'm Just Going Over There

I'm Mos' Dun Travelin' - see - I'm Almost Done Traveling

I'm 'Most Done Traveling - see - I'm Almost Done Traveling

I'm Runnin' on - see - I'm Running on

I'm So Glad Trouble Don't Last Alway - see - I'm So Glad Troubles Don't Last Always

I'm Troubled - see - I'm Troubled in Mind

In-a-Dat Mornin' - see - You May Bury Me in the East

In Dat Day - see - In That Day

In Dat Great Gittin'-up Mornin' - see - In That Great Getting Up Morning

In de Army - see - In the Army

In de Mornin' - see - In the Morning

In His Hands - see - He's Got the Whole World in His Hands

In That Beautiful World on High - see - I Hope My Mother Will Be There

In That Morning - see - You May Bury Me in the East

In the Army of the Lord - see - I'm a Soldier in the Army of the Lord

Inchin' Along - see - Keep Inching Along

Is Massa Goin' to Sell Us Tomorrow - see - Mother Is Master Going to Sell Us Tomorrow

I'se Mighty Tired - see - I'm Mighty Tired

It's Me - see - Standing in the Need of Prayer

It's Me O Lord - see - Standing in the Need of Prayer

It's Movin' Day - see - It's Moving Day

I've a Message F'om Ma Lord - *see* - I've a Message From My Lord

I've Been A-List'ning All de Night Long - *see* - I've Been Listening All Night Long

I've Been 'Buked - *see* - I've Been Rebuked

I've Been In de Storm So Long - *see* - I've Been in the Storm So Long

I've Been Toilin' at de Hill - *see* - I've Been Toiling at the Hill

I've Done What You Told Me to Do - *see* - I Done What You Told Me to Do

I've For a Mother in de Heaven - *see* - I've Got a Mother in the Heaven

I've Got a Home in the Rock Don't You See - *see* - I Got a Home in That Rock

I've Got a Mother in de Heaven - *see* - I've Got a Mother in the Heaven

I've Got a Robe - *see* - Going to Shout All Over God's Heaven

Jacob's Ladder Long an' Tall - *see* - Jacob's Ladder Long and Tall

Jedus Blood Done Mek Me Whole - *see* - Jesus Blood Done Make Me Whole

Jedus Done Just What He Said - *see* - Jesus Done Just What He Said

Jerusalem Mornin' - *see* - Sweet Turtle Dove

Jes' Gwine Ober in de Heabenlye Lan' - *see* - Just Going Over in the Heavenly Land

Jes Like John - *see* - Walk in Jerusalem Just Like John

Jesus Ain't Comin' Here t' Die No Mo' - *see* - Jesus Ain't Coming Here to Die No More

Jesus Gon Tuh Make Up My Dyin' Bed - *see* - Jesus Going to Make Up My Dying Bed

Jesus Heal' de Sick - *see* - Jesus Healed the Sick

Jesus Is Listenin' - *see* - Jesus Is Listening

Jesus Lock' de Lion' Jaw - *see* - Jesus Locked the Lion's Jaw

Jesus Rollin' In-er His Arms - *see* - Jesus Rolling in His Arms

Jine de Army ob de Lord - *see* - Join the Army of the Lord

Jine Them - *see* - Join Them

John Done Saw Dat Number - *see* - John Done Saw That Number

John Saw de Holy Number - *see* - John Saw the Holy Number

John Saw de Number No Man Could Number - *see* - John Saw the Number No Man Could Number

John Was A-Writin' - *see* - John Was Writing

John's Gone Down on de Island - *see* - John's Gone Down on the Island

John's on de Island on His Knees - *see* - John's on the Island on His Knees

Join de Heaven Wid de Angels - *see* - Join the Heaven With the Angels

Joshua Fight de Battle ob Jericho - *see* - Joshua Fought the Battle of Jericho

Joshua Fit de Battle ob Jericho - *see* - Joshua Fought the Battle of Jericho

Judgement Day Is A-Rollin' Around - *see* - Judgment Day Is Rolling Around

Judgment Day Is Tryin' Time - *see* - Judgment Day Is Trying Time

Just Let Me Get Up in the House of God - *see* - Let Me Get Up

Just Like John - *see* - Walk in Jerusalem Just Like John

Keep A-Inchin' Along - *see* - Keep Inching Along

Keep A-Moving - *see* - Keep Moving

Keep de Ark a Movin' - *see* - Keep the Ark Moving

Keep Me F'om Sinkin' Down - *see* - Keep Me From Sinking Down

King Jedus Is Muh Only Fr'en' - *see* - King Jesus Is My Only Friend

King Jesus Is A-Listenin' - *see* - King Jesus is Listening

King Jesus Sittin' on de Water Side - *see* - King Jesus Sitting on the Water Side

Kum Bah Yah - *see* - Kum Ba Yah

Lamb Blood Dun Wash Me Clean - *see* - Lamb's Blood Done Washed Me Clean

Lawd I Want Two Wings - *see* - Two Wings

Lawdy Lawdy Lawdy - *see* - Lordy Lordy Lordy

Lay Dis Body Down - *see* - Lay This Body Down

Leanin' on Dat Lamb - *see* - Leaning on That Lamb

Leanin' on de Lord - *see* - Leaning on the Lord

Let de Church Roll on - *see* - Let the Church Roll on

Let de Heb'n-light Shine on Me - *see* - Let the Heaven Light Shine on Me

Let Me Shine Shine Like de Mornin' Star - *see* - Let Me Shine

Let My People Go - *see* - Go Down Moses

Let Us Break Bread - *see* - Let Us Break Bread Together

Let Us Break Bread Togeder on Our Knees - *see* - Let Us Break Bread Together

Let Us Go Down to Jerden - *see* - Let Us Go Down to Jordan

Ligion So Sweet - *see* - Religion So Sweet

Li'l Boy Name David - *see* - Little Boy Named David

Lil' David - *see* - Little David

Li'l David Play on Yo' Hawp - *see* - Little David

Lil' David Play Yo Harp - *see* - Little David

Lis'en to de Lam's - *see* - Listen to the Lambs

Listed in de Field O' Battle - *see* - Enlisted in the Field of Battle

Listed in the Battlefield - *see* - Enlisted in the Field of Battle

Listen to de Lambs - *see* - Listen to the Lambs

Lit'l Boy - *see* - Little Boy

Lit'le David Play on Yo' Harp - *see* - Little David

Litte Wheel A-Turnin' in My Heart - *see* - Little Wheel Turning in My Heart

Little Black Train Is A-Coming - *see* - Little Black Train Is Coming

Little Chillun You Better Believe - *see* - Little Children You Better Believe

Little David Play on You Harp - *see* - Little David

Little Talk Wid Jesus Makes It Right - *see* - Little Talk With Jesus Makes It Right

Little Talk With Jesus - *see* - Little Talk With Jesus Makes It Right

Little Wheel A-Turning in My Heart - *see* - Little Wheel Turning in My Heart

Live A-Humble - *see* - Live Humble

Livin' Humble - *see* - Living Humble

Look-a How Dey Done Muh Lawd - *see* - Look at How They Done My Lord

Look Away - *see* - Look Away in the Heaven

Look Away - *see* - Some of These Mornings

Look What a Wonder Jedus Done - *see* - Look What a Wonder Jesus Done

Lord Have Mercy on Me - *see* - Lord Have Mercy

Lord I Can Not Stay Here By Mase'f - *see* - Lord I Can Not Stay Here By Myself

Lord I Cannot Stay Here By Myself - *see* - I Cannot Stay Here By Myself

Lord I Waih I Had A-Come - *see* - Lord I Wish I Had Come

Lord I Want to Be a Christian in-a My Heart - *see* - Lord I Want to Be a Christian

Lord I Want Two Wings - *see* - Two Wings

Lord Is Dis Hebben - *see* - Lord Is This Heaven

Lord Keep Me From Sinking Down - *see* - Keep Me From Sinking Down

Love an' Serve de Lord - *see* - If You Love God Serve Him

Love Come Tricklin' Down - *see* - Love Come Trickling Down

Ma Lawd's A-Writin' Down Time - *see* - My Lord's Writing Down Time

Ma Sister You'll Be Called on - *see* - My Sister You'll Be Called on

Ma Soul's Determin' - *see* - My Soul's Determined

Mah Brudder's Died an' Gone to Hebben - *see* - My Brother's Died and Gone to Heaven

Mah God Is So High - *see* - My God Is So High

Man Goin' Round - *see* - There's a Man Going Around Taking Names

Many T'ousand Go - *see* - Many Thousand Go

March Down to Jerdon - *see* - March Down to Jordan

Mary an' Martha Jes' Gone 'Long - *see* - Mary and Martha

Mary Don't You Weep Don't You Mourn - *see* - Mary Don't You Weep

Mary Had a Baby Aye Lawd - *see* - Mary Had a Baby

Mary Had de Leetle Baby - *see* - Mary Had a Baby

Mary Wept an' Marthy Moaned - *see* - Mary Wept and Marthy Moaned

Massa Gwine to Sell Us Tomorrow - *see* - Mother Is Master Going to Sell Us Tomorrow

May Be the Last Time I Don't Know - see - May Be the Last Time

Meet You in the Morning - see - Shine Shine I'll Meet You in the Morning

Member Me - see - Do Lord Remember Me

Members Don't Git Weary - see - Members Don't Get Weary

Milk-White Horses - see - Band of Gideon

Moanin' - see - Moaning

Moanin' Dove - see - Sometimes I Feel

Mone Member Mone - see - Moan Member Moan

Mos' Done Toilin' Here - see - Almost Done Toiling Here

Moses Smote de Water - see - Moses Smote the Water

Most Done Toiling Here - see - Almost Done Toiling Here

Most Done Trabelling - see - Almost Done Traveling

Mother Is Massa Gwine to Sell Us - see - Mother Is Master Going to Sell Us
    Tomorrow

Motherless Child - see - Sometimes I Feel Like a Motherless Child

Murmering Word - see - He Never Said a Mumbling Word

My Army Cross Over - see - My Army's Crossing Over

My Body Rock Along Fever - see - My Body Rocked a Long Fever

My God He Is a Man a Man of War - see - My God He Is a Man of War

My God Is a Man of War - see - My God He Is a Man of War

My God Is a Rock in a Weary Land - see - My God Is a Rock

My Good Lord Has Been Here - see - Good Lord Done Been Here

My Good Lord's Done Been Here - see - My Good Lord Done Been Here

My Head Wet Wid de Mid Night Dew - see - My Head Wet With the Midnight
    Dew

My Lawd Gawd Rockin' in De Weary Land - see - My Lord God Rocking in
    the Weary Land

My Lord Delibered Daniel - see - My Lord Delivered Daniel

My Lord Says He's Gwineter Rain Down Fire - see - My Lord Says He's
    Going to Rain Down Fire

My Lord What a Mornin' - see - My Lord What a Morning

My Lord What a Mourning - see - My Lord What a Morning

My Lord What Should I Do - see - My Lord What Shall I Do

My Lord's A-Ridin' All the Time - see - My Lord's Riding All the Time

My Lord's A-Writin' All de Time - see - My Lord's Writing All the Time

My Lord's Comin' Again - see - My Lord's Coming Again

My Lord's Goin' Move This Wicked Race - see - My Lord's Going to Move This Wicked Race

My Lord's Riding All the Time - see - My Lord Is Riding All the Time

My Ship Is on de Ocean - see - My Ship Is on the Ocean

My Soul Is a Witness - see - Witness for My Lord

My Soul Wants Something Dat's New - see - My Soul Wants Something That's New

My Soul's Been Anchored in de Lord - see - My Soul's Been Anchored in the Lord

My Soul's Determining - see - My Soul's Determined

My Soul's Goin' to Heaven - see - My Soul's Going to Heaven

Never Said a Mumbalin Word - see - He Never Said a Mumbling Word

No Devil in Our Lan' - see - No Devil in Our Land

No Hidin' Place - see - No Hiding Place

No Hiding Place - see - There's No Hiding Place Down There

No I Ain't Ashame - see - No I Ain't Ashamed

No Liar Can Stan' - see - No Liar Can Stand

No Mo' My Dear Brudder - see - No More My Dear Brother

No More Auction Block - see - Many Thousand Gone

No More My Brother - see - No More My Dear Brother

No More Rain Fall for Wet You - see - No More Rain Fall to Wet You

Nobody Knows de Trouble I See - see - Nobody Knows the Trouble I See

Nobody Knows de Trouble I've Seen - see - Nobody Knows the Trouble I've Seen

Norah Hist the Windah - see - Noah Hoist the Window

Nummer Me One - *see* - Number Me One

O Adam Where Are You - *see* - What a Trying Time

O Didn't It Rain - *see* - Didn't It Rain

O It's Goin' to be a Mighty Day - *see* - It's Going to be a Mighty Day

O Lord How Long - *see* - Lord How Long

O Lord Write My Name - *see* - Lord Write My Name

O Mary What You Weepin' About - *see* - Mary What You Weeping About

O Mary Where Is Your Baby - *see* - Mary Where Is Your Baby

O My Good Lord Show Me de Way - *see* - My Good Lord Show Me the Way

O Peter Go Ring-a Dem Bells - *see* - Peter Go Ring Them Bells

O Wasn't Dat a Wide River - *see* - Wasn't That a Wide River

O Watch the Stars - *see* - Watch the Stars

O Who Dat Coming Ober Yonder - *see* - Who's That Coming Over Yonder

O'er the Crossing - *see* - Over the Crossing

Official Song of the NAACP - *see* - Lift Every Voice and Sing

Oh By and By - *see* - By and By

Oh Dat Sun Gwine Down - *see* - That Sun Going Down

Oh de Robe - *see* - Oh the Robe

Oh Den My Little Soul's Gwine to Shine - *see* - I'm Going to Join the Great
    Association

Oh Gambler Git Up Off o' Yo' Knees - *see* - Gambler Get Up Off of Your
    Knees

Oh Hear Me Prayin' - *see* - Hear Me Praying

Oh Lawd How Long - *see* - Before This Time Another Year

Oh Little Chillun - *see* - Little Children

Oh Look-a Death - *see* - Never a Man Speak Like This Man

Oh Lord Answer Ma Prayer - *see* - Lord Answer My Prayer

Oh Lord Dese Bones ob Mine Comin' Together in de Mornin' - *see* - Lord
    These Bones of Mine

Oh Lord Have Mercy on Me - *see* - Lord Have Mercy

Oh Lord I Done Done - *see* - Lord I Done Done

Oh Lord I'm Hungry - *see* - Lord I'm Hungry

Oh Ma Lord What Shall I Do - *see* - My Lord What Shall I Do

Oh Mary Doan' Yer Weep - *see* - Mary Don't You Weep

Oh Mary Doncher Weep - *see* - Mary Don't You Weep

Oh Mary Oh Marthy - *see* - Oh Mary Oh Martha

Oh Mother Don't You Weep - *see* - Mother Don't You Weep

Oh My Little Soul - *see* - My Little Soul

Oh My Lord What Shall I Do - *see* - My Lord What Shall I Do

Oh My Lovin' Brother - *see* - My Loving Brother

Oh Nebbuh Me One - *see* - Never Me One

Oh Nobody Knows Who I Am - *see* - Nobody Knows Who I Am

Oh Peter Go Ring-a Dem Bells - *see* - Peter Go Ring Them Bells

Oh Po' Little Jesus - *see* - Poor Little Jesus

Oh Redeem' Redeem' - *see* - Oh Redeemed Redeemed

Oh Ride on Jedus - *see* - Ride on Jesus

Oh Rise an' Shine - *see* - Rise and Shine

Oh Rocks Don't Fall on Me - *see* - Rocks Don't Fall on Me

Oh Sinner Now Is the Time for to Pray - *see* - Sinner Now Is the Time for
    to Pray

Oh Sinner You'd Better Get Ready - *see* - Sinner You Better Get Ready

Oh Sister Git Yo' Ticket Right - *see* - Sister Get Your Ticket Right

Oh Wasn't Dat a Wide Ribber - *see* - Wasn't That a Wide River

Oh When I Git t'Heaven - *see* - When I Get to Heaven

Oh Won't You Sit Down - *see* - Won't You Sit Down

Oh Wrastlin' Jacob - *see* - Wrestling Jacob

Oh Yes I'm Goin' Up - *see* - Yes I'm Going Up

Oh Yes Oh Yes Wait 'Til I Git on My Robe - *see* - Oh Yes

Ol' Ark's A-Moverin' - *see* - Old Ark Is Moving Along

Ol' Man Devil Gotta Go Some - *see* - Old Man Devil Gotta Go Some

Old Ark - *see* - Old Ark Is Moving Along

Old Ark A-Moving Along - *see* - Old Ark Is Moving Along

Old Ark's A-Moverin' - *see* - Old Ark Is Moving Along

Old Ark's A-Moving Along - *see* - Old Ark Is Moving Along

Old Ark's A-Moving and I'm Going Home - *see* - Old Ark Is Moving Along

Old Sheep Know the Road - *see* - Old Sheep Done Know the Road

Ole Ark A-Moverin' Along - *see* - Old Ark Is Moving Along

Ole Ship Maria - *see* - Old Ship Maria

Ole Ship o' Zion - *see* - Old Ship of Zion

Ole-Time Religion - *see* - Old Time Religion

On Ma Journey - *see* - On My Journey

On My Knees - *see* - Communion

On the Other Side of Jordan - *see* - Going to Roll in My Jesus' Arms

One-a These Days - *see* - One of These Days

Opon de Rock - *see* - Upon the Rock

Paul and Silas - *see* - All Night Long

Peter Go Ring Dem Bells - *see* - Peter Go Ring Them Bells

Po' Heathens Are Dyin' - *see* - Poor Heathens Are Dying

Po' Li'l Jesus - *see* - Poor Little Jesus

Po' Little Jesus - *see* - Poor Little Jesus

Po' Me - *see* - Poor Me

Po' Mona You Shall Be Free - *see* - Poor Moaner You Shall Be Free

Po' Mo'ner Got a Home at Las' - *see* - Poor Mourner's Got a Home at Last

Po' Mourner's Got a Home at Las' - *see* - Poor Mourner's Got a Home at Last

Po' Pilgrim - *see* - Poor Pilgrim

Po' Sinner Fare You Well - *see* - Poor Sinner Fare You Well

Po' Sinner Man - *see* - Poor Sinner Man

Poor Me - *see* - Trouble Will Bury Me Down

Poor Mourner's Got a Home - *see* - Poor Mourner's Got a Home at Last

Praise de Lamb - *see* - Praise the Lamb

Prancin' Horses - *see* - Prancing Horses

Pray All the Member Pray All the Member - *see* - Pray All the Members

Pray Is de Key to de Kingdom - *see* - Praying Is the Key to the Kingdom

Pray Is the Key to the Kingdom - *see* - Praying Is the Key to the Kingdom

Pray on - *see* - In the River of Jordan

Prayer Is de Key - *see* - Prayer Is the Key of Heaven

Prayer Is de Key of Heaven - *see* - Prayer Is the Key of Heaven

Praying in de Land - *see* - Praying in the Land

Prepare Me - *see* - Prepare Me One Body

Put John on de Islan' - *see* - Put John on the Island

Raslin' Jacob - *see* - Wrestling Jacob

Redeemed Redeemed - *see* - Oh Redeemed Redeemed

Reign Massa Jesus - *see* - Reign Master Jesus

Reign Oh Reign - *see* - Join the Army of the Lord

Religion Is a Fortune I Really Do Believe - *see* - Religion Is a Fortune

Remember de Dyin' Lamb - *see* - Remember the Dying Lamb

Rise an' Shine - *see* - Rise and Shine

Rise Mourners - *see* - Rise Mourners Rise

Rise Shine for Thy Light Is A-Coming - *see* - Rise Shine for Thy Light
    Is Coming

Rise Up Shepherd - *see* - Rise Up Shepherd and Follow

Rise Up Shepherd an' Foller - *see* - Rise up Shepherd and Follow

Rock-a My Soul - *see* - Rock My Soul

Rock Oh My Soul - *see* - Rock My Soul

Rock o'Jubilee - *see* - Rock of Jubilee

Rockin' Jerusalem - *see* - Rocking Jerusalem

Roll an' Rock - *see* - Roll and Rock

Roll de Ole Chariot Along - *see* - Roll the Old Chariot Along

Roll Jerdon Roll - *see* - Roll Jordan Roll

Rollin' in Jesus' Arms - *see* - Rolling in Jesus' Arms

Room Enough in de Hebben - *see* - Room Enough in the Heaven

Roun' About de Mountain - *see* - Around About the Mountain

Roun' de Glory Manger - *see* - Round the Glory Manger

Run Mo'ner Run - *see* - Run Moaner Run

Samson's Wife Sot on His Knees - *see* - Samson's Wife Sat on His Knees

Satan's Camp A-Fire - *see* - Satan's Camp Fire

Save Me Jedus Save Me Now - *see* - Save Me Jesus Save Me Now

Sea Gwine Deliver Up Dry Bones - *see* - Sea Is Going to Deliver Up Dry Bones

Seek and You Shall Find - *see* - Seek and Ye Shall Find

Sen' dem Angels Down - *see* - Send Them Angels Down

Sen'er One Angel Down - *see* - Send One Angel Down

Set Down Servant - *see* - Sit Down Servant

Settin' Down by de Side of de Lamb - *see* - Sitting Down Beside the Lamb

Shine Shine - *see* - Shine Shine I'll Meet You in the Morning

Shoot dat Buffey - *see* - Trip to Raleigh

Shout All Over God's Heaven - *see* - Going to Shout All Over God's Heaven

Sing-a Ho That I Had the Wings of a Dove - *see* - Sing Ho That I Had the Wings of a Dove

Singin' Wid a Sword In Ma Hand - *see* - Singing With a Sword in My Hand

Singing on de Ol' Church Groun' - *see* - Singing on the Old Church Ground

Sinner Please Doan Let Dis Harves' Pass - *see* - Sinner Please Don't Let This Harvest Pass

Sinner You'd Better Get Ready - *see* - Sinner You Better Get Ready

Sister Mary Had-a But One Time - *see* - Sister Mary Had But One Child

Sitting Down Side Ob My Jesus - *see* - Sitting Down Side of My Jesus

Slav'ry Chain - *see* - Slavery's Chain

So High - *see* - My God Is So High

Some Come Cripple - *see* - Hail the Crown

Some o' Dese Days - *see* - Some of These Days

Some o' Dese Mornin's - *see* - Some of These Mornings

Some Will Lub Yo' and Some Will Hate Yo' - *see* - Some Will Love You and Some Will Hate You

Somebody Got Lost in de Storm - *see* - Somebody Got Lost in the Storm

Somebody Knockin' at Yo' Door - *see* - Somebody's Knocking at Your Door

Somebody's Calling My Name - *see* - Hush Somebody's Calling My Name

Sometimes I Feel - *see* - Sometimes I Feel Like a Motherless Child

Sometimes I Feel Like a Motherless Chile - *see* - Sometimes I Feel Like a Motherless Child

Sometimes I Feel Like I Wanna Go Home - *see* - Sometimes I Feel Like I Want to Go Home

Sometimes My Trouble Makes Me Tremble - *see* - Were You There

Soon A Will Be Done - *see* - Soon I Will Be Done

Soon in de Morning - *see* - Soon in the Morning

Soon One Mawnin' Death Come Creepin' In Yo' Room - *see* - Soon One Morning

Soon One Mornin' - *see* - Soon One Morning

Soon One Mornin' Death Come Creepin' - *see* - Soon One Morning

Soon We Will be Done - *see* - Soon I Will Be Done

Soon Will I Be Done - *see* - Soon I Will Be Done

Spirit o' the Lord Done Fell on Me - *see* - Spirit of the Lord Done Fell on Me

Stan' By Me - *see* - Stand By Me

Stan' Steady - *see* - Stand Steady

Stan' Still Jordon - *see* - Stand Still Jordan

Stand on the Sea of Glass - *see* - Standing on the Sea of Glass

Standin' in the Need of Prayer - *see* - Standing in the Need of Prayer

Standin' on de Sea ob Glass - *see* - Standing on the Sea of Glass

Stan'in' in de Need of Prayer - *see* - Standing in the Need of Prayer

Stars Begin to Fall - *see* - Stars in the Elements

Stars in the Elements are Falling - *see* - Stars in the Elements

Steal Away - *see* - Steal Away and Pray; Steal Away to My Father's Kingdom

Steal Away to Mah Father's Kingdom - *see* - Steal Away to My Father's Kingdom

Story of Norah - *see* - Story of Noah

Study War No More - *see* - I Ain't Going to Study War No More

Sun Don't Set in the Mornin' - *see* - Sun Don't Set in the Morning

Sund'y Mornin' Ban' - *see* - Sunday Morning Band

Sunshine Into My Soul - *see* - Sun Shine Into My Soul

Sweet Hebben - *see* - Sweet Heaven

Sweet Turtle Dove - *see* - Jerusalem Morning

Sweet Watuh Rollin' - *see* - Sweet Water Rolling

Swing Low - *see* - Swing Low Sweet Chariot

Takes a Little Bit ob Man to Rock Dan - *see* - Takes a Little Bit of Man to Rock Dan

Tall Angel at de Bar - *see* - Tall Angel at the Bar

Tell Bruddah Lijah - *see* - Tell Brother Elijah

Tell 'Em I'm Gone - *see* - Tell Them I'm Gone

Thank God I'm in the Feel - *see* - Thank God I'm in the Field

That Lonesome Valley - *see* - Lonesome Valley

The Crucified - *see* - Were You There

Then My Little Soul's Going to Shine - *see* - I'm Going to Join the Great Association

There Is a Balm in Gilead - *see* - Balm in Gilead

There Is a Meeting Here Tonight - *see* - There's a Meeting Here Tonight

There's a Great Camp Meeting - *see* - Walk Together Children

There's a Little Wheel A-Turning - *see* - Little Wheel Turning in My Heart

There's a Man Goin' 'Roun' Takin' Names - *see* - There's a Man Going Around Taking Names

There's a Meeting Here To-Night - *see* - There's a Meeting Here Tonight

There's No Hiding Place - *see* - There's No Hiding Place Down There

These All of My Father's Children - *see* - These Are All My Father's Children

These Bones Gwineter Rise Again - *see* - These Bones Going to Rise Again

They Look Like Men of War - *see* - Enlisted Soldiers

This is de Healin' Water - *see* - This Is the Healing Water

This May Be My Las' Time - *see* - This May Be My Last Time

This Old Time Religion - *see* - Old Time Religion

This Ole World's a Hell to Me - *see* - This Old World's a Hell to Me

This Ole Worl's A-Rollin' - *see* - This Old World's Rolling

Time Is Drawin' Nigh - *see* - Time Is Drawing Nigh

Tis Me - *see* - Standing in the Need of Prayer

Tis Me O Lord - *see* - Standing in the Need of Prayer

Tis the Old Ship of Zion - *see* - Old Ship of Zion

To See Gawd's Bleedin' Lam' - *see* - Want to Go to Heaven When I Die

To See God's Bleedin' Lamb - *see* - Want to Go to Heaven When I Die

Toll the Bell - *see* - Go Mary and Toll the Bell

Toll de Bell Angel I Jus' Got Over - *see* - Toll the Bell Angel

Tone de Bell - *see* - Towe the Bell

Tone de Bell Easy - *see* - Tone the Bell Easy

Trampin' - *see* - Tramping

T'ree Long Nights and T'ree Long Days - *see* - Three Long Nights and Three Long Days

Trouble's Gwine Ter Weigh Me Down - *see* - Trouble's Going to Weigh Me Down

Trubble Dun Bore Me Down - *see* - Trouble Done Bore Me Down

Tryin' to Get Home - *see* - Trying to Get Home

Until I Reach-a My Home - *see* - Until I Reach My Home

Up on de Mountain - *see* - Up on the Mountain

View de Road - *see* - View the Land

Wade in de Water - *see* - Wade in the Water

Wade In Nuh Watuh Childun - *see* - Wade in the Water

Walk Gawd's Hebbenly Road - *see* - Walk God's Heavenly Road

Walk in Jerusalem - *see* - I Want to Be Ready

Walk in Jerusalem Jus' Like John - *see* - Walk in Jerusalem Just Like John

Walk in Jerusalem Just Like John - *see* - I Want to Be Ready

Walk Jerusalem Jes' Like John - *see* - Walk in Jerusalem Just Like John

Walk Mary Down de Lane - *see* - Walk Mary Down the Lane

Walk Togedder Childron - *see* - Walk Together Children

Walking in de Light - *see* - Walking in the Light

Wasn' That a Wonder - *see* - Wasn't That a Wonder

Way Bye and Bye - *see* - Way By and By

'Way in de Middle of de Air - *see* - Away in the Middle of the Air

Way in the Heaven Bye-and-Bye - *see* - Way in the Heaven By and By

'Way in the Kingdom - *see* - Away in the Kingdom

Way Over in de Promise' Land - *see* - Wonder Where Is Good Old Daniel

Way Up on de Mountain - *see* - Way Up on the Mountain

W'at Harm Has Jesus Dun - *see* - What Harm Has Jesus Done

Wayfaring Stranger - *see* - Pilgrim's Song

We Am Clim'in' Jacob's Ladder - *see* - Jacob's Ladder

We Are Walkin' Down de Valley - *see* - We Are Walking Down the Valley

We Are Walking in de Light - *see* - Walking in the Light

We Shall Walk Thru the Valley - *see* - We Shall Walk Through the Valley

We Will March Through the Valley - *see* - We Shall Walk Through the Valley

Weary Traveler - *see* - Let Us Cheer the Weary Traveler

Weepin' Mary - *see* - Weeping Mary

Welcome Table - *see* - I'm Going to Sit at the Welcome Table

We'll March Down Jerden - *see* - We'll March Down Jordan

Well She Ask Me in de Parlor - *see* - Well She Ask Me in the Parlor

W'en I'm Gone - *see* - When I'm Gone

W'en Israel Was in Egypt's Lan' - *see* - Go Down Moses

We're Almost Home - *see* - We Are Almost Home

Whar' Shall I Be - *see* - Where Shall I Be

What is de Matter Wid de Mourners - *see* - Jubilee

What Yo' Gwine t' Do When de Lamp Burn Down - *see* - What You Going to Do When the Lamp Burns Down

What You Gwine to Do - *see* - What You Going to Do

Wheel in de Middle ob de Wheel - *see* - Wheel in the Middle of the Wheel

When de Saints Come Marchin 'In - *see* - When the Saints Go Marching In

When de Train Come Along - *see* - When the Train Comes Along

When I Come t' Die - *see* - When I Come to Die

When I Fall on My Knees - *see* - Let Us Break Bread Together

When I Git in Heben in Muh Elbow Chair - *see* - When I Get in Heaven in My Elbow Chair

When I Lay My Burden Down - *see* - Glory Glory Hallelujah

When I Rise Cryin' Holy - *see* - When I Rise Crying Holy

When Israel Was in Egypt's Land - *see* - Go Down Moses

When Jesus Brought de Light to Me - *see* - When Jesus Brought the Light to Me

When Jesus Met the Woman at the Well - *see* - Woman at the Well

When Moses Smote de Water - *see* - When Moses Smote the Water

When My Blood Runs Chilly an' Col' - *see* - When My Blood Runs Chilly and Cold

When the General Roll Is Called - *see* - General Roll Call

When the Saints Come Marching In - *see* - When the Saints Go Marching In

When the Stars Begin to Fall - *see* - My Lord What a Morning

Where Shall I Be When de Firs' Trumpet Soun' - *see* - Where Shall I Be

White Horse Pawin' in the Valley - *see* - White Horse Pawing in the Valley

Who Built de Ark - *see* - Who Built the Ark

Who Dat a-Comin' Ovah Yondah - *see* - Who's That Coming Over Yonder

Who Is Dat Yondah - *see* - Who's That Yonder

Who Is This A-Coming - *see* - Who Is This Coming

Who Lock de Lion's Jaw - *see* - Who Locks the Lion's Jaw

Who Love Ma Lord - *see* - Who Love My Lord

Who Shall Deliver Po' Me - *see* - Who Shall Deliver Poor Me

Who'll Be a Witness For My Lord - *see* - Witness for My Lord

Who'll Jine de Union - *see* - Who Will Join the Union

Who's Dat Yandah - *see* - Who's That Yonder

Who's Goin' to Close My Dyin' Eyes - *see* - Who's Going to Close My
Dying Eyes

Who's That a-Comin' Over Yonder - *see* - Who's That Coming Over Yonder

Why Don't You Let Gawd's People Go - *see* - Why Don't You Let God's
People Go

Why Don't You 'Liver Me - *see* - Why Don't You Deliver Me

Why He's the Lord of Lords - *see* - He Is the Lord of Lords

Wide River - *see* - Wasn't That a Wide River

Wish I Was in Heabum Settin' Down - *see* - Wish I Was in Heaven Setting
Down

Witness - *see* - Witness for My Lord

Woke Up Dis Mornin' - *see* - Woke Up This Morning

Wonder Where Is Good Ole Daniel - *see* - Wonder Where Is Good Old Daniel

Workin' on the Building - *see* - Working on the Building

Wrastling Jacob - *see* - Wrestling Jacob

Wretched Man - *see* - Wretched Man That I Am

Wring My Hands and Cry - *see* - Sometimes I Feel Like a Motherless Child

Yo' Better Run Run Run - *see* - You'd Better Run

Yo' Better Run to de City of Refuge - *see* - You Better Run to the City of
Refuge

Yo' Cyan' Find a New Hidin' Place - *see* - You Can't Find a New Hiding Place

Yo' Go I Go Wid Yo' - *see* - You Go I'll Go With You

Yo' Mus' Hab Dat True Religion - *see* - You Must Have That True Religion

Yo' Publican, Yo' Pharisee - *see* - You Publican You Pharisee

Yo' Sins Are Gonna Find You Out - *see* - Your Sins Are Going to Find You Out

You Better Git Religion Sinner Man - *see* - You Better Get Religion Sinner Man

You Better Git Yo' Ticket - *see* - You Better Get Your Ticket

You Better Run Run Run - *see* - You'd Better Run

You Can't Find a New Hidin' Place - *see* - You Can't Find a New Hiding Place

You Go I'll Go Wid You - *see* - You Go I'll Go With You

You Goin' to Reap Jus' What You Sow - *see* - You Going to Reap Just What You Sow

You Got to Walk That Lonesome Valley - *see* - Lonesome Valley

You Hear the Lams A-Crying - *see* - Hear the Lamb's Crying

You May Bury Me in de Eas' - *see* - You May Bury Me in the East

You Mus' Come in By an' Thro' de Lamb - *see* - My God Is So High

You Mus' Hab Dat True Religion - *see* - You Must Have That True Religion

You Must Come in By and Through the Lamb - *see* - My God Is So High

You'd Better Min' - *see* - You'd Better Mind

Young Lamb Mus' Fin' de Way - *see* - Old Sheep Done Know the Road

You're Going to Reap Just What You Sow - *see* - You Going to Reap Just What You Sow

You're Tired Chil' - *see* - You're Tired Child

Zekiel Saw de Wheel - *see* - Ezekiel Saw the Wheel

Zion Weep a-Low - *see* - Zion Weep Low

Topical Index

Admonition/Judgement

After a While
Almost Over
Are You Ready
At the Bar of God
At the Judgment Bar

Bear Your Burden
Belshazzah Had a Feast
Better Walk Steady
Blood Done Sign My Name
Blow Gabriel
Blow Your Gospel Trumpet
Blow Your Trumpet Gabriel
Brothers Don't Get Weary

Can't Hide Sinner
Can't You Live Humble
Come Down Sinner
Come Sinner Come
Come Unto Me
Coming Again By and By

Day of Judgment
Didn't It Rain
Don't Be Weary Traveler
Don't Let the Wind Blow
  Here No More
Don't You Weep After Me

Down in Hell
Downward Road
Downward Road Is Crowded

End of That Morning
Every Day

Gabriel's Trumpet Going to Blow
Gambler Get Up Off of Your Knees
Get in the Union
Get Your Ticket
God Don't Like It
God Knows It's Time
God's Going to Straighten Them
Going Home in the Chariot
Got to Go to Judgement
Great Judgment Day

Hail Sinners Hail-lo
Hammering Judgment
He Is Waiting
He's Got His Eyes on You
Hear Gabriel Blow in That Morn
Heaven Bell Ring
Hide Me
Hymn to Parnassus

I Ain't Going to Trust Nobody
I Got My Sword in My Hand
If I Have My Ticket Lord
If I Was a Mourner

I'll Be There
In That Day
In That Great Day
It May Be the Last Time
It's Going to be a Mighty Day

Jerusalem Morning
Judgment
Judgment Day Is Rolling Around
Judgment Day Is Trying Time
Judgment Will Find You So

Little Black Train Is Coming
Lord Bless the Name
Lord Have Mercy

Mighty Day
Moan Member Moan
Mother Don't You Weep
My Brethren Don't Get Weary
My Lord Is Riding All the Time
My Lord Says He's Going to
    Rain Down Fire
My Lord What a Morning
My Lord What Shall I Do
My Lord's Coming Again
My Lord's Riding All the Time
My Lord's Writing All the Time
My Mother Got a Letter
My Sister You'll Be Called On
My Time Is Come

No Hiding Place
No Liar Can Stand
Nobody Knows Who I Am
Number Me One

Oh Sinner
Only a Look
Other World Is Not Like This

Poor Sinner Fare You Well
Pure Religion
Put John on the Island

Remember Me
Restitution
Rock Chariot

Rocks Don't Fall on Me
Run Sinner Run
Run to Jesus

Satan's Camp Fire
Sea Is Going to Deliver Up Dry
    Bones
See the Signs of Judgment
Sin Sick Soul
Sinner Die
Sinner Man
Sinner Now Is the Time for to Pray
Sinner Please Don't Let This
    Harvest Pass
Sinner You Better Get Ready
Sinner You Know
Sitting Down Beside the Lamb
So Sad
Some of These Days
Somebody's Knocking at Your
    Door
Stand Up Like Soldiers
Stars Begin to Fall
Stars in the Elements
Stay in the Field
Sweet Turtle Dove

Talk About Me
Tall Angel at the Bar
That Sabbath Has No End
That Sun Going Down
There's a Handwriting on the Wall
There's a Mighty War in Heaven
There's No Hiding Place Down
    There
They Shall Receive a Blessing
This Old World's Rolling
Time Is Drawing Nigh
Tomorrow You May Die
Too Late
True Religion

View the Land

Wake Up Children
What You Going to Do
What You Going to Do When the
    Lamp Burns Down

Wheel in the Middle of the Wheel
Where Shall I Be
Woe Be Unto You
Working on the Building

Yes Yonder Comes My Lord
You Better Get Religion Sinner
  Man
You Better Run to the City of
  Refuge
You Can't Find a New Hiding
  Place
You Can't Stay Away
You Going to Reap Just What You
  Sow
You Shall Reap
You'd Better Mind
You'd Better Run
Your Low Down Ways
Your Sins Are Going to Find You
  Out

Aspiration

Am I a Soldier

Band of Music
Built a House in Paradise

Coming Down the Line

Dig Deep Children
Do Lord Remember Me
Do What the Spirit Say Do
Don't Leave Me Lord

Even Me

Free Free My Lord

Give Me a Clean Heart
Give Me Your Hand
Give Way Jordan
Going Lay Down My Life for My
  Lord
Going to Live Humble to the Lord
Gold Band
Good Lord Shall I Be the One

Good Lord Shall I Ever be the One

Heal Me Jesus
How Long
Humble

I Ain't Going to Study War No
  More
I Am Seeking for a City
I Belong to the Union Band
I Don't Want to Stay Here No
  Longer
I Know I Would Like to Read
I Stood Outside the Gate
I Want God's Heaven to Be Mine
I Want to Be Ready
I Want to Join the Band
I Want to Live So God Can Use
  Me
I Wish I Been There
If I Got My Ticket Lord
If I Had a Hammer
If I Had Died When I was a Babe
If You Love God Serve Him
I'm a Soldier of the Cross
I'm Going to Do All I Can
I'm Going to Stay in the Battlefield
I'm Running On

Just As I Am

Land I Am Bound For
Lead on O King Eternal
Leaning on the Lord
L'Envoi
Let Me Get Up
Listen to the Angels
Lord Don't Move This Mountain
Lord I Want to Be a Christian
Lord Touch Me

Move Me
My Brother I Do Wonder
My Soul Wants Something That's
  New
My Soul's Going to Heaven

Now Let Me Fly

Oh Mary Oh Martha

Reign Master Jesus
Reign Oh Reign
Roll Jordan Roll

Shine Shine
Shine Shine I'll Meet You in the
    Morning
Some of These Days
Standing on the Sea of Glass
Sweet Canaan

Tramping
Travel On

Until I Reach My Home

Walk in Jerusalem Just Like John
Wasn't That a Wide River
We Are Climbing the Hills of Zion
What Kind of Shoes You Going to
    Wear
What Shall I Render
When the Saints Go Marching In
White Marble Stone

Christmas

Amen

Behold That Star

Children Go Where I Send Thee

Glory Hallelujah to the New-Born
    King
Go Tell It On the Mountain

Mary Had a Baby
Mary Where Is Your Baby
Meet Oh Lord

New Born Baby

Oh Mary

Rise Up Shepherd and Follow

There Was a Babe
This Is the Christmas Time

What Month Was Jesus Born In

Church

Church of God

It Just Suits Me

Join Them

Let the Church Roll On
Let us Break Bread Together

Move Members Move

Old Time Religion

This Is the Trouble of the World

You Must Have That True Religion

Death

Ain't Going to Tarry Here
All Over This World
Almost Done Toiling Here
Am I Born to Die
Angel's Waiting at the Door

Before This Time Another Year
Burden Down
By and By

Coffin to Bind Me Down
Cold Icy Hand
Cross Me Over

Danville Chariot
Death Ain't Nothing But a Robber
Death Come to My House He
    Didn't Stay Long
Death Is in This Land
Death's Going to Lay His Cold Icy
    Hands on Me
Die in the Field

Don't You Grieve After Me
Done Found the Way at Last

Everybody Got to Die
Everybody Wants to Know Just
    How I Die

Farewell My Brother
Farewell My Dear Mother
Fold My Hands and Tie My Feet
For I Ain't Going to Die No More
From Every Graveyard
Funeral Chant

Getting Ready to Die
Go Mary and Toll the Bell
God's Going Wake Up the Dead
Going to Pull My War Clothes
Gone Along
Good Bye Mother
Graveyard

Hammer Keeps Ringing
Hush Somebody's Calling My
    Name

I Am Not Afraid to Die
I Feel Like My Time Ain't Long
I Got to Lay in Yonder Graveyard
I Know My Time Ain't Long
I Stood on the River of Jordan
I Want to Die Easy When I Die
I Want to Die Shouting
I Will Sleep Away
I'm Almost Done Traveling
I'm Mighty Tired
I'm Traveling to the Grave
In Some Lonesome Graveyard
In That Old Field
It's Getting Late in the Evening

Jesus Going to Make Up My
    Dying Bed
John Brown's Body

Last Call
Lay This Body Down

Like a Rough and a Rolling Sea
Lord How Long
Lord Remember Me
Lord Time Is Drawing Nigh

May Be the Last Time
My Brother's Died and Gone to
    Heaven
My Lord's Writing Down Time

New Burying Ground
No More Rain Fall to Wet You
Now We Take This Feeble Body

Oh Graveyard
Oh the Robe
One of These Days

Poor Mourner's Got a Home
    at Last
Poor Sinner

Rule Death in His Arms

Shall I Die
Singing on the Old Church Ground
Sit Down Servant
Somebody's Buried in the
    Graveyard
Soon I Will Be Done
Soon One Morning
Steal Away
Sun Mows Down
Sweetest Sound I Ever Heard
Swing Low Chariot

There's a Man Going Around
Taking Names
These Are My Father's Children
This May Be My Last Time
This May Be Your Last Time
Toll the Bell Angel
Tone the Bell Easy
Traveling Shoes

We Are Traveling to the Grave
Weep No More for Baby
We'll Die in the Field

When I Am Gone Gone Gone
When I Come to Die
When I Die
When I'm Dead
When I'm Gone
When My Blood Runs Chilly
    and Cold
When the Chariot Comes
When the Devil Comes Around
When the Train Comes Along
When You Hear My Coffin Sound
Who's Going to Close My
    Dying Eyes

You Can Dig My Grave

Deliverance

Ain't I Glad I've Got Out the
    Wilderness
All My Sins Done Taken Away
All Night Long
And I Cry
Anyhow My Lord

Babylon's Falling
Bless My Soul And Gone
By and By

Changed My Name
City of Babylon
Climbing Up the Mountain
Come Down
Come Down Angels
Come Out the Wilderness
Coming Here Tonight

Don't Come Oh Lord
Don't You View That Ship Come
    Sailing
Done Been Sanctified
Done Written Down My Name
Down By the Riverside

Every Day Will Be Sunday
Every Time I Feel the Spirit

Free At Last

Freedom Train Coming

Get on Board Little Children
Get on Board Old Ship of Zion
Give Me the Wings
Go Down Death
Go Down Moses
Go Elijah
Go Round Go Round
Going to Sing All Along the Way
Going to Write to Master Jesus
Good Bye City of Babylon
Good News the Chariot's Coming
Gospel Train

Has Anybody Here Seen My Lord
Ho Every One That Thirsts
How Long Has the Train Been
    Gone

I Ain't Going to Grieve My Lord
    No More
I Am Free
I Am Hunting for a City
I Done What You Told Me to Do
I Went to the Hillside
I'll Be Sleeping in My Grave
I'm Going Back with Jesus
In Bright Mansions Above
In That Great Getting Up Morning
Israelites Shouting

Join the Army of the Lord

Keep Me From Sinking Down
Kind Savior
Kum Ba Yah

Lamb's Blood Done Washed Me
    Clean
Lead Me to the Rock
Let Me Fly
Let Me Ride
Lord I Just Got Over

Many Thousand Go
March Along
March On

Moaning
My Army's Crossing Over
My Lord's Writing All the Time
My Name's Been Written Down
My Ship Is on the Ocean
My Sin's Been Taken Away

Nobody Knows the Trouble
    I've Seen

Oh Freedom
Oh Holy Savior
Old Ship Maria
Old Ship of Zion

Pilgrim's Song
Poor Moaner You Shall Be Free
Praise Chant

Roll Jordan

Same Train
Save Me Jesus Save Me Now
Save Me Now Save Me
Send Them Angels Down
Slavery's Chain
Soon and Very Soon
Spirit of the Lord Done Fell on Me
Steal Away to My Father's
    Kingdom
Swing Down Chariot
Swing Low Sweet Chariot

Tell Brother Elijah
Tell Them I'm Gone
That Same Train
Them Bones
This Train

Walk in Jerusalem Just Like John
Way Up on the Mountain
We Shall Overcome
Wear a Starry Crown
Where Shall I Go
Who Locks the Lion's Jaw
Who Shall Deliver Poor Me
Who Will Join the Union
Who's That Coming Over Yonder

Why Don't You Deliver Me

You Better Get Your Ticket
You Can't Cross Here

Easter

All the Way to Calvary
Angel Roll the Stone Away

Calvary
Calvary's Mountain
Christians' Hymn of the
    Crucifixion

Did You Hear How They Crucified
    My Lord
Did You Hear When Jesus Rose

He Arose
He Never Said a Mumbling Word
He Rose From the Dead

Jews Killed Poor Jesus
Jews They Took Our Savior

Last Supper
Look at How They Done My Lord

One Sunday Morning

They Led My Lord Away

Were you There

Faith/Assurance

Ain't Going to Tarry Here
Ain't You Glad You Got Good
    Religion
Amazing Grace
Amen
Anchor in the Lord
Angels Are Watching Over Me
Appolyon and the Pilgrim
Archangel

Balm in Gilead
Be With Me
Believer I Know
Bell Done Ring
Bell Done Rung
Black Sheep Where You Left
   Your Lamb
Blessed Hope
Blessed Quietness
By and By

Calinda
Certainly Lord
Children Do Linger
Children We All Shall Be Free
Children You'll Be Called on
Come All of God's Children
Come Here Lord
Come to Me
Come Trembling Down

Didn't You Hear
Done Found My Lost Sheep
Done Found the Way at Last
Don't Get Weary
Don't You Let Nobody Turn You
   Around

Faith of Our Fathers
Fighting On
Fisherman Peter
For My Lord

Galman Day
Get on the Boat Little Children
Give Me Jesus
Give Me Jesus When I Die
Glad I Got Religion
Go and I Go With You
Go in the Wilderness
God Be With You
God's Going to Set This World
   on Fire
Going to Set Down and Rest
   Awhile
Golden Altar
Good Bye Brother
Good Bye Brothers

Half Has Never Been Told
Happy New Year
His Eye Is on the Sparrow
Hold Out
Hold Out to the End
Holy Baby
Hope I Join the Band
House That's Built Without Hands
Hunting for a City
Hunting for the Lord

I Ain't Got Weary Yet
I Can't Stay Away
I Do Know God Don't Lie
I Don't Feel No-Ways Tired
I Got a Hiding Place
I Got a Home in That Rock
I Got a Light
I Know I Have Another Building
I Know My Jesus Loves Me
I Know That My Redeemer Lives
I Know the Lord
I Know the Lord's Laid His Hands
   on Me
I Saw the Beam in my Sister's Eye
I Shall Not Be Moved
I want Jesus to Walk With me
I Will Overcome
I'm a Child of Grace
I'm a Soldier in the Army of
   the Lord
I'm Going to Eat at the Welcome
   Table
I'm Going to Lay Down My Life
   for My Lord
I'm so Glad Jesus Lifted Me
I'm So Glad Troubles Don't Last
   Always
If Anybody Ask You Who I Am
If the Lord Calls You
If You Ask Him
In God We Trust
In the New Jerusalem
Is It True

Jesus Rolling in His Arms
John Saw the Number No Man
   Could Number

Just Above my Head

Keep Your Lamps Trimmed

Leaning on That Lamb
Little Children
Little Innocent Lamb
Little More Faith in Jesus
Little Talk With Jesus Makes
    It Right
Lord Heal Him
Lord Help Me to Hold Out
Lord I Done Done
Lord Is My Shepherd
Lord Until I Reach My Home

Made My Vow to the Lord
Members Don't Get Weary
Missionary Baptist Song
My Faith Looks Up to Thee
My Little Soul's Going to Shine
My Lord God Rocking in the
    Weary Land
My Lord's Going to Move This
    Wicked Race
My Mind Stayed on Freedom
My Soul's Been Anchored in the
    Lord
My Soul's Determined

Negro Lullaby
Never Leave Me Alone
No Man Can Hinder Me
Not Weary Yet

Oh Yes
On My Journey
Onward Christian Soldiers

Religion Is a Fortune
Religion That My Lord Gave Me
Remember the Dying Lamb
Remon
Ring the Bells
Rise Shine for Thy Light
    Is Coming
Rock My Soul
Rock of Ages

Roll and Rock
Roll On
Rolling in Jesus' Arms
Round About the Mountain
Run Moaner Run

Sail Oh Believer
Sailing Over Yonder
Seek and Ye Shall Find
Sitting Down Side of My Jesus
Soldier for Jesus
Solid Rock
Some Day
Some of These Mornings
Somewhere Around a Throne
Stand By Me
Stand Steady
Stand the Storm
Stand Up Stand Up for Jesus
Surely God Is Able
Swing Low Sweet Chariot

Thank God I'm in the Field
There is a Balm in Gilead
There Is Rest for the Weary
    Traveler
There's Room Enough
Trouble
Trying to Cross the Red Sea

Up on the Mountain
Upon the Rock

Walk About Elders
Walk God's Heavenly Road
Walk Through the Valley
Walk Through the Valley in Peace
Walk Together Children
Walk You in the Light
Walking in the Light
We Are Almost Home
We Are Building on a Rock
We Are Walking Down the Valley
We'll Overtake the Army
We'll Stand the Storm
We've Come This Far By Fatih
What Shall I Do
Wheel in a Wheel

When I Rise Crying Holy
When My Lord Calls Me I
    Must Go
When We Do Meet Again
White Horse Pawing in the Valley
Who Is on the Lord's Side
Who Is This Coming
Who's Been Here
Winter Will Soon Be Over
Woke Up This Morning

Yes God Is Real
You Go I'll Go With You
You Got a Right
You May Bury Me in the East

Heaven

Ain't That Good News
Angels in Heaven Going to Write
    My Name
Archangel Open the Door
Away in the Kingdom
Away in the Middle of the Air

Band of Angels
Bound for the Promised Land
Bright Sparkles in the Churchyard
Brother Guide Me Home
Brothers Don't Stay Away

Chatter With the Angels
Choose You a Seat and Set Down
City Called Heaven
Climb Up Ye Little Children
Come and Go
Comfort in Heaven

Deep River
Don't Call the Roll
Don't You Wish You Were
    in Heaven

Early in the Morning

Father Abraham

General Roll
General Roll Call
Go Chain the Lion Down
Go on Brother
Going to Ride Up in the Chariot
Going to Shout All Over God's
    Heaven
Going Up
Good Lord When I Die
Good News
Good News Angels Bring the
    Tidings
Got a Home at Last
Great Big Stars

He'll Understand and Say Well
    Done
Hear the Angels Singing
Heaven
Heaven Bells
Heaven Bells Ringing and I'm
    Going Home
Heaven Bells Ringing in My Soul
Heaven Is a Beautiful Place
Heaven Is Going to Be My Home
Heaven Is Shining
Hold Out Your Light

I Ain't Going to Die No More
I Am Going Over There
I Can't Stay Behind
I Don't Care for Riches
I Going Put on My Golden Shoes
I Going Try the Air
I Got a Home
I Got a Key to the Kingdom
I Got a Mother in the Bright
    Shining World
I Got Shoes
I Have Another Building
I Heard From Heaven Today
I Heard of a City Called Heaven
I Hope I'll Join the Band
I Hope My Mother Will Be There
I Saw the Light
I Want to Go Where Jesus Is

I Won't Die No More
If You Want to Get to Heaven
I'll Be There in the Morning
I'll Fly Away
I'll Meet You Way Up Yonder
I'm Crossing Jordan River
I'm Going to Join the Great
    Association
I'm Going to Live With Jesus
I'm Going to See My Loving
    Father When I Get Home
I'm Going Up to Heaven Anyhow
I'm on My Journey Home
I'm So Glad
I've Got a Mother in the Heaven
In the Army
In the Kingdom
In the Morning

John John
Join the Angel Band
Join the Heaven With the Angels
Just Behold That Number
Just Going Over in the Heavenly
    Land
Just to Behold His Face

King Jesus Built Me a House
    Above

Let the Heaven Light Shine on Me
Like a Feather in the Wind
Little Children Then Won't You Be
    Glad
Look Away in the Heaven
Lord Is This Heaven
Love Feast in Heaven

Marching up the Heavenly Road
Move Along
My Little Soul
My Mother's in Heaven
My Soul Wants to Go Home to
    Glory

Oh Glory
Over My Head

Peter Go Ring Them Bells
Plenty Good Room

Ride On
Ride on Conquering King
Road to Heaven
Room Enough
Room Enough in the Heaven

Shine Shine I'll Meet You in the
    Morning
Social Band
Somebody's Buried in the Graveyard
Stand Still Jordan
Sweet Heaven
Sweet Heaven Is a Handsome Place
Sweet Home

Tell It
Thank God I'm on My Way to
    Heaven
Them Charming Bells
There Is a Mighty Shouting
There's a Heavenly Home Up
    Yonder
This World Is Not My Home

View the Land

Wait a Little While
Wasn't That a Wonder
Way By and By
Way in the Heaven By and By
What a Beautiful City
When do we Meet Again
When I Get in Heaven in My
    Elbow Chair
When I Get to Heaven
When Shall I Get There
Wish I Was in Heaven Setting
    Down
Won't You Sit Down

Yes I'm Going Up
You Got a Robe

Zion's Children

Jesus

Amen
Angels Done Bowed Down

Blood Will Never Lose Its Power
But He Ain't Coming Here to Die
    No More

Christ Is All
Come Down My Lord
Conviction of the Wise Men in
    Jerusalem
Crowned Him Lord of All
Cruel Jews

Down By the River
Drinking of the Wine

Everywhere I Go My Lord

Fairest Lord Jesus
Footprints of Jesus

Hail John's Army Bend Down and
    Died
Happy Morning
He Is King of Kings
He Is the Lord of Lords
He's a Mighty Good Leader
He's the Lily of the Valley
He's the Lord of Lords
His Love Comes Trickling Down
His Name So Sweet
Hypocrite and the Concubine

I Believe This Is Jesus
I Know the Lord Has Laid His
    Hands on Me
I Look for Jesus All My Days
I Love the Lord
I Want Jesus to Walk With Me
Is There Anybody Here

Jehovah Has Triumph Messiah
    Is King
Jesus Ain't Coming Here to Die
    No More

Jesus Blood Done Make Me Whole
Jesus Done Bless My Soul
Jesus Done Just What He Said
Jesus Got His Business Fix
Jesus Healed the Sick
Jesus Is Risen From the Dead
Jesus Locked the Lion's Jaw
Jesus on the Waterside
Jesus Rides That Milk-White Horse
Jesus Sitting on the Waterside
Jesus Won't You Come By and By
Jesus Wore the Crown

King Emanuel
King Jesus Is Listening
King Jesus Is My Only Friend
King Jesus Is the Rock
King Jesus Sitting on the Water
    Side
King of Kings

Little Boy
Look What a Wonder Jesus Done
Love King Jesus
Love the Lord

Never a Man Speak Like This Man
Never Saw Such a Man

Poor Little Jesus
Prancing Horses
Pretty Little Baby

Reign Oh Reign
Ride on Jesus
Ride on King Jesus
Roll Away That Stone
Round the Glory Manger

Sinner Won't Die No More

Take My Mother Home
Tell My Jesus Morning
There's No One Like Jesus
These Are All My Father's Children
They Nail Him to the Cross
This Is the Man

Wasn't That a Mighty Day
What You Going to Name that
    Pretty Little Baby
When Christ the Lord Was Here
When Jesus Brought the Light
    to Me
When Jesus Comes
Who Do You Call the King
    Emanuel
Who's That Yonder

You Won't Find a Man Like Jesus

New Testament

Angel's Waiting at the Tomb

Divers Never Gave Nothing to
    the Poor
Dives and Lazarus
Dust and Ashes

He Raised Poor Lazarus

I Want to Die Like Lazarus
In the River of Jordan

John Done Saw That Number
John John of the Holy Order
John Saw the Holy Number
John the Revelator
John Was Writing
John's Gone Down on the Island
John's on the Island on His Knees

Paul and Silas
Peter on the Sea

Sinner-Man So Hard to Believe

Tell All the World John
There Were Ten Virgins
Turn Back Pharaoh's Army
Twas on One Sunday Morning

Way Over in the Egypt Land
We Need More Reapers

Zion

Old Testament

According to My Lord's Command
Adam in the Garden Pinning Leaves
Animals a Coming

Band of Gideon
Big Fish
Brother Moses Gone

Come Along Moses

Daniel Daniel Servant of the Lord
Daniel Saw the Stone
Daniel's in the Lion's Den
Didn't My Lord Deliver Daniel
Didn't Old Pharaoh Get Lost
Does You Call That Religion
Dry Bones

Elijah Rock
Ezekiel Said Here Was a Wheel in
    a Wheel
Ezekiel Saw the Wheel
Ezekiel's Wheel

Forty Days and Nights
Four and Twenty Elders

Gideon's Band
Go Down Moses
Good Lord Done Been Here

He's Just the Same Today
How Long Watchman

I Fold Up My Arms and I Wonder
I Heard the Preaching of the Elder
I Wish I Had Died in Egypt Land
I'll Make Me a Man
I'm Going Where There Ain't No
    More Dying

Jacob's Ladder
Jacob's Ladder Long and Tall
Job

Praise

He's Got the Whole World in His
  Hands
How I Got Over
Howdy Howdy
Humble Yourself the Bell Done
  Ring

I Ain't Going to Die No More
I Am Coming to a King
I Am the Light of the World
I Am the True Vine
I Am the Truth and the Light
I Do Love the Lamb
I Don't Care What the World
  May Do
I Don't Feel Weary
I Got a Letter This Morning
I Got a New Name
I Got My Religion on the Way
I Have a Leader Over There
I Heard the Angels Singing
I Love Everybody
I'm Going to Sing
I'm Going to Sit at the Welcome
  Table
I'm Working on the Building
I've a Message From My Lord
I've Been Toiling at the Hill

Jehovah Hallelujah
Jubilee

King Jesus Is My Only Friend

Let Us Cheer the Weary Traveler
Let Us Praise Him
Lift Every Voice and Sing
Little Children You Better Believe
Little Wheel Turning in My Heart
Lord Lord Lord
Love Come Trickling Down

Mighty Fortress in Our God
My God He Is a Man of War
My God Is a Rock
My God Is So High
My Name's Written on High
My Sister Ain't You Mighty Glad

No Devil in Our Land

Oh Holy Lord
Oh Shout Away
Oh the Sunshine
On to Glory

Praise God From Whom All
  Blessings Flow
Praise Member
Praise the Lamb

Reign My Savior
Reign Oh Reign
Religion So Sweet
Resurrection Morn
Rise and Shine
Rocking Jerusalem

Serving My God
Shine Like a Star in the Morning
Shout Away
Shout for Joy
Shout Jerusalem
Shout on Children
Singing With a Sword in My Hand
Sun Will Never Go Down
Sunday Morning Band

This Little Light of Mine
Trees

Who Love My Lord
Wondrous Love

You Publican You Pharisee

Zion Hallelujah
Zion Weep Low

Prayer

As I Went down in the Valley to
  Pray

Bow Low Elder
Brother You'd Better Be a Praying

Down in the Valley to Pray

Every Hour in the Day

Four and Twenty Elders

Go Down in the Valley and Pray
Guide My Head

Hear Me Praying
Holy Holy You Promised to
    Answer Prayer
How Can I Pray

I Couldn't Hear Nobody Pray
I Will Pray
I Won't Stop Praying
If I Keep Praying On

Jesus Is Listening
Lord Answer My Prayer
Lord's Prayer

Pray All Night
Pray All the Members
Pray On
Pray on the Way
Prayer Is the Key of Heaven
Praying in the Land
Praying Is the Key to the Kingdom

Sometimes I Feel Like I Want to
    Go Home
Standing in the Need of Prayer
Steal Away and Pray
Sun Don't Set in the Morning

There's Something on My Mind
This Is the Way I Pray
Time for Praying

We're Some of the Praying People

Rituals of Preparation for Renewal/Regeneration

Angel Done Changed My Name

Baptism
Baptizing
Baptizing Hymn
Be Still and Listen
Been Washed in the Blood
Book of Life

Chilly Water

Don't Be Weary Traveler
Drive Satan Away
Dry Bones Going to Rise

Fare Ye Well
Fix Me Jesus

Gift of God Is Eternal Life
Give Up the World
Going to Heaven
Going to Roll in My Jesus' Arms
Good Old Way
Got My Letter

Healing Waters
Holy Is My God

I Believe I'll Go Back Home
I Want to See Jesus in the Morning
If You Want to See Jesus
I'm Going to Wait Until the Holy
    Ghost Comes
I've Been Redeemed
I've Just Come From the Fountain

Just Now

Lamb Beautiful Lamb
Let Us Break Bread Together
Lord These Bones of Mine
Lord's Been Here

My Good Lord Done Been Here
My Good Lord's Been Here
My Head Wet With the Midnight
Dew

New Born Again
No Condemnation in My Soul
No I Ain't Ashamed

Oh Redeemed Redeemed
Old Sheep Done Know the Road

Poor Heathens Are Dying

Religion So Sweet
Ring Jerusalem
Run Mourner Run

Send One Angel Down
Show Me the Way
Steady Jesus Is Listening
Sweet Water Rolling

Take Me to the Water
This Is the Healing Water

Walking in God's Commandments
Where Do You Think I Found My
Soul
Why Don't You Come Along
Wide Deep Troubled Water

You Go I'll Go With You
You Must Be Pure and Holy

Satan

Hard to Rise Again
Hell and Heaven

I and Satan Had a Race

Old Man Devil Gotta Go Some
Old Satan

Roll Him Out Again

Towe the Bell

Wait Mr Mackright

Songs of Spiritual Journey

Ain't Got Long to Stay Here
Almost Done Traveling
Aye Lord Don't Leave Me

Been Down Into the Sea
Big Camp Meeting in the Promised
Land
Black Bird and the Crow
Blood-Strained Banders
Bound for Canaan Land
Bound to Go
Brother Have You Come

Come Along
Come and Go With Me
Come Down Angels
Come Let Us All Go Down

Did You Hear My Jesus
Do Don't Touch My Garment Good
Lord
Done Made My Vow To the Lord
Don't Be Weary Traveler
Don't You Want to Go
Dum-A-Lum

Eagle's Wings
Every Little Step Goes Higher

Foxes Have Holes in the Ground

Get on the Evening Train
Going Away to See My Lord
Going Over on the Other Side of
Jordan
Going to Follow
Going to Quit All of My Worldly
Ways
Good Lord I Done Good

Hand Me Down My Silver Trumpet
Have You Got Good Religion

Heaven-Bound Soldier
Hold the Wind Don't Let It Blow
Hold Your Light
How You Do Believer

I Am Bound for the Promised Land
I Am Going to Join in this Army
I Come This Night
I Done Been Home
I Don't Want You Go on and Leave
    Me
I Feel Like Dying in This Army
I Found Jesus Over in Zion
I Heard a Voice Couldn't Tell
    Where
I Know My Road Is Rough and
    Rocky
I Know When I'm Going Home
I Mean to Lift Up the Standard for
    My King
I Never Felt Such Love in My Soul
    Before
I Never Intend to Die in Egypt Land
I Wish I Have Had an Eagle's
    Wings
I'm an Everyday Witness
I'm Going Down to the River of
    Jordan
I'm Going Home
I'm Going Home on a Cloud
I'm Going to Join the Band
I'm Going to Walk With Jesus By
    Myself
I'm Just Going Over Jordan
I'm Just Going Over There
I'm Traveling to the Land
I've Been Trying to Live Humble

John the Bunyan

Keep in the Middle of the Road
Keep Inching Along
Keep Moving
Keep Your Hand on the Plow

Let Me Shine
Living Humble
Lonesome Valley

Lord I Want to Be a Christian
Lord Make Me More Patient
Lord Write My Name
Low Down Chariot

March Down to Jordan
Michael Row the Boat Ashore
Mount Zion
My Father Took a Light
My Good Lord Show Me the Way
My Little Black Star

No More My Dear Brother

Oh Jerusalem
Oh Redeemed Redeemed
Old Zion's Children Marching
    Along
Over Yonder

Prepare Me One Body
Prepare Us

Ride the Chariot
Rise Mourners
Rise Mourners Rise
Road Is Rugged But I Must Go
Rock of Jubilee
Rocks and the Mountains
Roll the Old Chariot Along

Sabbath Has No End
Sing Ho That I Had the Wings of a
    Dove
Sister Get Your Ticket Right
Soldier of the Cross
Some Will Love you and Some
    Will Hate You
Soon in the Morning
Stand on a Sea of Glass
Steamboat Song
Sun Shine Into My Soul

Takes a Little Bit of Man to Rock
    Dan
Tell Jesus
That Suits Me
These Are My Father's Children

Three Long Nights and Three Long
    Days
Tis Jordan's River
Trip to Raleigh
Turn Sinner
Turn Sinner Turn

Walk Mary Down the Lane
Watch the Stars
Way Over Jordan
We Shall Walk Through the Valley
We'll March Down Jordan
We'll Wait Til Jesus Comes
What Do You Say
When the General Roll Is Called

You're My Brother So Give Me
    Your Hand
You're Tired Child

Suffering

All I Do the Church Keep
    Grumbling
Away Down in Sunbury

Before I'd Be a Slave
Blind Man Lying at the Pool
Blind Man Stood on the Road and
    Cried

Come Here Jesus If You Please

Dark Was the Night
Do Don't You Weep for the Baby
Don't You Have Everybody for
    Your Friend
Down on Me

Going to Hold Out to the End

Hail Mary
Hammering
Hanging Over Hell
Hard Trials
He Knows Just How Much We
    Can Bear
Hear the Lamb's Crying

Holy Bible

I Cannot Stay Here By Myself
I Can't Stand the Fire
I Love My Blessed Savior
I Want to Go Home
I'm a Poor Little Orphan
I'm All Wore Out Toiling for the
    Lord
I'm Going to Tell God All My
    Troubles
I'm in Trouble
I'm Rolling
I'm Running for My Life
I'm Troubled in Mind
In This Field
In This Land
I've Been in the Storm So Long
I've Been Listening All Night Long
I've Been Rebuked

Listen to the Lambs
Lord Have Mercy
Lord I Can Not Stay Here By
    Myself
Lord I Wish I Had Come
Lord I'm Hungry

Mighty Rocky Road
Mother Is Master Going to Sell Us
    Tomorrow
Motherless Children Have a Hard
    Time
My Body Rocked a Long Fever
My Father How Long
My Loving Brother
My Merlindy Brown
My Trouble Is Hard
My Way's Cloudy

Never Me One
Nobody Knows the Trouble I Feel
Nobody Knows the Trouble I See
Nobody Knows the Trouble I've
    Had
Nobody Knows the Trouble I've
    Seen

Over the Crossing

Poor Me
Poor Mourner
Poor Pilgrim
Poor Rosy
Poor Sinner Man

Rain Fall and Wet Becca Lawton
Rough and Rolling Sea

Scandalize My Name
Shepherd Shepherd
Some Valiant Soldier
Somebody Got Lost in the Storm
Sometimes I Feel
Sometimes I Feel Like a
    Motherless Child
Sometimes I Feel Like I Wanna Go
    Home
Sorry to Tell
Standing in the Need of Prayer

That Lonesome Stream
These Dry Bones of Mine
This Is a Sin Trying World
This Old World's a Hell to Me
Trouble Done Bore Me Down
Trouble of the World
Trouble Will Bury Me Down
Troubled in Mind
Trouble's Going to Weigh Me
    Down
Trying to Get Home

Until I Found the Lord

Wasn't That Hard Trials
Way Down in Hell
What a Hard Time
What a Trying Time
What Harm Has Jesus Done
When You Feel Like Moaning
Winter
Wonder Where Is My Brother Gone
Wretched Man That I Am

Women

Mary and Martha
Mary Don't You Weep
Mary Wept and Marthy Moaned
Mary What You Weeping About

Run Mary Run

Sister Hannah
Sister Mary Had But One Child

Weeping Mary
Where Is Mary Gone
Woman at the Well

Yonder Comes Sister Mary

Work Songs

Baby Mine
Baby's in Memphis

Cotton Needs Picking

Day I Left My Home

Enlisted in the Field of Battle
Enlisted Soldiers

Glow Within
Grade Song
Green Trees
Grey Goose

Heave Away
Heave-A-Hora
Hint to the Wise
Ho-Ho
Hold On

I Thought I Had a Friend
If You Don't Like the Way I Work
It's Moving Day

Jay Gooze

About the Compiler

KATHLEEN A. ABROMEIT is the Conservatory Public Services Librarian at Oberlin Conservatory of Music in Oberlin, Ohio. An active member of the Music Library Association, she has written numerous reviews and articles for scholarly journals.